UNRAVELING INSANITY
AND OTHER STORIES

UNRAVELING INSANITY AND OTHER STORIES

Narratives of a Forensic Psychiatrist

By Albert Drukteinis, MD, JD

© 2020 by Albert Drukteinis, MD, JD

All rights reserved. This book or any portion thereof may not be reproduced or used in any manner whatsoever without the express written permission of the publisher except for the use of brief quotations in a book review.

ISBN: 9781708922641

*To Aldona and her great-grandchildren:
Lily, Daniela, Gavin, Mila, and Annika*

Your illusions are a part of you like your bones and flesh and memories.
—William Faulkner

Contents

Introduction: Creating a Narrative · 1
Blessed Death · 37
The Prince of Wales · 57
The Witch Is Dead · 71
Firefly · 89
The Good Night Motel · 109
Pops · 125
Nice Shoes · 141
Out of Africa · 159
Little Saints · 179
Insanity · 205
Conclusions: Narratives and Science · 223
Acknowledgments · 237
Notes · 239
Bibliography · 261

Introduction: Creating a Narrative

Figure 1. "Statue of Liberty," DigitalVision Vectors, photo: omergenc, Getty Images #165786950.

Ellis Island remains a landmark in my memory. I was three and a half years old when I landed there in 1949 with my father, mother, and grandmother after sailing from Germany to the United States on the army transport ship *General Howze*. Displaced by World War II from our homeland, my Lithuanian family was among the millions of huddled masses who for nearly half a century had found Ellis Island their entry point to freedom. In the 1980s, when Ellis Island was being restored, I saw photographs of its cavernous halls with startling recognition from my childhood: the large, semicircular windows near the ceiling, the dark wooden paneling, the rows of sleeping bunks…

But I have to stop here before going further, for I know my lovely wife will interrupt to say that I didn't sail to the United States on the *General Howze*; she did seven months later. My wife is probably right, but I continue to refer to the *General Howze* as the ship that brought me to America because I don't know the name of another transport ship used for that purpose after the war. More importantly, I don't think my story would be as good without the name of a ship. So, consciously or unconsciously, I "borrowed" hers. My wife is also Lithuanian, and with a similar family history, although she doesn't know if she landed on Ellis Island or not. Aha! At least I had that over her—or so I thought, until a few years before my father's death when I was telling him about the photographs I'd seen of the restoration of Ellis Island and all that I recognized in them. In his kindly way acquired from years as a beloved family physician, he said, "We didn't go through Ellis Island, Albert. We landed directly at Port Authority in New York City."

What!? How could that be? I clearly remember Ellis Island and the images in the photographs. Ellis Island was part of my personal identity as an immigrant who came to this country with his family carrying only two suitcases. At the time of this conversation with my father, I was a practicing forensic psychiatrist, retained as an expert in analyzing complex psychiatric cases, dissecting facts from fiction, and standing up to opposing lawyers and their experts in a trial. I was in the business of getting at the truth in highly contentious courtroom disputes. How could my memory of Ellis Island be so clear when it wasn't true?

I am sure my family discussed Ellis Island when I was growing up. My grandfather had immigrated to the United States at the turn of the century before later returning to his homeland. He went through Ellis Island. My aunt, uncle, and two of my older cousins also passed through Ellis Island when they arrived in the United States a year or so before we did. Of course, the story of my immigrant family and the famous portal that accepted us was relevant to who I am. Was it that much of a stretch to include Ellis Island or the *General Howze* in my version? Including those details did make for a better story—maybe a really good story. It connected me directly to the huddled masses—a visual of which I wanted to be a part. The story helped define me, just as our stories define each of us. Was

I fooling myself without knowing it? Ellis Island is only one of my stories. And I am now aware that some of the others are not completely true either.

This book is about forensic *narratives* that a psychiatrist encounters in courtroom work. However, it is really about stories. We all tell stories that are not completely true, sometimes knowing we are doing it, but much of the time not knowing. It may be hard to grasp the extent of this behavior, not to mention how unsettling it is once we find out how wrong our story was. It is not unusual to insist that our story is true even when it is falling apart because of truths that we can't accept. After thirty-five years of practicing forensic psychiatry and evaluating thousands of people who entered or were forced to enter criminal and civil litigation, I have learned that it is all about unraveling and testing their stories.

The difference between narrative and story, if any, is that *narrative* implies a choice as to which events are included and in what order the story is made up.[1] But in common usage, that may be a distinction without a difference. Take these examples:

- The governor's *narrative* was that he knew nothing of his campaign manager procuring illegal financial contributions in the last election.

- After he was caught with child pornography on his home computer, the defendant's *narrative* was that it streamed in accidentally when he was searching for erotic adult movies.

- The fourth grader's sob *story* to his teacher was that he left his finished homework on the steps while eating breakfast, and the dog ate his homework.

In these examples, the message behind the word *narrative* or *story* is the same: "Oh, that's a good story, but don't assume it's true," or "Nice try. You're not going to get away with it." Throughout this book, I use the words *narrative* and *story* interchangeably because, with either term, forensic psychiatry is about understanding how a narrative or story was created and why and whether it stands up to scrutiny in court disputes.

To get back to my Ellis Island narrative, I think it is a good immigration story, but I didn't tell it to get away with anything. Did I just make a mistake? Were the facts from that long ago not so clear, and I told the story to myself so often that it became true? Or was I motivated, consciously or unconsciously, to add Ellis Island and the name of a ship to my story because I perceived some benefit to myself? For example, would I want my listener to think, "Oh, that's an interesting story," and to see me as having a colorful background? Or would I want to leave the impression that I accomplished a lot even in difficult circumstances? My point is that our narratives may be created for various reasons and expectations, not all of which are apparent to the narrator or the listener. Therefore, we need to explore our motivations in order to understand our narratives. We must also realize that even if our narratives are unreliable, this form of organizing information and transmitting it is essential to who we are.

Tens of thousands of years ago, long before written language developed, our earliest ancestors in the African savanna told and retold stories about important events to members of their tribes for survival, to connect them to each other, and to make sense of their world. The old people of the tribe were the keepers of the information then, as they still are for some of their descendants who survive today, such as the Ju/Wasi bushmen. So valuable is the knowledge of the old people of this tribe that bushmen say, "The old person who does not tell stories just does not exist."[2]

Not only do their stories contain factual information but, more importantly, they relay cultural principles and lessons for life, as in this fable: "Python and Jackal were sunning by a quiet pool just outside of the thick jungle when Lion crept out of the jungle toward them. Python, who is sleek and serene, quietly slithered out of sight, but Jackal, who is nervous and screeches, jumped up and down making a racket. Lion devoured Jackal. Good things happen to serene Python, and bad things happen to screeching Jackal."[3] It is easier for younger members of the tribe to remember a story like this and apply it than if they were simply told, "Better to be serene than screeching in times of trouble."

Stories told around campfires brought to life dangerous encounters, acts of heroism, love found and lost, the traditions of the tribe, and instructions on how to deal with everyday circumstances. This story of a hunt on Africa's Serengeti Plain, for example, provides lessons for future hunters:

My younger brother, Kushe, and I were on our first hunt with father when we spotted four wildebeests standing in the tall yellow grass well out of range of our arrows. Father told us to stay where we were while he went around to the other side and bent below the grass so as not to be seen, downwind from the wildebeests. When the wildebeests caught a whiff of him, they looked up and spotted us. Thinking the scent was ours, they didn't move because we were so far away. Suddenly, out of nowhere, father sprang up and shot his arrow into the largest one. This had been his plan all along, but we didn't know it.[4]

The story may be amusing to the listener, but it wasn't to the brothers who had hoped for more action and glory of their own in the hunt. However, the story provided a hunting strategy that they would long remember, as well as a lesson to them and to those who may hear the story from them: "Don't be too trusting of others, not even father."

Stories also conveyed truths about the tribe and its members. Some of those stories evolved to become myths, superstitions, and parables of wisdom. The stories were not always true in a factual sense, but they served a necessary purpose: to provide an understanding of the human mystery. As an example from another part of the world, an ancient Indonesian myth relates a story about the origins of life:

In the beginning, our ancestors were not distinguished by sex. There were no births and no deaths; the people simply were. Then, one day, a great dance was held with such excitement that one of the dancers was trampled to death, his body torn to pieces. The pieces were buried. At the moment of his death, the sexes became separated so that death was now balanced by birth, and birth by death; from the buried pieces of the body, food plants grew. Time had come into being, birth and death, and the killing and eating of other living things, so that life could go on.[5]

Of course, there never was such a dance, and today we wouldn't accept such a fanciful explanation of how the sexes originated. However, the story is a metaphor about the cycle of birth, death, and birth again in which all living things participate. It also explains that it is necessary to consume other living things to keep the life cycle turning. The story is not true, but it is true enough to be meaningful and memorable.

Stories help people understand what has occurred in their lives and to make sense of it. Stories help people predict when similar situations might occur and decide what to do when that happens. Learning about a past experience helps us comprehend a new, similar one. This may be what intelligence is all about. If we didn't have a prior story to guide us, whether it is our own or someone else's, every situation in life would be brand new, and we would have no guidance for how to deal with it.

It is also easier to learn a lesson when it is told as a story, such as this mother's tales to safeguard her son:

- "Last July 4 in New Jersey, a twelve-year-old boy was setting off fireworks when one exploded in his hand. He will now have to wear a plastic hand for the rest of his life. Is that what you want?"

- "You know why Mr. Morrison is so short, don't you? He smoked cigarettes when he was young. He didn't listen to his mother."

These tales may not be entirely true, but they are a mother's illustrative warning to her children about an understandable concern. Life can be dangerous without stories of our own past experiences and those of others to guide us. Regardless of how we acquire knowledge, we become intelligent through stories.

Long before stories were written down, our forbearers painted pictures that represented stories about who they were and what their lives were like. For example, thirty thousand years ago, ancient artists painted giant pictures in a cave at Lascaux, France, depicting horses, bison, and hunters and suggested mysteries that those images represented, as in the unnamed picture in Figure 2.

Figure 2. "Lascaux Cave Painting," credit: AFP Story by Mira Oberman, Lifestyle-France-US-Archeology-Culture-Museum-Art-Tourism, photo: AFP/Stringer, Getty Images #164097579.

We can only guess at the stories they were telling, but they were sufficiently important for them to take considerable time in difficult conditions to paint them. Most artists tell stories in their paintings and other works of art. Some, like the nineteenth-century French postimpressionist painter Paul Gauguin, were very explicit, as seen in his sprawling work about Polynesian life, at the bottom of which he wrote, "Where did we come from, what are we, where are we going?" (Figure 3).

Figure 3. *Where Do We Come From? What Are We? Where Are We Going?* by Paul Gauguin, Hulton Fine Art Collection, photo: Leemage, Getty Images #168966546.

In contrast, the modernist painter Pablo Picasso, in an even larger and more disturbing depiction of *Guernica*, dramatically pulls the viewer into the story of the bombing of a Basque village in Spain by German and Italian warplanes during World War II. The beginning and the ending of the story can only be inferred in this tile reproduction, as seen in Figure 4.

Figure 4. Tile reproduction of (Pablo) Picasso's *Guernica*, © tichr, stock photo, 123RF Images #115996071.

No matter how large or complex a painting, like every oral or written story, it captures only a representation or a part of something, not the whole reality. This is perhaps why Picasso once said, "Art is a lie that makes us realize truth."[6]

Being in the audience of a musical production or dance gives us pleasure, a way to escape our everyday struggles, but the artists who created the production are also telling stories: the composer through sound and the choreographer through bodily motion. One example is Beethoven's Fifth Symphony, which has no words or obvious meaning but is divided into four movements that imply a story through the feelings that the music invokes:[7]

- sonata: dramatic, powerful opening—that is, fate at your door

- andante: lyrical, calmer, with some grand moments

- scherzo: thundering, slow march

- allegro: finale of joyful triumph and exhilaration

Beethoven does not confine us to a specific place or time; he allows us to use our imagination to find narrative meaning without words.

Consider a more contemporary song made famous by the late country singer Johnny Cash. "Ring of Fire" tells an explicit story through sound and lyrics, one that requires less imagination, though not everyone will interpret it exactly the same way:

Bound by wild desire
I fell into a ring of fire.
I fell into a burning ring of fire,
I went down, down, down and the flames went higher
And it burns, burns, burns,
The ring of fire, the ring of fire.[8]

Many forms of art—paintings, music, dance, and obviously literature—tell stories that take us to a place in which we see ourselves and life from a new perspective. Sometimes the stories sound similar to those we have heard before or have told to ourselves and about ourselves. At times they challenge our own stories and are unsettling. Most of our stories are not completely true, but we try to come up with good ones or at least better ones that we would like to believe are true and that we would like our listener to believe. The holiday letters many of us include in our greeting cards are a good illustration of this: "The Bradshaws had a great year. Glenn was promoted to district sales manager and broke eighty for the first time at our annual country club golf tournament. Megan was busy with gardening (you should have seen the tomatoes this year) and helping out at the soup kitchen when she had free time from her online antiques business. The twins made the honor roll, and their soccer team was runner-up in the city championship…" Rest assured that's not all that happened to the Bradshaws last year, but that's the story they chose to tell their friends and family, and a good one it is.

Consider next a more modern form of storytelling, Facebook postings: "I hate it when people on the street ask me if I'm a model," or "I'm so embarrassed that I finished reading *War and Peace* in only four days." This type of "humblebragging" is not considered good Facebook etiquette, but even without such transparent attempts to disguise bragging, a good deal of Facebook communication is people telling stories about themselves, which spread so conveniently and quickly, and which they want their "friends" to believe are true. In fact, they might be true, but not completely. Inevitably, some things are left out, and some are misrepresented.

My dear mother was a great storyteller. She could tell stories nonstop, sometimes redundant, often self-congratulatory. A highly educated woman, she taught German and Russian language studies and encouraged my curiosity and love of reading and learning. Intellect aside, some of her stories were whoppers, and not just the ones she told about herself. Here's one she told about me, when in a generous frame of mind: "The thing I always say, Albert, is that you didn't give me one day of trouble in my life."

Really? How could you say that, Mom? Don't you remember when the state trooper came to our house in the middle of the night and hauled me out to the back seat of his cruiser where my good friend Mike E. was already apprehended? How we had to clean up the broken beer bottles that we had thrown out of Mike's car earlier that night? And don't tell me you can't remember when I was suspended from college for celebrating my birthday with Tom T. and Tony V. on the roof of the Tri Delta sorority house without the girls' permission. Or…well, I better not go on with this.

I didn't reply to my mother's story about how I never gave her trouble. It was not that long ago and easier to accept her wishful memory. It was not so easy when I was younger. In those days, my brother Eddie and I, and sometimes our father if he felt courageous, would interrupt mother rudely in the middle of one of her stories to correct her with the "truth"—what we remembered happened or didn't happen. Needless to say, our corrections didn't go over well. My grandmother, who lived with us throughout my childhood, had her own way of correcting her daughter. She would audibly inhale through her nose, the implied message being that something mother said was not correct! That didn't go over so well either.

I thought for a long time that my mother was unique in the number of distorted stories she would tell, but over the course of my career conducting clinical and especially forensic psychiatric evaluations, I learned that most of our stories are distorted to a greater or lesser degree. At the same time, I have recognized how necessary those stories are and how we are drawn to them despite their inaccuracies.

We like stories not just because they are interesting and may be helpful to us but because that's the way we think: in story form.[9] This model of brain function, called "narrative thinking," may be at the core of what it means to be conscious.[10] If we step back and consider our thoughts at any given time, on any given day, what are they made up of? Unless we are reciting the names of the fifty states or the chemical composition of DNA (i.e., "semantic knowledge"), we are probably thinking in narrative, scrolling through memories of events that happened or could have happened (i.e., "episodic knowledge").[11] When done in private, however, narrative thinking occurs in a much more primitive form. It consists of fragments of stories, some that have concluded and others that have not, or fragments triggered from different, perhaps related, stories in a loose chain of thoughts without clear beginning or end. These fragments of stories emerge from what we are experiencing in that moment, from memories of other moments, or from fantasies of moments that could have been or still could be. Once we begin talking, narrating our thoughts, we must organize those fragments, or the listener won't understand what we are saying. But long before we begin talking, our minds are already swimming in a sea of our own or borrowed narratives in fragment form.

We can get a better sense of this by considering our dreams and how hard it is to describe them to ourselves or to others when we wake up because they are so jumbled and don't seem to make a lot of sense. They appear to be much different from our waking thoughts, when in fact they may not be. While awake, the same jumbled fragments of narratives are present in our minds. They are partially hidden by the sights, sounds, and other sensory experiences occurring at the same time, as well as by our attempts to shape what we may want to think about. In other words, as we are swimming in a sea of fragmented narratives, we are also trying to find direction.

At the beginning of the twentieth century, a number of writers tried to capture this primitive form of thinking before it becomes organized by purposeful shaping or by narrating to a listener. It is called "stream of consciousness," and it was used by authors such as Marcel Proust, Virginia Woolf, James Joyce, and others as an experimental form of writing to capture the multitude of thoughts and feelings that pass through our minds in a fast-moving stream.[12] A good example is this passage from Joyce's long and, for some, painful-to-read novel *Ulysses*, in which the main character, Leopold Bloom, reflects on an attractive young woman:

Wait hm. Wait. Hm. Hm. Yes. That's her perfume. Why she waved her hand. I leave you to think this of me when I'm far away on the pillow. What is it?…Roses, I think. She'd like the scent of that kind. Sweet and cheap: Soon sour. Why Molly likes opoponax. Suits her with just a little jessamine mixed. Her high notes and her low notes. At the dance night she met him, dance of the hours. He brought it out. She was wearing her black and it had the perfume of the time before. Good conductor, is it? Or bad? Light too. Suppose there's some connection. For instance if you go into a cellar where it's dark. Mysterious thing too. Why did I smell it only now? Took its time in coming like herself, slow but sure.[13]

Compare that to an excerpt from a contemporary of Joyce, Ernest Hemingway, in his novel *For Whom the Bell Tolls*, as his character Robert Jordan likewise reflects on an attractive woman:

So he thought about the girl Maria, with her skin, the hair and eyes all the same golden tawny brown, the hair a little darker than the rest but it would be lighter as her skin tanned deeper, the smooth skin, pale gold on the surface with a darkness underneath. Smooth it would be, all of her body smooth, and she moved awkwardly as though there was something of her and about her that embarrassed her as though it were visible, though it was not, but only in her mind. And she blushed when you looked at her, and she's sitting, her hands clasped around her knees and the shirt open at the throat…And as he thought of her, his throat was choky and there was a difficulty in walking.[14]

Joyce was trying to depict how we think before we organize our thoughts into a formal narrative. Because it is so heavily based on a stream of consciousness, it is challenging to try and construct a story from Bloom's reflections; nevertheless, it still conveys narrative thinking. Hemingway's depiction of Jordan's reflections is, in contrast, more straightforward and, therefore, easier to read; the narrative structure is obvious. If we reflect on our own thought processes as we rummage through the ingredients that make up our narratives, we may come to see that, as in our dreams, our everyday thinking is closer to Joyce's depiction than to Hemingway's.

We also think in narrative form because it makes it easier to remember events we have experienced or lessons we've learned or want to learn. Here's an example of facts we might take from a history book about Alexander the Great:[15]

- Alexander of Macedon (Alexander the Great)

- Born 356 BC, Pella, Macedonia

- Son of Philip II of Macedon, assassinated 336 BC

- Succeeded his father on the throne

- Invaded and ruled Asia Minor, 334 BC

- Defeated Darius III of Persia, 332 BC

- Liberated Egypt, 331 BC

- Married three times: Roxanna of Bactria, Stateira of Persia, and Parysatis II of Persia

- Undefeated in battle and considered one of history's most successful commanders

- Died 323 BC, Babylon, Iraq

Compare that to this narrative about Alexander: "Alexander the Great became king at only twenty years old, after his father was assassinated. By thirty, he had created one of the largest empires in the ancient world, spread Greek civilization, and named twenty cities after himself, including Alexandria, Egypt. Two of his three wives were Persian, human spoils of the Persian Empire, which he also conquered. In seeking to reach the ends of the world for his glory, he left a trail of blood and death. At thirty-three years old, he died, and his empire broke up."

Historically, the facts about Alexander's life are important to catalog. But those facts, even if well organized, are difficult to remember, whereas the narrative format not only relates facts about Alexander—for example, how young he was when he created his empire—but also shows that there may be more than one interpretation of his remarkable accomplishments. It may also contain a lesson. Some might say that I chose to present Alexander's accomplishments in an unfavorable light. But all historians form interpretations of their subjects by including certain details and leaving out others, even if this form of interpretation may not be obvious to the reader who is less familiar with the topic. For me, the Alexander story, although incomplete, is easier to remember and perhaps more meaningful than a mere catalog of facts. This is the case not just for history book information but also for personal information—what has happened in our lives, what we need to remember, and how best to remember it.

Telling Stories to Ourselves

One reason for using stories to help us remember personal information is that we are confronted every day with "too much information" about ourselves and our lives. Consider just for a moment all that happens to us in any one day, then multiply it by day after day. It adds up to an awful lot to remember. Here's an accounting from yesterday in Anthony's life:

- Woke at 7:00 to alarm clock.

- Went to bathroom and showered.

- Brushed teeth.

- Picked clothes to wear from closet.

- Dressed.

- Made coffee.

- Ate a banana.

- Drank coffee while checking emails.

- Carol confirmed that she's available for dinner this evening.

- Replied that I would meet her at 5:00 p.m.

It's obvious from this growing list that Anthony does not need to remember all that he did yesterday, since much of it is routine and unimportant. But over the course of every day, there will be important events that he wants to remember. He might, from all of yesterday's activities, single out one event that happened later that day:

- Got out of work early.

- Met Carol for dinner.

- We both ordered pasta Bolognese.

- She didn't like it as much as I did.

If that dinner happened just yesterday, the details from it would be easy to remember, and the short narrative above would make it easier to do so. If, however, that dinner took place last week or last month, the details would become much harder to recall. A year from now, that dinner might remain in Anthony's memory in a more condensed narrative:

- Carol didn't like what we had for dinner.

- Every time I take her out, it seems she's not happy with her meal.

Can Anthony be sure a year later that Carol was unhappy with dinner *every time*? How many times did he actually go out with Carol? Was he dissatisfied with his meal on some of those occasions too? Perhaps it is not necessary to answer those questions. Nevertheless, what remains of Anthony's narrative of dinner with Carol might be useful if he ever takes her out again: "Don't forget. She may not like the food."

One of the first things that happen to memories of events in our lives is that they undergo a "memory selection process"—that is, what is useful to remember is identified from among all the events that happened.[16] A narrative helps us remember those selected fragments even if some of the details are missing or we no longer recall them accurately. Memories of what is most useful are called *gist*, as in "I get the gist." The details are not as important and may change when we remember the events later, but the gist remains. Maybe Carol was not always unhappy with her meal when she and Anthony dined together, but that's what Anthony's gist is telling him, and so he might decide that he wouldn't enjoy eating out with her again. On the other hand, Anthony's gist may be shortchanging Carol. Perhaps he was too quick to decide that she's judgmental about restaurant food, or even if she is, maybe he could grow to enjoy her company for other reasons or in other circumstances. The point is, for better or for worse, we use gist to summarize our past in order to guide our understanding of ourselves and others and what the world is all about. Gist is, essentially, a short story that we pocket for easy reference. It gives us a quick way to assess our surroundings and to deal with them comfortably. In many cases, our gist may be right on. Research, in fact, shows that people who use gist often reason better than those with a greater storehouse of memories.[17] The price we pay for relying on gist, however, is that we lose the complexity of our world by coming to abbreviated conclusions.

We use gist to tell stories about ourselves, taken from memories we have selected from our personal experiences—the good or the bad, the successes or the failures—and what we believe identifies us. Whether or not the gist is accurate, it still may be useful. Freud's psychoanalytical contemporary, Carl Jung, said that our illusions (i.e., our misleading stories) are extremely important even if they don't reflect all aspects of reality, since all our actions and their results are because of them.[18] But we should recognize that those stories are rarely complete and often are chosen to reinforce what we already think or want to think about ourselves. In addition, it is not unusual for our stories to come into conflict with the stories of others, as in Marilyn's case: "They had no reason to fire me. I was the best nurse on the unit. All the patients loved me."

Obviously, someone does not agree that Marilyn was the best nurse on the unit. Even so, she may have been fired unfairly. However, Marilyn's gist about the quality of her work may have excluded incidents when she did not perform well in the eyes of others—perhaps much more often than her gist leads her to believe or that she would like to remember.

Next, consider Arthur's self-inflating gist about his artistic talent: "Of course, I'm an artist, so I see light much differently than other people do." Missing from Arthur's gist is information about what kind of artist he is. Is he someone who pursues art as a hobby, or has he studied art formally, or is he an acclaimed professional? Raising himself above others is important for him, but it may be on a weak foundation. Arthur's gist, like many of our own, shows how gist is important to our identity and is a source of self-esteem, so this gist is not easy to give up even when it may not be accurate. A study of college professors validated this; it showed that 90 percent believed they were more accomplished and better regarded than their colleagues.[19] If that is true, how many colleagues are left?

The reverse happens as well. We may misjudge ourselves in a negative way by excluding success stories, focusing instead on our failures. This may seem surprising, but psychologically, there are reasons for it, such as a predisposition to pessimism, negative early life experiences, or possibly having a depressive disorder. However, the result is the same: a distorted negative view of ourselves that we reinforce by telling a distorted story. Take this executive's lament: "Oh, I know I'm president of my company, and I have a lot of money, but if people really knew me, they would know I'm a fake."

Regardless of why we choose to remember positive or negative stories about ourselves, we do so partly because we can never remember every incident in our lives, so it's easy to exclude a lot of information. The exclusion process may be linked to a predisposed view of ourselves that, in turn, can make up the story of who we think we are.

Telling Stories to Others

Assume that we could overcome the hurdle of having a brain that forgets most of what has happened to us, and we didn't need to use stories as a way of retaining more important memories. Then take, from the earlier example with Anthony, someone else asking him the question "What did you do yesterday?" He could start by answering, as before:

- Woke up at 7:00 to alarm clock.

- Went to bathroom and showered.

- Brushed teeth.

- Picked clothes to wear from closet…

No, no, no! No one wants to hear all that. Again, it's "too much information." What if Anthony then countered with "Well, why did you ask the question?" But the question was not asked in order to learn every detail of his morning schedule. That implies there are rules to follow in speaking with others, to guide us as to what to say and not to say when providing information—rules that help us select information from all that we remember and choose what we think the listener may actually want to hear. Here's one way Anthony might answer the question "What did you do yesterday?": "Oh, nothing much; I went out to dinner with Carol. She didn't like her food—again."

Not everyone understands those rules—what story to tell or not to tell. For example, autistic savants remember much more than most of us do.[20] Some of them can actually recite in detail what happened a year ago yesterday. What they don't recognize is that we may not want to hear all those details. As a listener, I am much more likely to want to hear a good story about your day yesterday, one that is interesting, funny, or informative. I would not want to hear about it in comprehensive detail. As a narrator, however, I may not be sure which story you want to hear. Even as a psychiatrist, I can't always read a listener's mind. But that's exactly what most of us try to do when talking to people: we use clues from facial expressions and other body language to determine whether they're interested. This is an instinct that, in psychological terms, is known as *theory of mind*, a capability most of us have but autistic savants lack.[21] Autistic savants can't read subtle expressions on another person's face. If they could, they would notice that the blow-by-blow story they're telling is not interesting to the listener because it includes too much information. They might notice that the other person has stopped listening. Of course, it isn't only autistic savants who fail to read these signals. We all know people who go on and on with a story that is boring, and everyone has stopped listening. We all find ourselves at one time or another telling a boring story and losing our listeners—but not to the degree of an autistic savant. If we have a normally functioning theory of mind, we are able to "read" our listener's reactions or to anticipate their reactions and stop the boring story or tell one that better suits that listener. From reading the listener's reactions, we learn to select what to include in our story so that we can draw listeners into it so they become truly engaged with us as we tell it.

Telling stories or memories to others, therefore, is not just about us. Some memories may not be interesting and not worth telling at all. Other memories may place us in an unfavorable light if we tell them. Still others we may or may not tell depending on who the listener is. This simple process of including and excluding memories of our experiences and rearranging them to suit our needs and to gain the response we expect from our listener can lead to very different versions of the story we tell about yesterday. Consider Fred's three alternative narratives about his motor vehicle accident:

- To the auto mechanic: "I backed into my son's teacher. Her car was passing behind me in the school parking lot. Of course, I apologized, and she graciously accepted. I felt terrible for not looking more carefully. Fortunately, I was not cited by the police, but I'll pay for her repairs."

- To his wife: "Our son's teacher came out of nowhere behind me in her car as I was backing out of the school parking lot, and I ran into her. She knew it was her fault, but of course I took the blame. I was not cited or anything."

- To the insurance adjuster: "I had an accident at my son's school; I backed into his teacher's car in the parking lot. She was speeding, and my car has a blind spot on the right. Afterward, she stepped out of the car slowly, clutching her neck—what a joke. She could hardly look me in the eye."

Which is the true story of the accident Fred had yesterday in the school parking lot? Are any of the three stories completely true? Do any of them include all that occurred? Maybe not, but each one may be true enough for Fred's purpose in telling it. In addition, Fred may be convinced each version is true, even if it can't be.

Telling stories about ourselves and about others is also shaped in the telling. We may not realize how often we select memories, including some and excluding others and, once we have finished constructing the story, how it may seem to reflect the truth even if far from it. Stories we construct about ourselves and about others always contain limited information. For stories about ourselves, we have a larger storehouse of information from which to draw; for those about others, we have far less. Unfortunately, that does not stop us from "making up" stories that are often judgmental based on limited information. Once we construct the story, any other features are, in effect, lost to our story.

More often than not, we construct stories about ourselves to ensure that our listeners see us in a positive light, and just as often, we believe those stories. This form of self-deception may be the price we pay for being a social animal.[22] To be part of a social group, we must be accepted, and acceptance is easier if we appear cooperative, trustworthy, and sympathetic and if we can be counted on not to exploit the group.[23] So in order for us to be accepted and remain in the group, those features must be evident in the stories we tell about ourselves. Our character must be reflected in them. The problem is that it is difficult to deceive others in the group for long. Inevitably, people will realize that we are not being genuine in how we portray ourselves. That means we must first successfully convince ourselves before we can convince others. Because this process is for the most part unconscious, it is easy to convince ourselves of something we would like to believe. Here's an example of how this plays out: "When the woman lost control of her car and spun around in the face of oncoming traffic, I immediately pulled my own car over and got out to redirect traffic. I could never drive by and leave someone in such danger."

The heroic emphasis by the storyteller is plain. Unquestionably, this good deed is to be admired. But can we be sure this man would never drive by such a situation? What if he had been in a hurry, and traffic had been light? What if it had been a man who lost control of his car, and he looked like he could take care of himself? Regardless, our hero told his story in such a way as to make himself appear selfless and admirable. One gets the feeling he may like retelling it.

There is more than one way to tell every story, and tricks can be used to tell it better, although we may not recognize when we are using them. Since we can't remember everything that happened about an event or experience and may not want to tell everything even if we could, we need to find ways to make the story convincing—a good story that makes its point and won't be challenged. One way we do that is to use sweeping generalizations, like these: "I wouldn't go into that store. Everyone knows it's a rip-off," or "All the kids in her class are lazy."

In the first example, who is "everyone"? How can everyone know anything or the same thing? In the second example, is it really possible that "all the kids" in a given class are lazy? But saying that "some" of the store's prices are high or that "some" of the students are lazy may not be strong enough for the storyteller to make the point. A sweeping generalization accomplishes this much better. We all use such sweeping language when we need to make a point, often without realizing it. Oops! Did I just say "we all"? Maybe I should have said "most," or "many of us," or "at one time or another, all of us." Once we start listening for such generalizations in our own speech, we may hear them more frequently than we would like.

Another trick to make our stories convincing is using words that emphasize how certain we are, and then to say them in a tone that strengthens them. Strong adverbs and adjectives, in particular, serve this purpose well: "Maria was *always* at the top of her class," or "It was *certainly* the best movie he ever made," or "*Clearly*, Jack's honesty could *never* be questioned."

We use words such as *always, never, certainly, clearly*, and similar emphatic language in order to safeguard against any disagreement from the listener. We also hope to make our point without having to provide more specific information. The reality hidden behind the use of such language is that the person using it may not be so certain or so clear.

Another trick we use in storytelling is to include an *adage*, a saying most people accept as true, or an *aphorism*, a shortened self-evident example, to make our story believable. The saying or example may be one well known or one we make up; for example, if asked what I did yesterday, I might say, "I worked all day on my end-of-the-year report. My boss loved it. You know, if you don't put in the time, you can't get ahead."

The message in this statement is that I'm getting ahead, and I can prove it. Not only did I work all day, but people like me who do get ahead. So I must be getting ahead. Whether it's true that I worked all day, that my boss loved my report, or that I'm really getting ahead may not be completely true, but you don't have to take my word for it; take what we all know to be true.

Here's another example: "Whenever I go to visit Uncle Harold, he's mad about something, and then he wonders why I don't come by more often. No one wants to go into the doghouse when the dog is barking." My explanation for why I don't visit Uncle Harold more often might be enough for the listener to understand without the doghouse remark, but adding an image to which my listener could relate makes my reason more convincing. The image is a story within a story.

Perhaps more important than any device we use to construct a good story are two related decisions we must make before we tell it: where to start the story and where to end it. Our lives are in constant motion, with countless events occurring before the story starts, and countless events occurring after it ends. Some of those events before and after the story may have no connection to our story. But by deciding on a starting point and an ending point for our story, we automatically exclude other events. Not everyone may agree with us if they knew what those excluded events were and may believe the story should have started earlier or finished later to make it complete. Take Melissa's story about her sister Janey: "Last Saturday morning, after seventeen years of marriage, Janey's husband told her he wanted a divorce. She was devastated and called me sobbing. She said he wouldn't talk to her and that he just packed up and left. I'm afraid she might kill herself."

It is obvious from this story that Melissa felt sorry for her sister and wanted the listener to be sympathetic as well. To ensure that result, she may have left out important "before-and-after information," which gave the listener an incomplete picture of this event. Here's the story with some important before-and-after information included:

Janey and her husband have been fighting for years and have separated three times over her flirting when she has a few drinks. She insists that Friday night is her night out with the girls. Last Saturday morning, after seventeen years of marriage, Janey's husband told her he wanted a divorce. She was devastated and called me sobbing. She said he wouldn't talk to her and that he just packed up and left. I'm afraid she might kill herself. On Sunday, he emailed to tell her that if she stopped drinking and going out with the girls, he might reconsider, but she thinks it's too late.

Every story should raise two questions in the mind of the listener: what happened before and what happened after the events described? If asked, Melissa might have told the whole story. However, she might not have, especially if she felt she had to spare Janey any criticism and to ensure that her listener would be sympathetic.

Life Stories

My psychiatric training was in the days when Sigmund Freud and his psychoanalytic followers still held an influential place in helping psychiatrists understand why people think, feel, and behave the way they do. One of my favorite professors, a psychoanalyst, required all his psychiatric residents in training to spend many hours over a number of days exploring each patient's life history based on as many memories as the patient could provide. We were charged with bringing out these memories in a timeline through detailed probing, a process known as *anamnesis*. We were then instructed to write up each patient's life history and to develop an interpretation for us and the patient in order to discover how combinations of events in the patient's life had contributed to his or her psychological problems. What I found remarkable when I drafted these detailed life stories was the patterns I could see in each patient's experiences and behaviors that created a trajectory toward almost inevitable conflict and emotional distress.

Over time, various other psychiatric and psychological schools of thought won out over the Freudian approach for different reasons, and psychoanalytic interpretations are no longer the only way to understand mental disorders, though I believe they still have merit. Today in psychiatry there is a greater emphasis on biochemical changes in the central nervous system as an explanation for emotional distress. It is not that life events have no meaning, but only that there is less attention paid to them. Of course, some wild psychoanalytical ideas such as the Oedipus complex (which proposes that a young boy unconsciously wants to do away with his father and keep his mother for himself) have rightfully lost all credibility. However, the importance of the life story should not be underestimated, and patients and mental health professionals are not always aware of its significance. I believe that psychiatrists, psychologists, and counselors should treat people and their stories, not just their mental disorders. To do that, we need to know where patients came from, who they are, and where they are going. The patient's story gives us that vital information, as shown in this example: "Max was a successful middle-aged businessman who could not understand why he was depressed. He had everything to live for and denied having any stressors in his life. He asked for medication to treat his depression. Only when he was urged to provide a detailed life history did he report several major losses in the previous year: the resignation of his business partner, the death of his beloved dog, and the development of sciatica, which prevented him from playing racquetball. His previously well-ordered life was now out of his control, and he couldn't understand why."

Max not only needed treatment with antidepressant medication, but he also needed to address his distorted belief that he had control over his life by his wits and effort alone. He also needed to see that he was vulnerable to unexpected life changes like the rest of us and that they inevitably will occur.

Exploring life histories over multiple sessions became a standard part of my clinical practice and, later, of my forensic work. I think of this process as more of an art form, but unfortunately one that is not sufficiently encouraged in psychiatric or psychological training today. However, what I failed to appreciate fully either in my psychiatric training or in early clinical practice was that in exploring a detailed life history based on a patient's memories, I might not be hearing a true story, even if the patient believed it was true. Only years later, after I returned to school to study law and became a forensic psychiatrist, did I begin to realize how people's stories could be different—sometimes widely different—from those of others who witnessed or experienced the same events and how their stories about events could change over time. I learned, in short, that while a great deal of information is needed in order to understand a person, that person's memories may not be a reliable source of information. Oh, I can hear you asking me, "I guess you didn't get it. Remember your Ellis Island story?" You're right; we must all be careful with our stories, or the truth will sneak up on us. And we should realize that our stories will change over time. Consider how Rachel's story changed depending on when she was telling it and to whom.

- After graduating from high school at eighteen years old, she told her new college roommate, "My grades in high school were good—mostly As and Bs. I did best in English and history."

- After graduating from college at twenty-two years old, she told a prospective employer, "I was an A student in high school and took a number of advanced courses."

- After an auto accident at twenty-six years old, when she was seeking compensation for a head injury, she told lawyers in a deposition, "I had all As in high school; I was top of my class. I was in all the advanced courses. Now I can't even help my children with their homework."

If we were to obtain Rachel's early school records and discover that they contradicted her account, it would be easy to conclude that she was lying. But, in fact, changing an account of events in our life is so common that we'd be wiser to expect that it will happen. We must keep in mind that none of us can ever remember everything accurately about any of our experiences and that we reconstruct our memories continuously over time and for different reasons. One of those reasons stems from what takes place when we first form memories of an experience, how we feel at the time, and how we interpret it. Examples from two people who attended the same rock concert may show this process:

- The first concert attendee: "It was a great concert. The crowd was on their feet dancing and jumping to the music. The sound system and lights were dynamite."

- The second concert attendee: "There were too many people packed into the stadium. It was stuffy and hot, and you couldn't hear yourself think."

If we loved the concert, we may not remember how crowded it was in the stadium or that it was hot. If we hated the concert, we may not even remember that we went to it. Or, later, if we do remember and tell someone about it, we may leave things out that didn't matter to us, or we may make a big deal about those things that did matter. We may also exaggerate or exclude certain details, depending on why we are telling the story and to whom. Regardless, the original memory of the experience is not there anymore—at least not in the same form. It has been replaced by the story we tell about it. The second time we tell the story, the same thing happens again, and so the story—and in turn the memory—keeps changing. By the twenty-second time we tell it, there may not be much left of the original experience of the concert.

It is important to recognize that memories can change over a relatively short period of time, especially when the event has been traumatic or when the person who experienced it needs to emphasize some aspect of that event, as in these variations of a head injury:

- January 2013: "I slipped on ice in the parking lot last night and landed on my back and head, but I was more shocked than hurt."

- February 2013: "When I fell on ice last month in the parking lot, I hit my back and head really hard. I was dazed and confused for about a minute."

- August 2013: "What a fall I took last January on a very icy parking lot! I was knocked out for at least five or ten minutes and didn't know where I was when I woke up."

Memories that make up an individual's narrative change not only by how they are formed and how they are told but by a variety of other factors within the person and the person's environment. Among those factors are the person's cultural, political, and religious beliefs; wishful or imaginative thinking; inconvenient or otherwise damaging facts; and suggestibility from outside sources. In some cases, old memories may block new ones, or new memories may block old ones; trauma may cause the person to remember too much or too little, and experiencing mood changes, anxiety, and fear can disrupt memories. The aging brain is yet another factor to consider. I will explore in greater detail these factors and others through the forensic narratives that make up this book. For now just keep in mind that we must gather a large amount of information before we can begin to understand what actually happened in a person's life, when it happened, and why. We cannot merely rely on a person's memories. The challenge, of course, is that the more information we gather, especially from multiple sources, the more confusing it becomes to reach an understanding. Each of these sources will inevitably present a different version of the events, making it more difficult to uncover the true story.

Courtroom Stories

Lawyers practice their trade by presenting stories in court, taken from known facts in the case, which they use to persuade juries to their point of view. They know that juries rely on matching up the story presented in court with their personal experiences, and through that comparison, they will decide which version is the most reliable.[24] Judges are more sophisticated about legal issues, but even they consider the strength of the narrative presented. As part of their job, lawyers alter the stories they present not by unconscious memory selection as we might, but by purposely selecting and interpreting facts in the case to persuade juries and judges that theirs is the best story, the one most believable. Here's a case in point:

Margaret was walking through the jewelry section of a department store when she spotted a display of designer watches on a rack. She stopped and removed one and then another and tried them on, placing them on the counter afterward. She then tried on a third watch, which she also took off and placed on the counter with the others. Margaret looked briefly at other watches on the rack and then replaced two of the watches she had tried on. The third watch, which was next to her gloves on the counter, she picked up with her gloves and stuffed into her coat pocket. As she left the store, an alarm went off, and Margaret was confronted by a security guard who asked if she had anything in her pockets that might have set off the alarm. She reached into her coat pocket and pulled out her gloves, and the watch came out and dropped on the floor with its sales tag still attached. Margaret appeared shocked and apologized profusely, but the store had a strict shoplifting policy and pressed charges against her.

At district court, the prosecutor presented the case against Margaret with this narrative: "The defendant who is seated here in the courtroom stole a designer watch by a clever scheme of pretending to be trying on watches, conveniently placing them in a pile next to her gloves and then appearing to replace them on the rack when, in fact, it was always her intent to hide the third watch among her gloves and to leave the store with it. This is a devious plan that cannot be explained by anything but shoplifting, for which she must be found guilty."

Margaret's lawyer presented the facts in a different narrative and added new information that might be helpful to his client: "This is all a big mistake. My client had no intention of stealing anything. It is perfectly understandable that the third watch could have been picked up accidentally along with her gloves. Why would she be so willing to empty her pocket otherwise and then appear shocked and in disbelief? Furthermore, my client is married to a successful businessman in the community and has no need to steal watches. She may have been absentminded, but she is no shoplifter."

Lawyers have an ethical obligation to uphold the truth. For prosecutors, this means having a good-faith belief in the defendant's guilt. For defense lawyers, it means representing their clients zealously, though not assisting them in lying under oath. However, they must not allow their personal belief about whether their client is guilty or innocent to stand in the way of a vigorous defense. Both prosecutors and defense lawyers will inevitably try to do their job with alternative narratives.

Whether in criminal or civil litigation, every case can and will be interpreted differently, depending on which facts are emphasized. Or, to quote the commencement speaker at my law school graduation, "No matter how thin you cook a pancake, there is always another side."[25] Lawyers must find that other side and present it in its best possible light for their clients. To the layperson, the judicial process may seem twisted and misdirected at times, but its purpose is to come as close to the truth as possible—and as fairly.

Where does psychiatry fit in to this process? Do psychiatrists go to court to help their patients, or are they more like lawyers? The second question is easier to answer. No, psychiatrists are not like lawyers. Even as a forensic psychiatrist with a law degree, I know it is not my job to act as a lawyer. Answering the first question is much more difficult, for psychiatrists are often drawn into court to testify when their patients are in litigation, sometimes facing criminal charges, or embroiled in a civil lawsuit. It is awkward for psychiatrists who want to help their patients but who may be forced under oath to disclose sensitive information or to provide an opinion that could harm the patients' cases.

In Margaret's case, for example, let's assume that she admitted taking the watch on purpose and claims to not understand her own behavior. Her lawyer may know that she is being treated by Dr. Robert Jones, a psychiatrist, for chronic depression. So her lawyer might ask Dr. Jones whether her depression could have clouded her judgment when she took the watch. Dr. Jones, in a desire to support Margaret, may agree to come to court and testify on her behalf. Let's say he then provides the following clinical history and his opinion about her actions: "I have been treating Margaret for three years for deep depression. I have prescribed antidepressant medication, but it is only partly effective. Margaret continues to experience sadness, fatigue, and poor concentration. She has withdrawn from many of her friends. In her depressed state, she doesn't think through what she is doing very well. In my opinion, Margaret took the watch impulsively without stopping to consider the consequences, thinking only that it might give her some temporary pleasure. She would not have done this if she had not been depressed."

Every clinical history is a story, and here Dr. Jones provided a sad story about Margaret, which the judge might very well consider relevant, given Dr. Jones's professional standing and knowledge of human behavior.

Forensic psychiatrists, however, would avoid providing opinions on a patient they are treating, because the treatment relationship could be harmed and because it's difficult for them to be detached and objective about their patients. Furthermore, forensic psychiatrists typically obtain information from a number of sources beyond what a patient provides—records, witness statements, and other sources—in order to develop a more complete story before offering an opinion. Dr. Jones did not have that additional information, and would not have had it, because that is not what treating psychiatrists need for their clinical work. This lack of information, unfortunately, opens Dr. Jones up to a tough cross-examination by the prosecutor, who does have that information:

> PROSECUTOR: Dr. Jones, you did not see any police records in Margaret's case, did you?
>
> DR. JONES: No, I didn't.
>
> PROSECUTOR: So you were not aware that Margaret had been charged with shoplifting once before, five years ago?
>
> DR. JONES: No.
>
> PROSECUTOR: You were also not aware that Margaret told the security guard, once she started crying, that she doesn't know why she does "these things" and that she doesn't need "all that stuff"?
>
> DR. JONES: No, I didn't know that.
>
> PROSECUTOR: Doctor, did you ever speak to Margaret about why she needs to steal "stuff"?
>
> DR. JONES: No.
>
> PROSECUTOR: Isn't it fair to say, Doctor, that Margaret's behavior may not be an isolated impulsive act?
>
> DR. JONES: Yes, if that information is true, it may not be.

PROSECUTOR: Doctor, could this information change your opinion about why Margaret took the watch?

DR. JONES: Yes, it might.

Dr. Jones should not be faulted for his opinions about Margaret's depression nor his genuine belief that her depression made her act impulsively. His mistake was the same one that I made in the early years of my clinical practice—and that many psychiatrists make: he did not consider that her story might not be true or at least not completely true. With that, his opinion in the courtroom was substantially discredited.

When the prosecutor questioned Dr. Jones about Margaret's emotional admission that she does not know why she does "these things" and that she doesn't need "all that stuff," the implication was that not only did Margaret do this once or twice but that this is a pattern of behavior, which makes her more likely to be guilty. But what if she really doesn't understand her behavior, especially if she really doesn't need "all that stuff"? What if she has a closet full of items stolen that are still in their original packages and never have been used? Could that mean that Margaret is suffering from a mental illness that makes her criminally not responsible for taking the watch from the department store? That is more complicated.

First of all, *criminal responsibility* is defined by the two primary elements of a crime: *wrongful intent* and *wrongful act*.[26] In most criminal cases, both of these elements must be proven beyond a reasonable doubt by the prosecutor. Margaret may have committed a wrongful act, but did she really have wrongful intent? If she took the watch accidentally, she may not have had wrongful intent. If it was not accidental, was her mental capacity so impaired that she couldn't form sufficient wrongful intent for a crime? For example, if Margaret was intellectually disabled, functioning at the level of a child, she may not have had the same level of wrongful intent as she would as an adult with no such disability. Or, if she suffered from a severe mental illness that made her so confused that her actions were impulsive and random, she may not have even known she took a watch, much less stolen it. In that case, Margaret's lawyer would argue that she had *diminished capacity* to form wrongful intent, and there is no crime.[27]

However, if the prosecutor could show that Margaret had wrongful intent and that she committed a wrongful act, she may still have an excuse and is not criminally responsible. One such excuse is *insanity*.[28] Most people believe they have an idea of what insanity is and, if asked that question, are willing to offer an opinion. In Margaret's case, they might say, "She wasn't insane. She knew what she was doing," or "There must have been something wrong with her. Why would she take 'stuff' that she didn't need?" Most people may not really know what *insane* means in a clinical or legal sense. That's understandable, given that we often use the word as slang in our everyday conversation. For example, "The party was absolutely insane," or "He's insane if he thinks I'll loan him money again." There was a time in the psychiatric profession when the terms *insanity* and *mental illness* meant the same thing; they were both terms for a severe mental condition. If someone was insane, he or she was mentally ill, and vice versa. Insane asylums were built to protect such individuals and to protect everyone else from them. Until the second half of the twentieth century, if someone had been involuntarily committed to an insane asylum, by then referred to as a hospital, that person was said to be insane even if he or she committed no crime.

Today, *insanity* and *mental illness* have different meanings. In criminal law, we use the term *insanity* to mean that someone was not responsible for his or her unlawful acts because of a mental illness. But this is where it gets really complicated, because a person may have a mental illness yet still be criminally responsible. In addition, the meaning of *insanity* varies depending on where the crime was committed and where the defendant will go to trial (i.e., the *jurisdiction*).[29] Usually that means the state where the crime was committed, unless it's a federal crime. Every state has its own definition of insanity, as does the federal government. So before we can answer the question "Was Margaret insane?" we need to know the definition of insanity that applies in the jurisdiction where she allegedly committed the crime and where she will be tried. Once again, it's not enough to just say she was mentally ill. Note that I say "was" because with insanity, we are talking about when the crime occurred, not necessarily her mental state before or after the crime.

Most definitions of *insanity* fall into one or both of two categories. The first category is when a mental illness makes a person, in one way or another, *unable to think rationally*.[30] The second category of *insanity* is when a mental illness makes a person *unable to control him- or herself*[31]—even though the person knew what he or she was doing. Essentially, it means that the person knows better but can't control the criminal behavior. It's not surprising that this category of insanity is controversial. How do we distinguish between someone who truly couldn't control him- or herself and someone who just didn't? There are psychiatrists who believe it is never possible to make that distinction with certainty. What's more, after a serious crime, defendants frequently look back on their actions with surprise or disbelief, swearing, for example, "I could never have done something like that." In Margaret's case, it appears that she was aware of her actions and what she had done but could not explain them. Does that mean she was unable to control her actions? This is where forensic psychiatrists come in: to determine if the person was mentally ill when she committed the crime, and if so, whether she was unable to think rationally or unable to control herself. Their opinions, after a personal psychiatric evaluation and a dissection of Margaret's and Dr. Jones's narratives, will either support the narrative or show that the narrative does not hold together—that the story doesn't work.

Wait, wait! This can't be just about storytelling, you say. Psychiatry is a medical science. These are doctors who diagnose and treat patients with mental illnesses. They have gone through years of scientific training. They must have more to offer from their science—and I've been saying how stories can easily be distorted and are not completely true—so shouldn't we expect more than a story?

Of course, psychiatry is a science, and especially in the last few decades, great advances have been made in our understanding of the brain and its effect on mental processes and behavior. Psychological research has also shown improved methods of quantifying human behavior and formally testing it. However, except for neurological disorders, there is little objective evidence to confirm that someone has a mental illness and what kind it is. There are no X-rays, scans, or blood tests and no autopsy findings. Psychiatrists diagnose a mental illness by taking a clinical history from the patient (or sometimes from a family member or someone else who knows the patient), by carefully observing the patient during an interview for signs of psychiatric disturbance, and by matching up these findings to symptoms of known mental illnesses.

The science of psychiatry establishes which symptoms belong to which illnesses, how the symptoms start and develop, and how to treat those illnesses. The clinical history that the patient provides and that the psychiatrist records is a story, and how accurate the story is may determine how well the treatment goes. Patients have an incentive to provide an accurate history to their treating psychiatrist because the success of their treatment will depend on it. So, even if there is limited objective evidence, the partnership between the patient and the psychiatrist is likely to have the same goal, and the story can be reliable for that purpose. In fact, the importance of stories in a clinical relationship has recently led to a new discipline, *narrative medicine*, which seeks a deeper understanding of patients and their suffering beyond identifying symptoms.[32]

In forensic psychiatry, however, the patient's clinical history has another goal, a potential benefit not related to treatment but to a legal outcome. In criminal cases it may be to avoid guilt or punishment; in civil cases it may be to gain financial compensation or disability. So the incentives for the patient are quite different, and the story is often colored for the desired legal outcome. In cases of severe mental illness, a diagnosis may be obvious, but in most cases, there is a dispute not only about the diagnosis but also how it applies to the legal issue. That is why dissecting and questioning—unraveling the story—are most important.[33] To that end, scores of psychological tests have been developed to increase objectivity and aid in the process, many of which can be helpful, but rarely are they sufficient for a forensic psychiatrist to reach an opinion "within reasonable medical certainty."[34] Other than neuropsychological measures of brain function, psychological tests are often questionnaires that patients answer, and those answers can be unreliable, even when validity measures are included.[35] Therefore, forensic psychiatry must include attention to narratives and whether the proposed narrative is consistent with factual information and with the science of mental illness.

Truth is masked by the stories we tell, so it is understandable that trying to determine truth in the courtroom is complicated, as it is in "real life." The forensic narratives that I share in this book will show just how complex and fragile stories can be and how hard it may be to find the truth. Often more questions than answers come to light, some of which I have presented for consideration. You may have other questions. The narratives are taken from countless stories I have confronted in my forensic work, along with alternative nuances and outcomes I have imagined. The cases presented were inspired by real events that are part of police and other public records, but the stories presented are composites from different sources. My focus is on human struggles and the stories people tell or want to tell to describe and explain those struggles. While science is the foundation of forensic psychiatry, much of the work is in unraveling stories, challenging their consistency and reliability, and, once again, finding a story whose version is closest to the truth. There is no doubt, in reading these narratives, that you may believe that an alternative version is more compelling than the ones I suggest. That's okay. Perhaps yours is a better story.

Blessed Death

Figure 5. "Statue of a Sitting Angel," Moment, photo:
Douglas Sacha, Getty Images #547103184.

Warren looked down at the gray rushing river hundreds of feet below him, holding tightly onto the rail behind his back. He guessed he climbed over the rail about an hour ago. The state trooper had been talking to him for at least half an hour from a good ten feet away, but Warren didn't hear much of what the trooper said. He wasn't looking at the trooper. He kept repeating, "We all have to die. We all have to die."

The cars on the bridge crawled along in one of the two east-bound lanes, since police cruisers and first-responder vehicles blocked the other lane. As they passed by him, drivers caught a glimpse of Warren leaning out over the water. The state trooper saw Warren clearly; his alcohol-flushed face stood out in the gray of the morning, and his eyes were wide with fear. He looked as if any second he might just collapse in midair.

The trooper wanted to grab him but was afraid to come too close in case Warren panicked and let go. Warren just shook his head from side to side. He didn't answer the trooper. After what seemed like a long time to the trooper, Warren began to sob. Now the trooper felt he had no choice. He approached closer to Warren and in a slow but deliberate movement firmly took hold of his arm. With the help of another first responder, he eased Warren back over the rail. Warren was still crying and looked bewildered. The trooper then asked him, "Are you Warren Andrews?"

"Yeah," said Warren.

"You're the guy from Columbia Heights who called 911 a couple of hours ago?"

"Yeah."

Warren didn't struggle as he was handcuffed and read his rights. The trooper and his partner led Warren to their cruiser and placed him behind the cage-like barrier in the back seat. They drove away slowly with their lights flashing as the cars on the bridge moved over to let them pass. Without any prompting from either of the troopers,[1] Warren began to speak.

"I wanted you guys to find them. That's why I kept the door open, so you'd have no trouble getting into the house. I hope they give my note to her parents. I told them I was sorry. I left one for my parents too, but that's in my car…What will happen to my car?…I guess it doesn't really matter, but there's only fifteen thousand miles on it…We all had to die, you know. The only way I could think of for me was to jump off the Memorial Bridge. No one could survive that. It was so clear what I had to do, until I climbed over the rail…then I froze. I just froze. I've never been so scared in my life. If I wouldn't have looked down…It was so high. I have always been afraid of heights. Why didn't I think of that before?"

When the local police had arrived at Warren's home earlier, they found his wife Ann's body in her bed. She had purple bruises on her neck from apparent strangulation. The motionless bodies of his twin sons, Tommy and Timmy, who were not yet two years old, were in their own beds in another room. They had no marks on them. Police suspected that they died by suffocation. Warren was charged with three counts of first-degree murder and remained in custody at the county jail. Weeks later, his lawyers filed a plea of insanity[2] with the court. They decided this was the defense they must use. What else could have caused someone to commit such a horrible act?

Warren Andrews was forty-two years old at the time of his arrest, although he looked much older than that. He was weathered by years of physical labor in a home supply warehouse and by even more years of daily bourbon and ginger ale. His father had been a hard man with his own alcohol problems who believed in corporal punishment for his four sons and for their mother if she was "out of line." All of Warren's brothers drank heavily, and one committed suicide. Warren hadn't finished high school. Instead, he took a job at an auto body shop, where he made enough money to buy himself a Ford Mustang. He thought life was good then.

"I was busy partying and chasing girls. But I never got in trouble with the law, except for a couple of speeding tickets. And I wasn't violent. I never hit a girl or a woman, and I was never in a physical fight in my life. I saw too much fighting from my father and hated him for it."

When he was twenty years old, Warren married his first wife, Florence, and had three children by her. He found the warehouse job not far from where they lived. By working nights at higher pay, he enabled his family to live comfortably. However, he and Florence both drank way too much, which inevitably led to screaming arguments and two lengthy separations before they finally divorced after ten years of marriage. Warren explained it this way.

"Florence was hysterical and jealous—a crazy woman. She didn't appreciate how hard I worked and how good she had it. After I caught her cheating on me, that was it. I still loved her, but I couldn't live with her."

Florence had a different version.

"Warren lies, so you can't trust anything he says. He cheated on me from the first year of our marriage and probably before we were married. Yes, I had a fling with Jason, the laundryman, when we were separated, but it didn't mean anything. Warren got so mad, I had to get a restraining order against him. Then there's his sex problem. When he wants sex, it has to be now. He has raped me more than once. One Thanksgiving Day, when I refused to go to bed with him because he was so drunk, he slammed my head into the wall and then dragged me into the bedroom by my feet and forced sex on me. I still have panic attacks every Thanksgiving."

After their divorce, Warren provided support for his children, but they were never close to him. Every now and then, he met Florence for a coffee at Dunkin' Donuts. He looked forward to those meetings. They occasionally held hands.

Warren met Ann six years ago at an Alcoholics Anonymous meeting. Florence had made him go to meetings under the threat of leaving him. Ann brewed the coffee for the meeting and giggled when he called her "Sergeant." After the meeting, they sometimes went to McDonald's for a cheeseburger, but Warren didn't attend meetings often, so their relationship was slow to progress. Once Warren was in the process of divorce from Florence, he began going to Alcoholics Anonymous regularly just to see Ann. But he was still drinking. He kept it from Ann until one night when she skipped a meeting, and Warren went to her apartment and found her drinking. They both got drunk, and Warren spent the night with her. They swore they would not drink again. They married four years ago, and within three months, Warren and Ann were drinking regularly. She only cut back during her pregnancy because she didn't want to harm the baby. Warren felt that Ann was his partner and soul mate.

"I felt a love for Ann like I have never felt for anyone before. She took care of me. She understood me. I know we drank too much, but we had such hot nights together. Oh, I could tell you some stories. But after Tommy and Timmy were born—we had twins, you know—I thought she was pushing me aside. It was always about them. We weren't having fun. Of course I loved those boys, but I needed her too," he said.

By the time the twins were almost a year old, Warren had become increasingly frustrated with Ann. He called Florence and asked her to meet him for coffee. "I had to talk to someone," he said.

Florence agreed to meet Warren, and after their third cup of coffee, they held hands. Warren began to cry and told Florence he really missed her. Florence invited him to move back in with her and their children. He agreed. "I felt like the weight of the world dropped to my feet. She wanted me back. We were going to make it work. I went back and told Ann, 'There's not enough of you to go around; I'm going home.'"

Returning to Florence didn't go so well. The children would not warm up to him and didn't accept his discipline, and Florence constantly demanded more money. He was paying twice as much for their household expenses than what he had paid after the divorce when he was not living there. So he had to scale back what he gave to Ann for her support. Ann was not working because she wanted to stay home with the twins, and she was having difficulty making ends meet. She was growing more and more desperate. By then Warren hated living with Florence. When Warren asked Ann if he could return, she only agreed out of necessity. There was not much left of their love, at least as far as she was concerned.

During Warren and Ann's separation, she had started seeing an old boyfriend, Darrell, and flaunted it at Warren when he visited the twins. She continued talking about Darrell even after Warren returned to their house but denied that she was still seeing him. Warren didn't believe her. He became suspicious when she was at the store longer than expected, if she didn't return straight home after visiting her sister, or whenever he didn't know where she was. He drank more, and when he did, he accused Ann of lying to him. They argued constantly. Warren said, "I was trying to reason with her. I was very hurt. Why was she trying to break up our family? The twins needed their mother and their father, not some stranger, in their lives."

Ann vented her frustration to her sister: "I can't stand his yelling and screaming. He threatened to cut me with a razor and another time to 'buy me a bullet.' He forces himself on me. I wake up and find him naked on top of me, trying to have sexual relations. He's pitiful. I wasn't scared of him before—more annoyed that he was such a wimp. But now I don't know…It's worse. I don't know what he might do."

The tension between them grew, and eventually Ann told Warren she wanted a divorce. He pleaded and argued with her but finally agreed to it if she would give him a few weeks to find a place to live. But Ann couldn't wait. She filed for a restraining order against him, claiming that she was afraid for herself and the children. Warren had to be removed from their house by the police. He went to live with his parents.

Within a few months of their separation and after several letters of apology from Warren, Ann cooled off and was more civil toward him. She dropped Tommy and Timmy off every other week at Warren's parents' home for visitation. She would chat with him on the front porch for a few minutes when she came. She accepted Warren's telephone calls if he inquired about the twins but would hang up if he was the least bit argumentative. Ann stopped denying her interest in Darrell, and Warren realized they were seeing each other again. Warren occasionally drove by their house, looking for Darrell's car. He didn't try to go into the house. One evening, however, Ann caught Warren hiding in the bushes outside her living room window. She refused to accept his telephone calls for a few weeks after that. In the meantime, Warren discovered where Darrell lived and went to talk to him.

"I didn't threaten him in any way. I only asked him to consider what he was doing to our family. He was polite and said he would think about it. We shook hands at the end of our conversation," Warren said.

For a while, things seemed to improve. Warren and Ann stopped arguing on the telephone, and he was seeing Tommy and Timmy more frequently and not just at his parents' house. He and Ann were able to chat amicably when exchanging the children. Warren continued to hope for a reconciliation but didn't voice this to her. A few times, Ann let him come into their house for coffee before picking up the children. On returning them, Warren would buy a six-pack of Bud Light, the brand Ann liked, and they would have a couple of beers together before he left. There were even romantic moments, from Warren's point of view, when Ann would giggle as she listened to Warren talk of their courtship. When he left, however, Warren felt empty inside, an emptiness he believed only Ann could fill.

As time went on, Warren became progressively more depressed. He drank even more and called in sick to the warehouse. He called in sick so often that his boss gave him a letter of warning for excessive absences. Still providing for two families, Warren didn't have a clue as to what he would do if he lost his job. He decided to write a letter to Ann's parents in which he told them that he still loved her and wished it hadn't come to this. He hoped they might urge her to save the marriage: "I am truly sorry that I left Ann to go back to my first wife. That was a big mistake, which I realized very quickly. But I guess the damage is done. Now I'm losing my second family. You know Ann is the only woman I really loved," he wrote.

Warren also told his best friend, Jack, that he was very mixed up and that he was thinking of suicide: "At times I want to die, but I don't want someone else bringing up my children…I'd either kill her and take the kids or kill us all, you know…well, not really…but sometimes I feel like that."

The week before Warren's life changed forever, he bought a shotgun at the Walmart sporting goods department and asked the salesman to show him how to use it. He was prepared to kill himself. He had never owned a firearm before. He put the gun into the trunk of his car, bought a six-pack of Bud Light, and went to see Ann, he thought for the last time. She let him in, and as they drank together, he began to cry and told her that he was considering suicide and that he had bought a shotgun. He recalled how tender she was.

"Ann was shocked and seemed genuinely concerned for me. She hadn't been that nice for a long time. She told me that she and the twins needed me and talked me into taking the gun back to the store. I felt hope that maybe this doesn't have to happen. She also asked me to come over the following Saturday to stay with the twins while she went shopping with her sister. She said I could do my laundry there if I liked. She even gave me a hug as I left," he recalled.

Warren returned the shotgun to Walmart the next day. For the rest of the week, he looked forward to Saturday. With frequent bouts of joyful tears, he made new plans for himself and his family. Maybe they could buy a bigger house with a yard for Tommy and Timmy. Maybe he could get a second job to make their lives better. Maybe they could plan for a big Christmas celebration and invite both sides of the family.

On Saturday morning, Warren showed up at Ann's with the usual six-pack of Bud Light for later when she returned from shopping with her sister. He also gave her a couple of lottery tickets that he bought at the 7-Eleven convenience store along with the beer. As Ann was getting into her sister's car, he gave her twenty dollars so the two women could have a nice lunch.

Warren had a good day with Tommy and Timmy. Sure, they were a handful, but somehow he didn't mind. He did his laundry and picked up around the house. He vacuumed the carpet. Later in the day, he cooked macaroni and cheese for the twins and then made a salad to accompany the leftovers, which would be dinner for him and Ann when she returned home.

Late in the afternoon, Warren heard a car pull up to the house and looked out the window. It was not Ann's sister's car, but he thought he recognized it. Ann got out of the car and came inside. She had seen him looking out the window. She gave him a quick hello as she walked past him straight to the twins, who were all over her as they normally were after she'd been away. When Warren asked her whose car that was, she answered curtly, "A friend's…I mean…thanks a lot for watching the kids and all that…but look, I have my life now. You have to try to accept that."

Warren continued to press her about the "friend." She didn't answer. When he asked her directly if it was Darrell's car, she ignored the question and told him that she was taking the twins upstairs for their baths and to put them to bed. Almost as an afterthought, she turned back to him and said he could stay for supper. While waiting for her to come back downstairs, Warren drank a couple of the beers and then went looking for something stronger. He found a three-fourths empty bottle of Jim Beam in the cupboard and a can of ginger ale and fixed himself a bourbon and ginger.

Ann recognized as soon as she came downstairs that Warren was drinking bourbon. She cracked open a Bud Light for herself but was clearly upset and refused to eat the macaroni and cheese or the salad he'd prepared. Warren didn't eat any either. The telephone rang, and she picked it up. Warren heard Ann say, "Yes, he's still here…Yes, I think he does…I can't talk now."

Warren asked Ann, looking straight into her eyes, if it was her sister on the phone. She didn't answer. He pushed: "Was it Darrell?" She nodded that it was and admitted that they had been together all afternoon. She then changed the subject and told Warren that he had too much to drink and should not drive home. He could spend the night on the couch. She went upstairs to bed, and Warren finished the bourbon. He related what he was feeling at the time.

"I don't know what I was feeling. I was mad that she had lied to me, especially since she had been so nice the last time we were together. This threw me for a loop. Was I stupid? How did I think that we might still get together? I still wanted her so much. I thought about her lying in bed alone upstairs and how great it would be to lie next to her. I had a couple more beers and decided to go up to her room. I crawled into bed with her. She didn't push me away. She didn't even stop me from making love to her. When I was done, though, she pulled her nightgown down over her knees with such disgust. I don't know if she had pictured Darrell in her mind or what…I thought she wanted love, then at the end…it's like I was a piece of shit.

"I went downstairs and watched TV for a while. I didn't feel drunk. I guess I don't know for sure if I was or not. But I remember everything. I remember getting madder and madder about Darrell and thinking about Ann and Darrell together. I was confused. I thought everything was going good, and then this.

"I went back up to her bedroom, and somewhere along the way, I made the decision to kill her. I should have just left the house, but I kept thinking about her and Darrell and her taking the kids away from me. She had threatened not to let me see the kids in the past, and I thought she would do it again. These were my kids. I looked at her sleeping in bed and then got on top of her. I put my hands around her neck and began strangling her. She woke up and tried to fight me off, but I held her arms down with my knees so she couldn't move. She then stopped moving. I took her pulse to make sure she was dead, because I knew that I had cut off the oxygen to her brain, and I didn't want her to still be alive and a vegetable. That wouldn't be right. I remember all of this and everything that I did, but it was like someone else was doing it.

"I sat on the side of Ann's bed with her body next to me and thought that all I wanted was to die, but then Tommy and Timmy would grow up without parents or with someone else. It was like she was still taking them away from me. No! We're all going to die tonight. We all have to die. No more pain for any of us. I never considered that I had committed a crime, since I was going to die too; we were all going to die anyway. And this was the right thing to do.

"I went to the bathroom, and all I could find was the twins' sippy cups. I filled one with water and then went into their room. They were sleeping soundly. I went up to Tommy and put a pillow over his head and began to smother him. He kicked and tried to pull my hands off of him, but it was over quickly. I then poured some water from the sippy cup onto his forehead and made a cross there with my thumb; I baptized him. They had not been baptized yet, and I remembered that the nuns who taught me in school said you could do this if there was no priest available. I then went over to Timmy and smothered him. This went faster. I baptized him the same way. I remember thinking that I was sending them both to paradise, and this made me feel good.

"I went back into Ann's room, covered her up, and kissed her on the cheek. It was cold. I then went downstairs and wrote her parents a note to tell them that I was sorry but that I had to do it because Ann was going to leave me and take the twins from me, and I couldn't handle it. I put the note on the kitchen table and threw the macaroni and cheese down the garbage disposal. That's when I decided to jump off the Memorial Bridge. I grabbed my laundry, which I had done during the day; left the door open for the police; and drove off. About halfway to the Memorial Bridge, I pulled over and called 911."

Was Warren insane when he killed Ann and his children? That's what his lawyers say. When we look at the two traditional categories of insanity, the first question would be whether Warren suffered from a mental illness that made him "unable to think rationally" at the time of the killings.[3] Suppose Warren had a mental illness, one that made him falsely believe that Ann was planning to kill him, and he killed her to prevent her from doing what he falsely imagined. In that case, his lawyers might argue that he was unable to think rationally because of a false belief and was, therefore, insane. Of course, his lawyers would have to prove that Warren, in fact, believed he was protecting himself and did not have another reason for killing her. That reason would not explain why he killed Tommy and Timmy. The second question would be, Did Warren suffer from a mental illness that made him "unable to control himself," even though he could think rationally and may have known what he was doing?[4] This question is very difficult to answer, and that's why the category is so controversial. How can we know that Warren really couldn't control himself or that he just didn't? It's not as if he's saying, "That's not me. I could never do something like that," but he did say something similar: "I remember all of this and everything that I did, but it was like someone else was doing it."

Warren's statement suggests a mental process known as *dissociation*, in which there is a split in a person's awareness of him- or herself—of what the person is thinking, feeling, or doing.[5] It can be as simple as being so engrossed in thought that you've driven for half an hour and took the correct exit off the highway without remembering having done it. It can be as complex as traveling to another state and assuming a new identity without remembering who you really are. Does this explain Warren's statement?

Warren's case for insanity is more complicated—or perhaps less complicated depending on one's point of view—because he killed his wife and children in the jurisdiction for Columbia Heights, a community in Washington, DC, where he will stand trial. In Washington, DC, at the time, the definition of insanity was arguably the most straightforward in the country and did not include the traditional categories of insanity. Instead, insanity was determined by the answer to this question: were his actions the "product of a mental illness"?[6]

As it turns out, the definition is not straightforward at all. Psychiatrists, for example, talk about and refer to mental illness every day in their work, but they can't easily define what a mental illness is—at least not with any consistency. I know this from thirty years of teaching forensic psychiatry to psychiatric residents in training and posing that question. So if we can't agree about what a mental illness is, how can we say with reasonable certainty that Warren's actions were or were not the product of a mental illness? Psychiatrists regularly turn for help to a reference book called the *Diagnostic and Statistical Manual of Mental Disorders* (*DSM*),7 but it was compiled to address clinical treatment, public health concerns, and research, not to guide legal decision-making—an important distinction. The *DSM* has undergone seven revisions in the last forty years. Now in its fifth edition (*DSM*-5), it has grown to include almost four hundred mental disorders, ranging from very serious conditions such as schizophrenia, bipolar disorder, and delusional disorder to tobacco-induced sleep disorder, spouse or partner neglect, and gambling disorder. Are all four hundred of these disorders mental illnesses? So, despite what is included in the *DSM*, professionals may still be stuck in defining what mental illness is and, therefore, in determining whether a person's actions, like in Warren's case, were the product of a mental illness.

More alarming is that the judges and lawmakers in Warren's jurisdiction who arrived at the product of mental illness definition of insanity weren't concerned whether there was a good definition of mental illness around or not. Nor were they concerned whether juries even considered the testimony of psychiatrists in making their decisions. Instead, they instructed jurors that it was entirely up to them to decide whether the defendant suffered from a mental illness, by any definition they chose, and if they concluded that the defendant did have a mental illness, they could find him insane. That's a heavy responsibility to impose on a jury. It can lead to inconsistent and unjust verdicts. One jury may find a defendant insane on very little evidence of a mental illness, whereas another may reject insanity even in the face of a well-documented mental illness. And, once again, psychiatrists testifying for or against Warren's claim of insanity may not agree as to what a mental illness is.

Some attempt has been made more recently in a jurisdiction that still uses the product of mental illness test for insanity to help jurors by guiding them to ask themselves relevant questions that apply to serious mental illnesses (e.g., was the defendant suffering from hallucinations or delusions?).[8] But, even with that, those instructions do not confine the jury and can be rejected out of hand. The definition of insanity in most jurisdictions refers to mental illness as a *mental disease* or *mental defect* (also not that helpful) but may provide juries with a formal definition of insanity, typically from one or both of the categories discussed above, (i.e., whether the defendant was unable to think rationally or whether the defendant was unable to control him- or herself). Although Warren's jurisdiction does not provide a better definition than the product of a mental illness, it does give us an opportunity to examine the way his lawyers will try to prove to the jury that Warren's actions must have been due to a mental illness. Their running theme will be to ask, "How else could his actions be explained?" Consider this cross-examination of the prosecution's expert, well-known forensic psychiatrist Dr. Phyllis Webber, by one of Warren's lawyers:

> LAWYER: Doctor, would you agree that Warren was very depressed on the night of the killings?
>
> DR. WEBBER: Yes, I do.
>
> LAWYER: His world was collapsing around him?
>
> DR. WEBBER: Yes.
>
> LAWYER: He was losing his wife and children and saw no future?
>
> DR. WEBBER: Yes.
>
> LAWYER: He was suicidal too?
>
> DR. WEBBER: Yes, he was.
>
> LAWYER: He almost jumped off the Memorial Bridge?
>
> DR. WEBBER: Yes, that's true.
>
> LAWYER: He didn't go to his house that day to kill anyone?

DR. WEBBER: No, he was babysitting and hoping for more contact with his wife that evening.

LAWYER: He didn't plan to kill his wife?

DR. WEBBER: Well, he decided to kill her; it was not just a moment of rage during a fight.

LAWYER: But, Doctor, we're talking about minutes, not hours or days?

DR. WEBBER: It's not clear even to him when he decided to kill her, but he was going back up to her bedroom with that in mind.

LAWYER: But wouldn't you agree, Doctor, that this was abnormal behavior?

DR. WEBBER: Most homicide is abnormal, but he was not out of contact with reality. He knew what he was going to do and what he did, and he wrote a note to her parents apologizing.

LAWYER: What is a delusion, Doctor?

DR. WEBBER: Psychiatrically it means "a fixed, false belief."[9]

LAWYER: Now, wouldn't you agree that killing his children and then baptizing them so they would go to paradise sounds delusional?

DR. WEBBER: No. Wanting them to go to paradise is a belief that many normal people have. It was not because he was out of contact with reality. And even if his thinking was distorted, he killed them so they wouldn't be raised by strangers. Most of all, he felt that if he couldn't have them, no one else would, and they would all have to die.

Lawyer: Isn't that abnormal, Doctor?

Dr. Webber: Yes, of course it is abnormal, but not because of a mental illness.

Lawyer: So what is your definition of mental illness?

This is where it gets tricky. The expert knows that mental illness is not defined in that jurisdiction, but she has to give a definition anyway:

Dr. Webber: The American Psychiatric Association, in an official statement a number of years ago, wrote that mental illness is a "serious mental condition that grossly and demonstrably impairs an individual's ability to perceive or understand reality, and is not based on voluntary intoxication."[10]

Lawyer: You understand, Doctor, that this jury does not have to accept your definition or the definition of the American Psychiatric Association?

Dr. Webber: Yes, I do. It's just a guide for psychiatrists.

Lawyer: What "insane" means is up to the jury?

Dr. Webber: Yes.

Lawyer: You mention "not based on voluntary intoxication." How is that relevant?

Dr. Webber: Well, we know that intoxication reduces one's control mechanisms, but as public policy, you can't excuse yourself of a crime if you drink to the point of intoxication.

Lawyer: So when someone is intoxicated, they lose some of their ability to control themselves?

Dr. Webber: Yes, they may.

Lawyer: Isn't it fair to say that if Warren hadn't been depressed and intoxicated, he wouldn't have killed his wife and children?

Dr. Webber: That helps explain his state of mind, but neither depression nor intoxication made him do it.

Lawyer: But it was harder for him to control his actions?

Dr. Webber: Yes, it was.

To further show that Warren was mentally ill on the night that he killed Ann and his children, his lawyers will also try to demonstrate that the events of that night were totally unexpected, not typical of his character or usual behavior, and therefore must have been the consequence of an abnormal mental state. Warren believes that about himself, or at least that's what he led others to believe when he said, "And I wasn't violent. I never hit a girl or a woman and was never in a physical fight in my life. I saw too much of that from my father and hated him for it."

Warren's narrative, however, is not entirely corroborated. His first wife, Florence, gave her account of what happened one Thanksgiving Day, which may have left doubt in jurors' minds about just how violent he could be. "When I refused to go to bed with him because he was so drunk, he slammed my head into the wall and then dragged me into the bedroom by my feet and forced sex on me," she said.

Ann, Warren's deceased wife, claimed she had become afraid of him, too, and had previously given her account in a restraining order that also contradicts his narrative: "He threatened to cut me with a razor and another time to 'buy me a bullet.' He forces himself on me."

Warren's narrative was also contradicted by his behavior a week before the crime, when he bought a shotgun and took it over to Ann's, even though he said it was only to kill himself. After all, he had considered killing Ann, and possibly the children, based on what he told his friend Jack: "I'd either kill her and take the kids or kill us all."

Another question raised by the prosecutor was whether killing Tommy and Timmy was motivated less by Warren's concern about their future—living with strangers—than by a longstanding anger he felt toward them. The prosecutor argued that from the day they were born, Warren resented the time and attention Ann gave them—time that was taken away from him. These feelings were fueled by Warren's alcohol abuse, coupled with depression over losing his family, and may have led him to conclude that his future was bleak. But was that insanity?

Taken together, do these circumstances explain what Warren did? The vast majority of people who suffer from depression following a divorce—even if they are intoxicated—do not kill their spouses and children. Perhaps Warren's actions can be better explained by examining his personality. For example, it appears he had longstanding problems with relationships. He was sexually driven and showed poor control of his impulses, and he blamed others for his behavior. He lost his first family, and then his second. He faced serious financial problems and was on the verge of losing his job. Warren's distorted view of himself only intensified these problems. In his mind he had sacrificed for the good of his family, only to be punished by both of his wives. Remember, the trigger for Warren's rage on that fateful night was when Ann humiliated him by appearing disgusted as she pulled down her nightgown after he made love to her, making him feel like "a piece of shit."

Warren's actions might be understood in many ways, among which was the damage to his ego, a narrative called *narcissistic injury*,[11] coupled with a need for *righteous slaughter*.[12] If Warren could not have his family, no one else could. He was not about to give up something that was rightfully his. Yes, depression played a part in his reaction, but humiliation and rage may have been the real triggers. Still, Warren knew intuitively that humiliation and rage were a poor excuse for his actions even to himself, so he focused instead on depression. He may have known that preparing to commit suicide by jumping off the Memorial Bridge would dramatically highlight his depression. And the note Warren left for Ann's parents said nothing about killing himself, only that he was sorry for what he did. Doesn't it seem odd that a person about to kill himself would take his clean laundry with him? True, doing so could have been just automatic behavior, like throwing the macaroni and cheese in the garbage disposal before he left. Nonetheless, he may have thought about running away and only later realized it was futile. Do we know how much time went by between the killings and his appearance on the Memorial Bridge? Finally, did he really forget his fear of heights when he was on his way to the bridge?

As for the jury, given that they were bound by no legal definition of mental illness or insanity, how did they define it for themselves? Did they base their decision on a narrative that was favorable or not favorable to Warren? Without knowing it, as happens with many jury decisions, the jurors could have decided between "outrage and sympathy."[13] In my experience, weighing outrage against sympathy often predicts the outcome in a jury verdict. In this case, outrage against Warren for killing Ann and his twin sons may have been greater than the sympathy they might have felt for him because Ann rejected him and because he fell into depression.

The jury rejected Warren's claim of insanity and found him guilty on three counts of first-degree murder. He was sentenced to life in prison without the possibility of parole. Was that verdict fair to someone who suffers from depression, alcoholism, and probably a personality disorder?[14] Aren't those mental illnesses? Why not? Is Warren a cold-blooded killer when he expresses so much emotion?

It's worth noting that the jury might have had more sympathy for Warren if he had killed only his wife, Ann, and if they believed that killing her was unplanned. He might not have been found insane but may be guilty of only second-degree murder or manslaughter.[15] It was the murder of his sons, Tommy and Timmy, that the jurors appear to have found unforgivable; they weren't moved by his statement that he was "sending them both to paradise." For that matter, was he baptizing them to send them to paradise, or did he say this to himself so he could feel he did something holy, something good, and leave himself a less tainted narrative of who he was? Was this why he also didn't want Ann to be a vegetable—he needed to be sure she was dead—because that "wouldn't be right"? Don't we all have conflicting narratives about ourselves, among which we can choose when the need arises? Warren had two other conflicting narratives: one that his real love was Florence, and the other that it was Ann. Did he truly believe each when he needed to? Are our love narratives so fickle?

The Prince of Wales

Figure 6. Camillo Borghese, sixth prince of Salmona, DigitalVision Vectors, photo: duncan 1890, Getty Images #94413266.

Frankie had been waiting for three days. There was still no word from Ron, not that Ron owed him a phone call, but he could be more considerate. When Frankie heard a car driving into the parking lot of their apartment building, he ran to the window—it wasn't Ron. Near suppertime, Frankie left the apartment and went outside to have a cigarette. He sat on the front steps casually smoking, pretending he was only there to smoke. On the afternoon of the third day, he had several cigarettes and stayed outside even when it started to rain. He thought he heard someone calling to him: "Get out of the rain." Maybe that was Ron? Maybe he took the back entrance? Frankie ran inside and up the stairs to their apartment, but no one was there. Fifteen minutes later, Ron came through the door, drenched, just like Frankie. Frankie was glad to see him. Ron smiled sheepishly and went into his bedroom to change into a sweat suit. Frankie went into his own bedroom and put on pajamas. He thought he heard Ron jabbering to himself but couldn't make out what he said. Frankie came out first and set the supper table for the two of them. When Ron came out, he went to the refrigerator, took out a steak, and pointed it at Frankie, asking whether he wanted one too. Frankie nodded, then said, "I'll get the steak knives."

As Frankie was rinsing off one of the knives, Ron bent over to get the large frying pan from the oven drawer. When Ron stood up, Frankie was behind him and stabbed Ron in the neck with the steak knife. Ron stood dazed, then slumped to the floor on his knees. Frankie jumped on him and continued stabbing. He stabbed him three times, four times, while Ron whimpered, "Frankie, this is me, Ron."

It didn't matter what he said. With a last burst of energy, Ron crawled into the living room to get away from Frankie, but Frankie crawled after him, stabbing furiously all over his body until Ron stopped moving for good. Dropping the knife on the ground, Frankie went back to the kitchen in his blood-soaked pajamas and called the police. When the police came, Frankie was sitting at the kitchen table with his head down and his hands dangling at his sides. He asked the police, "Am I the Prince of Wales?"

The police looked puzzled and took Frankie into custody to the police station, where he agreed to be interviewed. He did not say much but only that he had killed Ron with a steak knife and didn't know why. The evidence at the crime scene told the rest of the story, even if not the explanation. Frankie signed his written statement "Francis Townsend." This was unusual since he hated the name "Francis" and was embarrassed when his mother called him that—no one else did. Frankie did tell the police about his psychiatric treatment and that he was being seen at the local mental health center. He also reported that he had tried to kill himself in the past and felt like killing himself now. After his history of psychiatric treatment was verified by the police, and with Frankie looking quite dazed, he was brought directly to the psychiatric unit at the county jail.

A well-known forensic psychiatrist, Dr. Robert Gleason, was retained by Frankie's lawyer to evaluate him. He learned that Frankie has bipolar disorder, a serious mental illness previously known as manic-depressive disorder, in which patients have dramatic mood changes. At times, they are depressed, hopeless, and without a will to live; at other times, they are manic (or hypomanic, which is just short of manic) and have excessive energy, inflated beliefs about themselves and their abilities, racing thoughts, and rapid speech. In some cases, they are *psychotic*[1]—out of touch with reality—and may say things like "Everyone knows I have special powers," or "I'm going to be president of the United States," or "Women fall in love with me if I blink my eyes three times." Bipolar disorder often runs in families and is frequently associated with alcohol or drug abuse. Frankie's father, a successful owner of a small chain of grocery stores, was a functioning alcoholic, and Frankie's father's mother had been in a psychiatric institution years ago, where she received shock treatment for suicidal depression. Frankie's two older brothers graduated from college and had no mental disorders. They were successful businessmen and were much more accomplished than Frankie—certainly in their father's eyes. Frankie's father wanted him to become an accountant so he would at least have a stable job in his grocery business; he doubted Frankie could work elsewhere. Frankie graduated from high school and began studying accounting at the state university but hated it. He dropped out after his second year. His father let him work as a bookkeeper at one of the grocery stores. Before long, Frankie had his first mental breakdown. Frankie reported the details to Dr. Gleason at the jail.

"My real love was theater. My father wanted me to join the speech club when I was in high school so I could build up some confidence in myself. But, on sign-ups, I went into the drama club room by accident, and from there I began competitive drama recitations. This took me to school tournaments all over the state. I also joined a community theater group later—not that I got the lead roles all the time, but people thought I was good. I was totally into my characters. That's what happened before my first breakdown. I was playing the role of Montresor in Edgar Allan Poe's *Cask of Amontillado*—that's the guy who chained up his enemy Fortunato and buried him alive behind a brick wall in the wine cellar. I started thinking I really was Montresor and that I was so powerful I could read people's minds…After one of my performances, my father and mother took me out to a late dinner. I kept standing up and sitting down at the table because

I thought my father wanted me to give a speech. Then the waiter smiled at me. I thought he was making a pass, so I grabbed a knife from the table and went after him. The police were called, but they let me go since they knew my father. I felt so guilty that I drank a bottle of iodine later that night to kill myself, but it only made me vomit. Then I took a kitchen knife and cut off the tip of my small finger at the knuckle and buried it in the backyard. I said a prayer and promised that this would never happen again. My parents freaked out when they saw my hand."

Frankie was psychiatrically hospitalized for eight weeks, where for the first time he was diagnosed as having bipolar disorder and prescribed mood-stabilizing and antipsychotic medication. He was advised not to continue in the community theater group. In his therapy, he discussed his feelings of failure and also his sexual confusion. Frankie had a girlfriend, Janice, with whom he was intimate, although it was not satisfying, and he didn't believe she loved him. Yet he liked walking down the street with her, pretending in his mind that he was her gigolo. Frankie had one brief gay relationship in college and told his father, knowing that his father would be horrified. He was. That relationship did not last, but what followed was a series of uncommitted gay encounters, which continued even while he was dating Janice. He eventually asked Janice if she would like a threesome to include one of his male friends. Janice was shocked, and that was the end of Frankie and Janice's relationship. Being free of Janice was a relief, but it led to his second psychiatric hospitalization.

"I was living on my own then. That was better since being around my parents was too stressful. My mother would try to approach me cautiously about my 'plans.' She would say things like, 'Francis, how much money do you have saved?' I'd go bonkers. When I picked up the table lamp and held it over her head one night, they got scared and let me move out, but living on my own, I had too much time to myself. I started to have these 'waves of fear,' especially when I used a knife. It was like I might do something bad with it. I remember when I was a kid, my father made a ritual of sharpening knives at home with an electric sharpener, and I never liked it. I don't know if I was afraid because of what he might do with the knives or what I might do. Now that same feeling was coming back to me. I saw my father frequently when he came by the grocery store to check on things.

He didn't say much to me and left me alone to do the bookkeeping. I worked in an office on a landing a few steps above the floor with a plate-glass window wrapped around the office so you could overlook the store. The store manager left me alone too. I guess they both thought I was safe there. I did feel safe there, more than at home or in my apartment. I'd look through the window into the store and think that I was in an interplanetary transporting chamber that magically took me from one galaxy to another. I'd visit black holes and land on planets where only worms lived. Time passed by without my knowing it.

"Then one of the younger male cashiers, Jimmy, started coming up to the office to say hi or to get advice about something. He wasn't much more than five years younger than me. He seemed interested in me and was very polite. So one day I asked him if he would like to go out after work for a beer. He said okay, and we went out. Somehow, we started talking about my office and how I was away from everyone else, and I told him about the interplanetary transporting chamber. I could see his face change, and I knew I said too much. A few minutes later, he politely indicated he had to go home and said, 'See you tomorrow,' but I knew he wouldn't come up to the office again. At my apartment, the thoughts about knives streamed in like a movie playing at fast-forward, faster and faster each night. Knives were all around me. I was dodging them, but they weren't real and couldn't hurt me. So why was I so afraid? I took out several knives from the kitchen drawer, placed them on the table, and forced myself to look at them to try and get over my fear. Then I tried to decide which one I should use on myself and where to cut. I took a serrated bread knife, placed it against my forearm, and began slowly sawing into my skin. The pain felt good; it was even thrilling. Could I go all the way? I did it with my finger before. Why not? Just then the telephone rang. It was my mother checking on me. She didn't call me 'Francis'; she just said that she was concerned. I broke down and told her what I was doing. She begged me to stop and came over with my father."

Frankie was psychiatrically hospitalized the second time for almost three months. He was placed on larger doses of antipsychotic medication and an antidepressant, one safer to use for bipolar disorder (some antidepressants can kick someone into a manic state). When he was about to be discharged, Frankie was advised not to live alone and consider finding a roommate. Frankie's parents agreed. With the help of a social worker, they identified a young man who was also a patient at the mental health center. He was said to be very stable. He and Frankie could be a support for each other, both having dealt with mental illness, and their case manager could check in on both of them from time to time. A couple of weeks later, Ron Davis moved in.

Ron was gay, but he and Frankie had no sexual relations together. Ron had his own circle of friends and viewed Frankie only as a roommate. Ron was messy and scattered his things all over the apartment, and he could be moody. Sometimes Frankie thought Ron was taking advantage of him. Frankie did not confront him directly but wrote Ron a letter outlining his concerns. Ron read the letter and apologized. Their relationship improved. They each discussed it with their therapists and the case manager from the mental health center and were complimented on how well they resolved the issue. Frankie and Ron had no conflicts over the next several months. Frankie continued working at the grocery store during the day, and Ron worked the second shift as a nurse's aide. When Ron went out with his friends, he didn't always return to the apartment the same night. The next day, he might show up at noon and would not say much to Frankie about where he had been. Ron did mention to Frankie, however, that there was a man in whom he was interested and who had been taking him to church.

A week before Ron's death, Frankie brought over a number of personal items and some furniture from his parents' home to his apartment. In a box of documents was an old scrapbook that his father kept with pictures and other mementos of Frankie's life. As Frankie paged through the book, he began feeling depressed. He thought that he should not have turned out this way, that he was a failure, and that he was all alone. Even Ron found someone.

"Our relationship became only functional; it would never be close. I was never attracted to Ron sexually, but I thought we might be closer. He didn't need me as he did before. He didn't need me at all…I started becoming delusional.[2] At the grocery store, when customers walked by my office window, I thought they were laughing at me, toying with me. The store manager said, 'It will all be different when the store is renovated,' and I thought to myself, how will it be different? Will I have a new role? A woman customer who was way overdressed for grocery shopping looked at me and nodded so formally. She was like royalty, and the other customers were like her servants following her out of the store. They knew who she was. She seemed to know who I was. But who was I? What did she know? I held a ballpoint pen holder out in front of me with two hands like a chalice, then released it and let it drop to the floor. It crashed with an echo. This was a sign. Maybe we should go to war with France. Maybe we should launch our ships. I remember lying down on the floor in the office meditating, trying to discover who I was. Then it came to me: I was the illegitimate son of Queen Elizabeth. The store manager came up and saw me on the floor and told me to go home, to take a few days off. But when I came home, Ron was not there. Was he in England? Was he my father? I remember sitting on the kitchen floor crying and placing a slice of white bread on my forehead, holding it with the fingertips of my right hand, like I was about to cross myself with it. Was this my coronation? I heard a voice say, 'Francis Townsend. You will be the next king of England.' I then went to the computer to type my thoughts. As I typed, I believed the computer was directly connected to the royal family at Buckingham Palace.

"The next two days are all jumbled, and I don't remember everything. I know I started to feel that the world was ending and that there was no hope. Then I thought that I alone could save the world. A voice—I don't know whose—told me that I had to kill something, and someone answered the voice and said, 'If thy will be done, Lord.' It frightened me, so I went for a walk. When I came back, the two voices were still there along with the thought of killing, and the knives started streaming in really fast, and the voice said, 'Be there.' I couldn't eat. I couldn't sleep.

"When I sat on the front steps and heard someone call, 'Get out of the rain,' I was overjoyed that Ron was home—but he wasn't. When he did come back, it was like no big deal to him. I was glad he was back, but killing was still in my head. I felt, I've got to do this, I just got to…and then a feeling, or a voice, or a thought—Princess Anne…a female bitch—and I attacked Ron," Frankie said.

Other than asking the police, "Am I the Prince of Wales?" when they first arrived, Frankie did not report any of his beliefs about being royalty during the interview with police after his arrest. Their reports noted that he was oriented to his surroundings and accurate in the information he provided about himself, his family, where he worked, and where he lived. The video recording of the interview did show him to be withdrawn, stunned, or dazed, and he paused before he answered each question as if the question was confusing. In the psychiatric unit at the county jail, he appeared to the staff to be withdrawn and depressed, but he reported no voices and no bizarre or irrational beliefs. They were concerned he might be suicidal. However, he assured the staff that he would not harm himself. He did not need additional psychiatric medication. Within a few days, he was transferred to the general inmate population at the county jail, awaiting trial for the murder of his roommate.

Dr. Gleason, the psychiatrist retained by Frankie's lawyer and who diagnosed him as having bipolar disorder, testified at the trial that Frankie was psychotic, that he was out of touch with reality, and that he didn't know what he was doing when he killed Ron.

"Mr. Townsend's bipolar disorder is well documented in his psychiatric records from two hospitalizations. There are times when he becomes profoundly depressed and suicidal and engages in self-mutilating behavior. At other times, he is manic. He feels he has special powers and can travel the universe in an interplanetary transporting chamber. He also began to believe he could read people's minds and that he was someone important.

"In the days before he killed Ron Davis, Mr. Townsend had a grandiose delusion, a fixed false belief that he was royalty, the illegitimate son of Queen Elizabeth, the Prince of Wales. This was clearly psychotic thinking. He believed he was to be the next king of England but also that the world was ending, and he needed to save it. To do so, he had to kill something. There is no evidence that he had any animosity toward Mr. Davis to justify violence, much less a killing. They were just roommates. Mr. Townsend's mind raced faster and faster. He heard voices telling him to kill, and Mr. Davis was just in the wrong place at the wrong time. What Mr. Townsend was thinking didn't make sense. His actions were all because of his psychotic mental illness. In my opinion, Mr. Townsend did not know what he was doing and did not know that it was wrong; he was just trying to save the world. He was insane at the time he killed Mr. Davis."

Was Frankie suffering from a mental illness when he killed Ron? If so, was this insanity?[3] Both are not easy questions to answer. However, in the jurisdiction where the crime occurred, the law helped define what it takes, beyond mental illness, for someone to qualify as insane. In defining insanity, the law selected from one of the two traditional categories of insanity—that is, was the person unable to think rationally?[4] Dr. Gleason also knew that definition of insanity had two options in that category, and he used them both in his testimony by saying that Frankie "did not know what he was doing" and "did not know that it was wrong."[5] He believed that both applied, which made his opinion that much stronger.

Dr. Gleason faced one big obstacle in forming his opinion; as in all psychiatric evaluations of insanity, he did not evaluate Frankie at the time of the killing for obvious reasons. He wasn't there; how could he have been? He saw Frankie days or maybe weeks later. The only person besides Frankie who was there at the time of the killing was Ron, and obviously he can't be a witness. So Dr. Gleason relied on what Frankie told him: that he believed he was the Prince of Wales and was confused about who Ron was. How does he know Frankie's story is true? Did Frankie really believe he was the Prince of Wales? Was he really trying to save the world by killing Ron? Psychiatrists often rely on their ability to know who's telling the truth when they hear it, but they can be wrong just as often. What helped Dr. Gleason form his opinions in this case was that Frankie had a documented history of a mental illness, bipolar disorder, and he had similar unusual beliefs in the past when he wasn't facing a murder charge. What also helped is that Frankie's description of what he was thinking at the time was so bizarre that it might be hard to make up.

Dr. Gleason's next obstacle was Frankie's inconsistent early statements. When police first came to Frankie's apartment, he did ask them, "Am I the Prince of Wales?" But in his interview with the police, he knew who he really was and did not say he was royalty. He signed his correct name on his written statement; he didn't sign it "Prince of Wales." He knew his correct address when he called 911; he didn't say it was "Buckingham Palace." He also didn't describe any further "delusions" about royalty to the staff at the county jail. How could these delusions, which sound psychotic, end so abruptly once he killed Ron? Forensic psychiatrists frequently face this issue, and prosecutors usually don't believe claims of insanity that end right after the crime was committed—namely, *temporary insanity*.[6] It's easier to claim temporary insanity than it is to prove it. Temporary insanity is not a separate condition, it just means that the acute symptoms of a mental illness were brief and, perhaps conveniently, limited to the time of the crime. Juries in general don't accept insanity claims easily either, particularly temporary insanity, because the evidence comes mainly from what the defendant says he was thinking or feeling, and, by law, once the defendant raises the issue of insanity as an excuse for the crime, he has to prove it.[7] That's different than what the prosecutor has to prove beyond a reasonable doubt in a criminal case—that is, that the defendant had the wrongful intent and committed the wrongful act.[8] With the insanity defense, the defendant has to prove that he is not responsible even though he committed the crime and may have wanted the result—in this case, to kill Ron—which is not easy to prove. That's why only one out of ten criminal defendants consider raising insanity as a defense and why only one out of ten of those are successful.[9] What actually happens in a trial is that once the jury has heard all the evidence, the judge will instruct them that they can only find Frankie was insane when he killed Ron if he has proved to them that he was. It is not up to the prosecutor to prove that Frankie wasn't. Since prosecutors know how hard this is, they may not hire their own psychiatrist to evaluate Frankie to provide a rebutting opinion. They may choose instead to put holes in Dr. Gleason's testimony on cross-examination. If the jury does not believe Dr. Gleason, they may not believe Frankie either. In many cases, however, prosecutors do hire their own psychiatrists who will have the right to personally evaluate Frankie and come to their own conclusions about his insanity. Because Frankie has raised his mental state as an issue, he can't say, "I'm not going to talk to the prosecutor's psychiatrist," or "I don't want the psychiatrist to know everything about me." Once a person opens the door by claiming insanity, then his mental state, his life history, and his other personal information all become fair game. It is not possible to understand someone's mental illness by looking only at what happened when the crime was committed. The person's whole story needs to come out, and this may not be what Frankie wants.

The bottom line in criminal cases, regardless of what defense is used—insanity or some other defense—juries want to understand what really happened and why it happened. At Frankie's trial, there was no disagreement as to what happened; he killed Ron. But there was disagreement about why he did it. Does Frankie's story explain his actions best? It's a difficult story to follow and does not tie together well. However, if Frankie was psychotic and was not thinking rationally, then his story wouldn't be rational either. It's not unusual for psychotic people to jump around from one topic to another, and only they may understand the connections. For example, it makes no sense that Frankie thought he may be the Prince of Wales but also had to kill Ron to save the world. But, taking Frankie's story as a whole, seeing the customer at the grocery store and thinking she was Queen Elizabeth, thinking he would be the next king of England, and calling Ron "Princess Anne…a female bitch" as he was killing him sounds pretty crazy, so he must have been insane, right? How could someone who wasn't insane make up that story? Also, there is no evidence that Frankie made up the delusions that led to his prior psychiatric hospitalizations, and he did have a history of a serious mental illness. However, was it serious enough to cause him to kill Ron? In any case, we do know that in this jurisdiction, just having a mental illness isn't enough for an insanity defense. The question is, did Frankie not know what he was doing or that it was wrong?

A forensic psychiatrist, hired by the prosecutor to evaluate Frankie, Dr. Phyllis Webber, provided a different opinion on Frankie's mental state at the time of the crime.

"Mr. Townsend does suffer from a chronic mental illness, bipolar disorder, and has had episodes of psychotic delusions that impair his ability to *think* rationally. However, even if he is psychotic, it does not mean that everything he does is psychotic or that every moment he is just as psychotic. Mr. Townsend may have had delusions about being royalty and may or may not have believed that he needed to save the world by killing something or someone, but immediately after he killed Mr. Davis, he telephoned the police and knew who he was and what he had done and that it was criminal. He did not continue to believe that he was royalty and did not require additional psychiatric treatment, beyond the medication he had already been taking prior to the killing, in order to recover.

"Mr. Townsend's behavior cannot be separated from his feelings about Mr. Davis, how Mr. Davis stayed out all night, how he had formed a relationship with another man, and how he had not returned for three days. Mr. Townsend denies that he had any sexual interest in Mr. Davis, but his actions and the rage that accompanied the killing suggest very intense feelings toward Mr. Davis, possibly accompanied by a sense of jealousy and betrayal.

"While Mr. Townsend has a history of mental illness, he was also a skilled actor in the earlier part of his life, with experience in drama. His description of how he believed he was connected to the royal family has a dramatic flavor and could represent exaggeration, which makes at least part of his story unreliable. Of course, it would be difficult for someone to make up a story that sounds so psychotic, unless…they had been through a psychosis before and could use those memories to create a psychotic story—more psychotic than he actually was at the time.

"This does not mean that Mr. Townsend is necessarily malingering or lying about what he *experienced*. However, in my opinion, he has not shown that his actions were because of a royalty delusion, when more ordinary feelings of jealousy and betrayal could explain his rage."

Frankie did not testify in his trial, and he did not interact much with his lawyer. Most of the time, he looked down at the table in front of him with his hands dangling at his sides. The jury rejected Frankie's claim of insanity and convicted him of first-degree murder. Frankie was unable to prove that he was insane—that his delusional story explained his actions better than another motive. He was sentenced to life in prison. In the course of the next four years, he was hospitalized on the psychiatric unit at the prison three times for psychotic delusional thinking. In the last of these hospitalizations, the treatment team believed that he was exaggerating his symptoms and transferred him back to the general inmate population after only two days. The next morning, Frankie was found dead in his cell. He had slashed his throat with a shank he constructed from a metal spoon stolen from the cafeteria.[10] Did Frankie commit suicide because of his mental illness? Did he still think he was royalty? Does it make a difference? If Frankie was psychotic when he killed Ron and wasn't lying about having delusions, could he have created the royalty story after the killing to give himself an excuse for what he did? Was a part of Frankie enraged at Ron, but the other part of Frankie didn't know it? Which part would be guilty of murder?[11]

The Witch Is Dead

Figure 7. "The Witchcraft at the Stake," Hulton Archive, photo: Fototeca Storica Nazionale, Getty Images #924753252.

On Monday, October 12, Melville police drove up to Marcel and Phyllis Lambert's farmhouse. The Lamberts had just returned from a long weekend visiting Phyllis's brother, and Marcel was bringing the suitcases into the house. The sergeant and his partner stepped out of the cruiser and asked Marcel if his son Dennis was home. Marcel hadn't seen Dennis yet, but his car was there, so he assumed that Dennis was home. Marcel said, "He would be in his apartment over the garage. Is anything wrong?" The sergeant said he just wanted to ask Dennis a few questions, so Marcel pointed to the outside stairway that led up to the apartment. The apartment was built three years earlier after Dennis and his father had their last physical altercation in which Phyllis had to pull Dennis off his father as they rolled around on the floor punching each other. Dennis was just out of high school and couldn't live on his own, but he couldn't live with them any longer either. The sergeant and his partner climbed the stairway and knocked on the door. Dennis opened it. He had a cigarette in his hand, and the television was on in the room. He didn't appear rattled by their presence and simply said, "Yeah?" They asked if they could come in and talk to him about Sally Duchesne. He let them in, and they all sat down on chairs in the small living area. The sergeant told Dennis that Sally never made it to her aunt's house in South Carolina and asked Dennis when he had last seen her. Dennis told them that he dropped her off at the bus station Saturday morning, and he didn't know any more than that. The sergeant asked him what their relationship was like. Dennis explained.

"We were sort of going together—kind of like a girlfriend, not really, more of a friend. She was into all that Wicca stuff…weird…She and some friends would have, like, these black masses; they thought they were witches or something. She said she could talk to spirits. I didn't pay much attention to all that.

"We smoked weed together sometimes, but she really liked acid, and I wasn't into that. I dropped some once or twice, but I didn't like it. Made me paranoid.

"She said she wanted to go to South Carolina to see her aunt—maybe stay there. I was cool with that. She was gonna take the bus Saturday morning and asked me to take her down to the station. I said, 'Why don't you spend Friday night with me here?' My parents were going away anyhow, not that it's a big deal, I do pretty much what I want. She said okay.

"I picked her up about five o'clock Friday afternoon, and she told me she had a surprise for me, but she wanted to eat something first. We stopped by McDonald's, and then I drove her back here. She had a suitcase with her and a plastic bag with some brownies that she made, she said just for me. We sat down by the TV and ate the brownies. She kept smiling at me funny as we ate, and then I knew she had baked something in 'em. At first, I thought it was just some weed, but it seemed a little stronger…We just chilled out together, got it on, and fell asleep. It was a great night. The next morning, I drove her to the station, and that was that. She asked me to visit her in South Carolina sometime if I had a chance. She didn't get along too well with her parents and was hoping to live with her aunt, but she wanted to try it out first.

"That's about all I can tell you. With Sally, you never know what she'll do. She may have just gone off somewhere else or with someone else."

The sergeant questioned him further, but Dennis insisted that he had not heard from Sally since he dropped her off at the bus station and didn't know where she was. They thanked him and asked if he would be around for the next few days in case they had any more questions. He said he would be and would help in any way he could.

The Lambert farm had been in the family for more than three generations since their relatives came from Quebec and began raising dairy cattle there. The farmhouse was much the same structure as originally built, but the garage was a later addition. It was built for one automobile and a small tractor but was so cluttered with rusting machinery, odd-sized lumber, tools rarely used, and just plain junk that Marcel's car was parked outside. There was a door from the garage into the kitchen of the farmhouse. There was no indoor access to the second floor of the garage, which had been for storage but was remodeled into Dennis's apartment. Dennis insisted that there should be only one entry, the stairway on the outside, to discourage his parents or anyone else from going into his space. Dennis's car was parked outside as well. The old barn stood some hundred feet down a dirt path. There had been no dairy cattle in it for years. The building was dilapidated, and its wood-plank floor was rotted, exposing worm-infested earth below. Marcel's parents could not do the farmwork anymore, and Marcel had no interest in dairy cattle. Marcel worked at the Pitney Paper Mill where Dennis also worked. They drove to and from work separately to limit their contact with each other and avoid altercations. Marcel was a righteous, inflexible man who could be violent. Phyllis had learned to keep quiet and not challenge him out of fear of his temper. Dennis, however, spoke out and unintentionally or intentionally provoked his father. Marcel's first marriage ended in a messy divorce; there was a restraining order prohibiting him from having contact with his ex-wife or unaccompanied visits with his daughter, Marie. However, once he married Phyllis, Marie was allowed to spend weekends at their farmhouse. Marie became close to Phyllis and loved helping with Dennis when he was a baby. Marie and Dennis were sister and brother even though they had different mothers.

Dennis was a troubled kid and a poor student. By middle school, he began skipping classes. At the end of almost every school year, he was short on credits and needed summer school to be promoted to the next grade. In high school, he took technical classes and had some aptitude for automotive mechanics. He also worked at a gas station. He smoked a lot of weed.

Sally Duchesne was a townie who went to the same high school as Dennis, although they hardly knew each other the first couple of years. When she began driving, she stopped for gas where Dennis worked. He thought she was hot. She was a rebel like he was, and an acidhead. They hung out together, but she also had her own circle of friends. Dennis thought her friends were weird. They talked about Wicca and got together to chant, use "magical tools," and burn incense. That could have turned him off, but Dennis was totally into Sally, so he didn't talk about it with her. She began spending Friday or Saturday nights at his apartment, telling her parents she was with one of her girlfriends. Sally's parents did not approve of her behavior, but they approved less of Dennis. Dennis wished that Sally would stay with him every weekend night. He wanted to be more than just her boyfriend and spoke to her of his plans to move away to someplace warmer once he saved enough money; he wanted her to come with him. Dennis would get mad if she told him that she was going to be with her Wicca friends that weekend, and several times he stopped seeing her for a week or two; then he called her again. After they graduated from high school and he was hired at the Pitney Paper Mill, Dennis began talking more seriously about their future together. Sometimes her eyes would glaze over, which he thought was because of the acid. He asked her to stick to weed with him, but he could tell she was still dropping acid.

On Wednesday, October 14, Melville police officers came back to the Lambert farmhouse with a search warrant that gave them access to all the structures on the property. Dennis was named as a suspect in Sally's disappearance, since he was the last to see her, and she had spent the night before with him. It was likely there was evidence on the property that could help in the search. Four police officers in two squad cars arrived, one of them with a veteran K-9, Amos. Amos smelled Sally's clothing that her parents provided and became excited as he was led up to Dennis's apartment over the garage. Other than a bong for smoking weed and cigarette papers in one of Dennis's dresser drawers, not much else was found. However, when Amos and the officers went back down the stairway, the dog began pulling hard against his leash toward the direction of the barn. Amos led the officers to the barn, and when the barn door was opened, he immediately dashed to an abandoned calving pen. Its floor was covered with rotted planks, broken cattle headlocks, and a decaying mattress. When the officers moved the debris to the side, they saw fresh dirt in one corner of the pen. Amos began digging into the dirt. An hour later, Sally Duchesne's hacked corpse, wrapped in bedsheets and a plastic mattress cover, was taken away by the coroner. Dennis Lambert was arrested that same afternoon at the Pitney Paper Mill.

As soon as Dennis saw his foreman and the police officers coming down the hall, he knew it was over. It was like the blood ran out of him, and he had no energy to resist, explain, or argue. Two state troopers from the major crime division drove him to their police barracks, brought him into an interview room, and read him his Miranda rights. Although he was hesitant at first, he agreed to be interviewed. They advised him that the interview was being audio and video recorded. He didn't object. He gave them only short answers at first without much detail but then acknowledged that he knew why he was arrested. Dennis relaxed a bit and began telling his story of what happened to Sally.

"Like I told the cops before, she wanted to spend the night with me and said she had a surprise. But she had this smile on her, so I knew something was up. So she brought out these brownies she baked. She ate two, and I ate two. I was starting to feel really mellow, so I knew she had put something in them. I figured it was some really good weed. Okay. That's all right. So we had the TV on, but we're not, like, watching the show—just kind of letting it happen. Then I started feeling nervous like butterflies in my stomach or something and feeling a little scared. I didn't know why. I wasn't scared of her or nothing, at least not yet, but just scared, you know. Like something bad could happen. I closed all the blinds on the windows, not like anyone could look in or anything; I just didn't want them open. I made sure the door was locked too, but I couldn't stop the butterflies.

"Then she got on the bed in this cross-legged position with her eyes closed and started humming…then chanting something I didn't know. Now I was getting a little scared of her. She had, like, this halo all around her body, and the halo was turning different colors. She just kept chanting. What was she trying to do? My bed that she was sitting on looked like it was starting to melt, like she was sitting on top of some kind of lava, white lava. I didn't know what she was going to do next. She still had her eyes closed and was chanting. It was like she wasn't even there. But she was there. She was turning colors and all. I went over to the cabinet underneath my sink where I kept some tools, my flashlight, stuff like that, you know. I had a small hand ax that I bought for protection, being that I'm alone in my apartment a lot of times, and my parents are gone. Never had to use it and didn't think I was going to use it then. But just in case anything weird happened, you know.

"So I was just sitting there thinking where she was going with all of this. Her eyes were still closed, and then they slowly opened. Great, she was coming out of it. But that didn't happen. They weren't her eyes anymore. They were, like, purple, and she was still, like, riding on this white lava cloud, and I looked at her face, and it was getting wrinkly like she started growing old right there in front of me. She did not look good. It wasn't even her. She'd been into that Wicca stuff and all, but I always thought it was her imagination or that it gave her and her buddies something to do when they were dropping acid. But now she looked like she was turning into a witch. I was really freaked out. I didn't know who she was anymore. I tried calling to her, 'Sally, Sally, cut it out. That's enough.' Nothing happened, but her head slowly turned to me, and this was an old woman now with deep-purple eyes. I knew right then I wasn't getting out of there alive. I didn't even think of running out the door. I'd never get away from this creature. Then I jumped out of my chair and ran over to the bed, lifted my ax over my head, and swung down on her with everything I had. I kept swinging, and she kept moving. It seemed like forever.

When she stopped moving, I stepped back. Her whole body was melting into the white lava and all the different colors too. The purple in her eyes became larger like pancakes with a wavy edge, and then her whole face was purple. I was wiped out. I hardly had the strength to walk over to my chair. I closed my eyes so I wouldn't have to see it anymore.

"When I woke up, it was getting on to morning, and all I could think of is that I had this really spooky dream. But when I looked over at the bed, there was Sally, all bloodied with her eyes open but not moving. My ax was right next to her. Now I really freaked out. It was no dream. It really happened, and I really killed her, but it wasn't her I was killing; it was something from another world. I had an awful headache. No one would believe my story. I knew that, so I wrapped Sally's body up in the bedsheet and mattress cover and tied her all up with some cable that I found in the garage. I took off all my clothes 'cause they had blood on them and put them in a plastic sack. I stuck the ax in there too. I put on a new set of clothes and put new sheets on the bed. Then I left the apartment and left Sally there, too, and drove with the sack down to Kmart, which hadn't opened yet, and threw the sack in one of their dumpsters.

"I came back to my apartment hoping that somehow Sally had disappeared, but there she was all wrapped up. I kept thinking how this could have happened. She shouldn't have made those brownies. It wasn't just weed in there. It was acid. She wanted me to go tripping with her on our last night. She shouldn't have started that Wicca stuff either…When it got dark, I dragged Sally's body down the steps and put it into a wheelbarrow. I grabbed a shovel and wheeled her down to the barn where I buried her. Look, I know I killed her, but she shouldn't have done that—mixed that acid in there. I wish I could have told somebody what happened, but I was scared. It was just too crazy. No one would believe me."

At this point, Dennis began crying and saying how sorry he was for what happened to Sally. He also told the troopers he was too tired to go on with the interview and thought he should speak to a lawyer before he said anything else.

Dr. Felix Mosley was a prominent psychiatrist and addictionologist who was an expert on hallucinogens, including LSD. He was a full professor at a prominent East Coast university and had an impressive résumé. He had written five books, as well as chapters in another twenty. He had over 165 publications in peer-reviewed journals, more than half of which directly or indirectly touched on LSD. He was asked by the Food and Drug Administration to chair a task force composed of well-known addictionologists throughout the country to address the types of mental disorders that are a consequence of hallucinogens. While not a forensic psychiatrist, Dr. Mosley had testified in a dozen criminal cases about the effects of LSD on a criminal defendant's behavior.

Dennis's lawyer contacted Dr. Mosley to see if he would be willing to testify at the trial about the impact of LSD on Dennis on the night that he killed Sally Duchesne. In addition to Dr. Mosley testifying about LSD and what it can do to a person, the lawyer would send Dr. Mosley the audio and video recording of Dennis's interview with the state police, so that Dr. Mosley could provide an opinion on whether Dennis's description of what he experienced that night was consistent with hallucinations caused by LSD. Dennis's lawyer did not file a notice of an insanity defense. Instead, he planned to argue that Dennis had *diminished capacity*[1] on the night he killed Sally and was not guilty of homicide, much less first-degree murder as he had been charged. More specifically, he would argue Dennis was experiencing psychotic hallucinations brought about by involuntary intoxication with LSD. In order to be convicted of this crime, the prosecutor had to prove two elements: that Dennis was the one who committed the wrongful act and that he had wrongful intent when he did it.[2] These elements had to be proved beyond a reasonable doubt. Dennis admitted that he killed Sally, so he was the one who committed the wrongful act. But did he have wrongful intent? There are several levels of wrongful intent in the crime of homicide, the highest being premeditation and deliberation, which is needed for first-degree murder. Essentially that means that Dennis had planned the killing. He did not have to plan it far in advance, but it wasn't just a sudden impulsive act. Something less than premeditation and deliberation to kill Sally might still be enough for second-degree murder, killing her in the heat of passion for voluntary manslaughter, or negligently causing her death for involuntary manslaughter. By presenting expert testimony about LSD and its effects, Dennis's lawyer hoped to muddy the waters, making it harder for the prosecutor to prove the level of wrongful intent needed in first-degree murder—or possibly any intent to kill Sally; after all, it was the witch he was killing, right? Besides, Sally's the one who spiked the brownies with LSD. Dennis's lawyer might want to avoid the insanity defense because even if Dennis was found to have been insane, he could face a long commitment at a psychiatric institution—perhaps longer than a sentence for voluntary or involuntary manslaughter.[3]

Once Dr. Mosley reviewed the recording of Dennis's interview, he notified Dennis's lawyer that the description Dennis gave of what he experienced that night was entirely consistent with LSD and that he would be glad to testify on Dennis's behalf. Ahead of his actual testimony, Dr. Mosley produced a report of his findings, which was disclosed to the prosecutor. The prosecutor, in turn, said he would petition the court to allow a psychiatrist of his choosing to evaluate Dennis, since Dennis raised his mental state as an issue by bringing in a psychiatrist as his expert witness. Dennis's lawyer responded to the petition by saying that Dr. Mosley did not personally evaluate Dennis and having a psychiatrist interview him would be like forcing a confession when Dennis had every right to remain silent.[4] Also, he said that Dr. Mosley had no intention of interviewing Dennis, and the prosecution could bring in their own LSD expert if they wanted to. Before the judge could rule on the petition, the prosecutor withdrew it and decided to just challenge Dr. Mosley's opinions on cross-examination without an expert of his own. At the trial, Dr. Mosley presented himself as a very poised and authoritative witness. Going through his credentials alone took half an hour. When asked to provide his opinion, he did so with confidence.

"Lysergic acid diethylamide, or LSD as most people call it, is a powerful hallucinogen that produces changes in auditory and visual perception, dissolution between the individual and the outside world, loss of identity, irrational fears, and short-term psychosis. In most cases, the psychotic condition is self-limiting, but there are instances when it persists long after the drug's half-life in the system. LSD is known to cause individuals to behave irrationally, even to become self-injurious. It is not unusual for individuals to become aggressive, especially when confronting what they believe is a threatening situation.

"Mr. Lambert's description of his perceptions on that night, as he provided to the state police in a recorded interview, is consistent with the effects of LSD and with the diagnosis of substance-induced psychotic disorder.[5] Mr. Lambert denied any animosity toward Ms. Duchesne, and it is my understanding that he had no prior history of criminal violence. Mr. Lambert's actions were caused by LSD, which, unbeknownst to him at the time, had been spiked by Ms. Duchesne in the brownies that she made. Just like many individuals who are under the influence of LSD, Mr. Lambert's memory is not complete for his actions, but his description of the colors surrounding Ms. Duchesne on her face, the melting of the bed underneath her into a white lava form, and then seeing her aging in front of his eyes to become a witch are graphic and credible depictions of the LSD experience and show why he was frightened of her. He was not killing Ms. Duchesne that night. He was killing the hallucination of a witch."

Following Dr. Mosley's direct testimony, the prosecutor began his cross-examination. He first established that Dr. Mosley had not conducted a personal interview with Dennis and that Dr. Mosley in his clinical practice always interviews the person before making a diagnosis. He also established that Dr. Mosley did not read the criminal records, witness statements, and other evidence gathered by state police.

> PROSECUTOR: Dr. Mosley, are you aware of any laboratory test on Dennis Lambert that showed traces of LSD in his system?
>
> DR. MOSLEY: No. LSD is rapidly removed from the body, usually within twenty-four to forty-eight hours, so even if urine toxicology had been done on the day he confessed to the killing, it would not have shown LSD. That is why his description of symptoms that he experienced is so important.

PROSECUTOR: But you're assuming that LSD had been in his system only from his report. Isn't that right?

DR. MOSLEY: Yes, but his report is credible and consistent with the types of hallucinations LSD causes. He wouldn't have been able to make that up.

PROSECUTOR: He would if he had used LSD before and remembered how he felt. Isn't that true?

DR. MOSLEY: I suppose, but someone would have to be very sophisticated to mimic those hallucinations as well as he did.

PROSECUTOR: Dr. Mosley, earlier you testified that you had not reviewed any police investigation records about this case except for the recording of Mr. Lambert's interview. Isn't that correct?

DR. MOSLEY: Yes, it is.

PROSECUTOR: Then you did not review statements provided by Mr. Lambert's mother, Phyllis, did you?

DR. MOSLEY: No, I did not.

PROSECUTOR: Let me show you a report that outlines what his mother told police…Would you be so kind as to read the second paragraph?

DR. MOSLEY: Sure, "That's why we built an apartment for Dennis over the garage; the fighting between him and his father was horrible. Marcel has not always been good to me, but when Dennis got mad at him, he flew into a rage and would jump on his father and start pummeling him. It was all I could do to pull him off. I never called the police because I didn't want Dennis or Marcel to get into any trouble."

PROSECUTOR: Doesn't that show that Dennis did have a history of violence?

DR. MOSLEY: I was referring to a criminal record of violence, which it is my understanding he does not have.

PROSECUTOR: Well, a criminal record or not, this young man is capable of violence. Isn't that right?

DR. MOSLEY: It is some evidence, but I do not believe it is relevant.

PROSECUTOR: Because you didn't review any investigation reports, you also didn't see the statement provided by Dennis's sister, Marie, did you?

DR. MOSLEY: No.

PROSECUTOR: Would you be so kind then, Doctor, to read the last paragraph of this report?

DR. MOSLEY: Okay. "About two weeks before all this happened, I told Dennis that I saw Sally walking hand in hand with some older guy at Victory Park. I thought it was her old boyfriend, Jack Hebert. I never liked that girl and thought that she was using Dennis. I hoped that this would convince him not to have anything to do with her. He got mad at me and thought I was lying because I didn't like Sally. He pretended like it didn't bother him, but I could tell it did. He was so stupidly in love with her and was upset that she was going to South Carolina."

Prosecutor: Thank you, Doctor. Doesn't this report show that Mr. Lambert could have had a motive to kill Sally?

Dr. Mosley: Just because someone is mad, if he was, does not mean he is going to kill a person.

Prosecutor: That's true, but saying that it was because of LSD that he killed her assumes he had no motive, correct?

Dr. Mosley: In my opinion LSD was the stronger factor regardless of what he said to his sister.

Prosecutor: Dr. Mosley, you did know that Mr. Lambert put his bloody clothes and the ax in a plastic sack and threw it in one of Kmart's dumpsters?

Dr. Mosley: Yes, he said that in the interview.

Prosecutor: But were you aware that police searched the town landfill where the contents of dumpsters from Kmart are deposited?

Dr. Mosley: No.

Prosecutor: Well, the sack was found, and the ax was confirmed from analysis of bloodstains to be the murder weapon. Is that new information for you?

Dr. Mosley: Yes, it is.

Prosecutor: Well, let me provide some additional information. The brand of ax was sold at Kmart, and sales records showed that brand of ax was sold on Tuesday, October 6, just three days before Sally's death. You didn't know that?

DR. MOSLEY: No.

PROSECUTOR: When films taken from a security camera inside Kmart were recovered from October 6, the purchaser of the ax was identified as Dennis Lambert. Is that information you also didn't have?

DR. MOSLEY: I did not have that information.

PROSECUTOR: And did you know that Mr. Lambert purchased a plastic mattress cover that day?

DR. MOSLEY: No, I didn't.

PROSECUTOR: Wouldn't you say, Doctor, that purchasing the murder weapon just three days before the crime is evidence of planning the crime?

DR. MOSLEY: Well, I don't know about all that; all I know is that if it wasn't for LSD, he wouldn't have done this.

PROSECUTOR: And wouldn't you say that purchasing a plastic mattress cover in which Sally was wrapped shows what Mr. Lambert had in mind?

DR. MOSLEY: That's not for me to say.

PROSECUTOR: But you would agree that it will be up to the jury to decide if Mr. Lambert planned on killing Sally or not, correct?

DR. MOSLEY: Yes, of course.

Science is imperfect, including the science of mental disorders, especially when it tries to explain human behavior. There is no medical instrument or testing procedure to identify if someone has a mental disorder or not. It might have been helpful to Dennis if blood or urine analysis found the presence of LSD in him after the killing,[6] which could have made Dr. Mosley's opinions more convincing. Instead, Dr. Mosley relied on reported symptoms, which can't be verified. This doesn't mean that the science of LSD has no value. Knowing what the symptoms of a mental disorder are and how people behave when they have such symptoms helps, but by itself it isn't enough. It's necessary to also know the facts surrounding the crime, which include not only the defendant's behavior when the crime was being committed but also the facts in evidence before and after the crime from as many factual sources as possible. With that, a story can be constructed as to what the evidence suggests happened, and then that story can be compared with the scientific story of what happens when someone has a mental disorder. Does Dennis's scientific story match the evidence? Is it a good story, meaning is it a reliable one? Scientists who criticize narrative may forget, whether they acknowledge it or not, that they are also telling a story. Dr. Mosley's story, taken from Dennis's story, is that just because Dennis hacked Sally to death with a hand ax does not necessarily mean that he wanted to hurt or kill her. Dr. Mosley's story goes on to imply that Dennis had no reason to harm Sally, and this odd, unexplainable event would not have occurred if Dennis was not hallucinating on LSD. Dennis could not have been in his right mind to do something so bizarre and so awful, but for LSD. Being a nationally known expert on LSD, Dr. Mosley had confidence in his own understanding of what LSD does to a person, so he didn't think it was relevant to know all the facts surrounding the crime. When the prosecutor presented him with those other facts, Dr. Mosley stuck to his story:

- The defendant had no criminal history of violence.

- The defendant had no rational reason for his actions.

- The defendant ingested LSD because Sally put it in the brownies.

- The defendant's description of his hallucinations was so characteristic of LSD that he couldn't have made it up.

- The defendant's actions are best understood by his frightening hallucination of Sally turning into a witch.

The prosecutor's story is a more ordinary explanation:

- The defendant has a history of violence not related to LSD, as shown in his extreme physical aggression toward his father.

- The defendant's sister reported that he was upset when he learned that Sally was holding hands with her old boyfriend, and he did not want Sally to go to South Carolina.

- The defendant bought the hand ax and a plastic mattress cover just three days before the killing, so he must have planned it.

- Other than his own report, the defendant has no evidence to show he had ingested LSD, and he did not tell police about his LSD experience when first questioned.

- The defendant buried Sally in the barn and got rid of incriminating evidence of the crime because he knew he was guilty.

It is possible that if Dr. Mosley had questioned Dennis about the incriminating evidence, there could have been some other explanation besides what the evidence suggests—namely, that he was mad at Sally and wanted to kill her. However, because Dr. Mosley did not address those facts, his testimony in spite of his expertise on LSD was not convincing. Dr. Mosley was correct to agree that it is up to the jury to decide whether Dennis planned this murder. It is also up to the jury to accept or not accept that Dennis was under the influence of LSD. However, a psychiatric opinion that does not consider the facts, or what the timeline of the defendant's behavior might show, is hollow and will not be helpful to the jury.

Psychiatrists can't decide which facts are true and which are not; that is also up to the jury when facts are in dispute. But psychiatrists shouldn't get too comfortable with their science alone. If the prosecutor had called a psychiatrist who did review all the evidence to testify in rebuttal to Dr. Mosley, the psychiatrist's opinion might have been something like this.

"Whether or not Mr. Lambert was under the influence of LSD when he killed Sally is a factual matter, which cannot be psychiatrically determined. His description of Sally's face looking like a witch may or may not have occurred. Mr. Lambert's account is subjective and unverifiable, but if reports are accurate that he has a history of violent behavior not associated with drug ingestion, that he believed Sally was not faithful to him and against his wishes was leaving for South Carolina, that he bought a hand ax and plastic mattress cover just before the killing, and that he buried Sally's body to cover up evidence of the crime, then his explanation for his actions being from the toxic effects of LSD is not supported. Instead, the timeline of events would be consistent with motive and planning for the killing and not the unproven effects of LSD on Mr. Lambert."

Remember that Dennis's lawyer did not raise the insanity defense, so he did not have to prove that Dennis was insane because of LSD. Instead, the prosecutor had to prove beyond a reasonable doubt that Dennis had wrongful intent for the crime of murder. Was he able to do that when a nationally recognized expert so confidently testified about the effects of LSD? Yes, but only in part. The jury found Dennis guilty of second-degree murder. The jury did not believe beyond a reasonable doubt that Dennis premeditated and deliberated the murder to be guilty of first-degree murder. They weren't completely sure that LSD played no role. This is why psychiatric testimony on diminished capacity is not recognized in many jurisdictions and why in those jurisdictions it is only allowed if insanity is raised as a defense.[7] Then, the defendant must prove that he was insane. Dennis was sentenced to fifteen to twenty-five years in state prison. He would be released from prison by middle age. Dennis's father was never convicted of a crime for his violence. Is there a connection between them for violent behavior? Is it in their genes? Is it what Dennis experienced growing up? Without the issue of LSD, could Dennis have had a basis for the insanity defense based on those factors? Maybe he couldn't control himself.

Firefly

Figure 8. "Boy Reaching Out through a Fire," DigitalVision Vectors, photo: jc_design, Getty Images #1088445548.

At about nine o'clock in the evening, several hours after she returned to her apartment from work at Jeff's Tire Warehouse, Roxie Marsh poured a glass of merlot from a three-liter box in her refrigerator. She gulped it down, then returned to Jeff's in her Ford Escort, parking behind the building. She got out of the car and walked over to the rear entrance of the building, which was accessed by a wooden stairway that led to a small deck in front of the door. She didn't climb the stairway but went over to a metal rubbish barrel underneath the stairway. She carried a green garbage bag from which she took a blue-striped bath towel that was rolled up into the shape of a log and soaked with canola oil. She dropped the towel into the barrel. The barrel was more than half-full of empty oil cans, discarded cartons, and greasy paper wrappings. Old tires were stacked along the back wall of the building, and there were many new tires inside. Roxie knew that the tires would be hard to ignite on their own. However, if the fire got hot enough, the tires would eventually burn and be hard to extinguish. She took out a book of matches, lit one, and set the rest of the book on fire, then threw it into the barrel. She watched the fire as it grew up the sides of the barrel, then inflamed the wooden stairway up to the door and into the building. Roxie's heart raced, and her breath quickened, but she was not afraid. She was excited. She returned to her car and drove down Beech Street to Victory Drive, where she turned right and parked in a lot next to the First Presbyterian Church. From there, she had a good view of Jeff's Tire Warehouse, which was across Victory Park. She shut off her headlights and the engine and waited. Soon fire trucks with sirens blaring arrived from all sides and encircled the warehouse. The commotion of the firefighters was electric. Roxie hadn't been this happy for months. Seeing the flames spread was like a long climax.

Just as Roxie predicted, once the tires began to burn, it was hard to extinguish the fire. As fast as the water from the fire hoses dampened the blazing building, the burning tires rekindled it. Within a few hours, Jeff's Tire Warehouse was a complete loss, but the smoke from the burning tires lasted for days and the smell for weeks. Roxie returned late to her apartment and slept well. When she awoke, she turned on her television set, where the news of the fire was extensively broadcast. She made herself a pot of coffee and enjoyed the fire all over again.

Roxie's family life had not been good. Her mother was addicted to pain pills that were prescribed for a chronic low-back condition that began when she was pregnant with her last child, Rebecca. The back pain with her other three pregnancies went away once the children were born, but not with Rebecca. She spent most of the day in bed or in her recliner. Roxie, who was the second child, took on many of her mother's responsibilities. Her older brother, Robert, and younger brother, Randall, were of no help. Roxie's father was a lieutenant in the Grafton Fire Department and a workaholic. However, the extra hours he worked may have been just to get out of the house. When Roxie was not yet in elementary school, she asked her father if she could go along on his fire truck when he went to a fire. She couldn't, of course. But when she was older, she clipped out newspaper articles with pictures of fires to which her father had been called and saved them in a blue two-pouch folder. Each of the pouches was full, and she never tired looking through them.

Roxie's older brother, Robert, was a heroin addict who spent much of his adult life in jail for drug-related crimes. When they were younger, Robert made Roxie play "doctor" with him; he was the doctor. Years later, he apologized to her, but it had not interfered with their relationship. Roxie idolized Robert and did anything she could to get his approval. Roxie didn't have many friends, so Robert became very important to her. Her brother Randall and her sister Rebecca also abused drugs, especially pills, which they sometimes stole from their mother, but they didn't have Robert's legal problems. Roxie was not as close to them; perhaps she resented having to raise them.

Roxie was moody from early childhood. Her moods changed quickly and made her unpredictable. As a teenager, the moodiness was worse, with long periods of depression during which she wouldn't call or see her friends. Roxie didn't like herself at those times and tried stopping the pain of her depression by smoking marijuana, drinking beer, or cutting herself. She wasn't trying to kill herself, at least not then, but she wanted to feel alive. Sometimes she would burn herself with matches by letting the match burn down to her fingertips or by pressing the lit match into her arms and thighs. She wore long-sleeved blouses to hide the burns on her arms. She later talked to a psychiatrist.

"I don't know why I liked watching matches burn, but I could go through a whole box of matches in an hour sitting alone in my room. By the time I was in high school, I wanted to feel the fire on me, to burn me…One time, I lit a pack of matches behind our high school, just to see it burn; I had this feeling like I was 'zoning in' on the flame, wanting it to get bigger and bigger, so I lit the field behind the high school that stretched all the way to the river. The long grass was brown, and the fire spread easily. I ran away and hid behind a dumpster where I could watch it. Fire trucks came, and the fire was put out. I liked it when the fire trucks came, and I told Robert about it afterward. He said, 'That's cool.' Another time, I lit a fire in back of the Hoyts' garage. They lived next door to us. The garage burned pretty good but didn't burn down. I really liked the fire trucks coming in on that one because I could see the whole thing from the boys' bedroom window. I told Robert about it later too, and he really liked it because he always hated the Hoyts. They didn't let their kids play with him. I had the same 'zoning-in' feeling when I lit the garage, like nothing could stop me, like nothing could hurt me."

Roxie became pregnant and dropped out of high school. It was her boyfriend Keith's baby. He hadn't finished high school either and worked as an assistant auto mechanic at a Ford dealership. When the baby was old enough for day care, Roxie went to work as a nurse's aide at St. Theresa's Manor, a local nursing home. She didn't like the second shift, and the work was very physical. She came home at midnight exhausted. She dreaded that Keith might be awake and would want sex. If she didn't go along with him, he screamed at her. She thought Keith was addicted to sex. He made her do things she didn't like. When Keith's best friend Lance and his wife Beth came over, they all drank a lot and then watched adult movies together. At first, it ended with the couples having sex with their own spouse in the same room, but later Keith insisted that they change partners. Roxie hated this but was too afraid of Keith to say no. He wouldn't physically hurt her, but she couldn't stand his screaming. After several months, Beth became uncomfortable too, so they stopped watching the movies together. There was no more having sex in the same room and no more changing partners. Roxie never got over her humiliation and blamed Lance and Beth as much as Keith. Several years later, when they were invited to a restaurant celebrating Lance and Beth's son Mark's bar mitzvah, Roxie lit a fire in the wastebasket of the women's restroom. Fire alarms sounded, and the sprinkler system turned on. Fire trucks came from all over. The event was a disaster for everyone but Roxie.

Roxie worked at St. Theresa's for nearly eight years in spite of hating the job. After a new nursing supervisor, Maureen, was hired, things got worse. Maureen was critical of Roxie for just about everything she did, and Roxie's performance evaluations suffered. Roxie was afraid she might be fired. One evening when Maureen screamed at her for trying to transfer an obese patient from the bed to a wheelchair alone, Roxie was furious. She didn't say anything to Maureen except that she had to leave early because she was sick to her stomach and might vomit. On the way out, Roxie lit a fire in a cleaning-supply closet and was off premises before the fire trucks arrived. She bought an ice cream sundae at Friendly's and ate it in her car. The smoke from the closet had been spotted early, and there was no significant damage, and no one was hurt, but Roxie felt satisfied. Fire investigators could not prove that the fire was started by someone because there were so many greasy rags in the closet and exposed electrical lines. The coincidence of Roxie leaving just before the fire was not unnoticed. The next day, Maureen fired Roxie for leaving her shift early when no replacement was available.

Shortly thereafter, Keith learned that Jeff's Tire Warehouse was looking for a receptionist and called his friend Jeff to see if he would hire Roxie. Roxie resented how Keith controlled her life. Their relationship deteriorated further. Roxie already had difficulty bonding with their son Jackson, who reminded her of Keith in his physical mannerisms and in his attitude. Keith and Jackson were bonded and inseparable. Once again, Roxie felt alone and depressed. One day, she decided to kill herself when Keith was at work and Jackson was in school. She went into their garage and started her Ford Escort, leaving the garage door closed. She opened all the windows in her car and sat in the front seat waiting to die. Unexpectedly, Keith returned home during his lunch break and found her passed out in the car with a strong scent of exhaust fumes in the air. He quickly opened the garage door, carried her out, and called 911. Roxie was taken by ambulance to Good Samaritan Hospital. She was treated with oxygen and medically stabilized. She survived without physical injury but was admitted by involuntary certification to the psychiatric unit of the hospital because of her suicidal ideation. She remained on the unit for about a week, where she discussed her depression and marital problems. She did not talk about her love of fires. At the end of the week, the chief psychiatrist had a conference with Roxie and Keith. Roxie and Keith spoke of the tension in their marriage, and Keith admitted he wanted a separation. Roxie felt some relief.

Keith found Roxie a small apartment but kept Jackson with him. He allowed her to see Jackson on weekends. Keith did not know of Roxie's love of fires, although she told him when they were younger that she used to cut and burn herself. Keith had thought it was a bit odd that Roxie was at the bar mitzvah and St. Theresa's when both of those fires broke out, but he didn't pay much attention to it. However, when he heard about the fire at Jeff's Tire Warehouse, where Roxie worked, he became suspicious and called Roxie. She denied having any part in the fire, but she sounded almost giggly, which was different than her voice of doom in recent months. Although Keith did not want to live with Roxie, he still had feelings for her and didn't want her in trouble. Also, he could not let her be a danger to someone else. After their phone conversation, he drove over to the Grafton Police Department.

About a week after the fire at Jeff's Tire Warehouse, Grafton police called Roxie, told her they were interviewing all employees, and asked whether she would mind coming to the station. She didn't mind. The lead investigator told her that even though the interview was being recorded, this was just routine questioning and that she wasn't a suspect or anything like that, but they wanted to know what time she left Jeff's that night and what she did afterward. Did she see anything? Did she have any information that might be helpful to them in the investigation?

> Roxie: Well, I don't really know anything about it, but I left maybe a little after six o'clock. I don't think anyone was there anymore, so I locked the back door. The front door was already closed for business. I always make sure the doors are locked. Jeff's real concern is that kids in the area may try to break in. There's been a lot of vandalism in that neighborhood, so you can't take any chances. It's too bad kids are like that these days…I then went home, ate some cold chicken, had a glass of merlot, and watched an old movie. I never left my apartment after that and didn't know anything about the fire until I saw it the next morning on the news.

INVESTIGATOR: What movie did you see?

ROXIE: You know, I don't even remember now; I think I fell asleep before it ended. I was pretty exhausted.

INVESTIGATOR: So you never left your apartment that night after you came home?

ROXIE: No, I didn't.

INVESTIGATOR: What kind of car do you have?

ROXIE: A Ford Escort. It's several years old but runs pretty good. My husband, Keith, looks after it. We're separated now.

INVESTIGATOR: Are you a religious person, Roxie?

ROXIE: Well, I grew up Catholic, and I believe in God, but I haven't gone to church for years. You know, come the weekend, I'm always pretty exhausted.

INVESTIGATOR: So you don't attend the First Presbyterian Church on Victory Drive?

ROXIE: No, I don't. I don't have anything against Protestants, but if I was to go to any church, it would be a Catholic church.

INVESTIGATOR: Is your Ford Escort a beige color?

ROXIE: Yes, it is, but it's so dirty, I hate to say, that it looks much darker.

INVESTIGATOR: Do you know a Pastor Williamson from the First Presbyterian Church?

ROXIE: No, I've never heard of that person.

INVESTIGATOR: There wouldn't have been any reason for you to go over to visit Pastor Williamson that night?

ROXIE: No, of course not; where're you going with this?

INVESTIGATOR: Well, Pastor Williamson was at his church that night, getting some things ready for a funeral service the next day. We talked to him because his church is in the neighborhood of Jeff's Tire Warehouse. Pastor Williamson said when he heard the fire sirens, he looked out the window and saw that there was a fire at Jeff's. He also said that he saw a beige car in the church parking lot and wasn't sure why it was there. Could that have been your car, Roxie?

ROXIE: Of course not. I told you I was in my apartment and didn't go anywhere. I had no reason to be at any church that night.

INVESTIGATOR: Well, let me ask you this, Roxie. Do you have a Confederate flag decal on the back window of your car?

ROXIE: I, uh…uh…So what does that prove? Lots of people have Confederate flag decals. I see them all the time—all kinds of flags.

INVESTIGATOR: Really? I don't see them all the time. And Pastor Williamson said that's what struck him about the car right away—that it had a Confederate flag decal. Roxie, we're here to get the truth, and I don't think you're giving us the truth. We need to find out what happened that night, and you're the person who can help us. This is the time to be honest. Look, what are the chances that someone who works at Jeff's Tire Warehouse just happens to be in the parking lot of a church that she does not attend, with her lights off, watching the raging fire across Victory Park? We know that you were in the car watching, Roxie, because Pastor Williamson saw the car drive off not long after, and no one had gotten into the car before it drove off. That means you were there. You were in that car. Let me ask you this, Roxie. What was your relationship like with Jeff?

At the mention of Jeff, Roxie's face changed from defiant and irritated to expressionless. She sat quite still as if she was in her own world. Then, her eyes filled with tears, and she began to weep. The experienced police investigator let her cry without interruption for a good fifteen minutes. When it seemed she couldn't cry anymore, he continued.

INVESTIGATOR: Would you like to tell me about it?

ROXIE: I hated him. He was a pig, just like Keith. They're all pigs. Keith got me this job. For all I know, he told Jeff that I was hot and can do more things than just a receptionist. He's sick. You wouldn't believe the things he's made me do. It was a relief when he said we should separate. He'll probably make my son Jackson into a pig too.

INVESTIGATOR: What about Jeff?

ROXIE: He was a pig. He'd tell me how my clothes looked good on me and brought out my "assets." He'd emphasize the "ass" part of it. Then, if I went to the bathroom, he'd tell me to call if I needed any help, or he'd lean down behind me when I was working at my desk, with his hot air breathing on my neck. If I said something to him, like I don't like this kind of stuff, he would just laugh. He'd ask me about my sex life with Keith. He told me that Keith was a lucky man. That's what made me think Keith may have said something to him. I told Jeff it was none of his business and to leave me alone. I dreaded coming into work, but I had no choice. Keith was paying for my apartment but expected me to support myself otherwise from my own salary. He said he was already paying for all household expenses in order to raise Jackson. I was stuck having to go through this every day with the pig.

INVESTIGATOR: So what happened?

ROXIE: Nothing. It was the same thing every day. I hated Jeff. I'd think how good it would be if he had a heart attack and died. I had fantasies about how I could kill him and get away with it. These are fantasies, you know; I'd never do something like that. But when you're so stuck, you don't know what to do. So you think these things that don't make any sense.

INVESTIGATOR: So when did you get the idea to burn down the place?

ROXIE: It wasn't an idea. It just happened. The tire warehouse was Jeff's whole life. He had big dreams of opening another warehouse in the city, maybe more. He'd talk about how wealthy he was going to be. He thought he was such a big shot. He said something to me that day about how if I hooked up with him, I'd go places too. It was just a bunch of crap. He was married. He just wanted to use me. I left work so pissed. I cried all the way home in my car. I ate cold chicken that night and had a glass of merlot, and then I went into a "zone." I didn't feel anything anymore. I knew what I had to do. I was going to start just a little fire, just to get him upset. I've never done anything like this before. I'm not a violent person. I went back to Jeff's behind the building and threw a match into a rubbish barrel by the stairway. Even as I threw the match in the barrel, I asked myself, What are you doing? Then I just drove off. I hoped that the fire would not get going at all and just die out in the barrel. So I stopped at the church parking lot to make sure that it was going out. When the fire started to spread, I got really scared. I didn't want all that to happen, but it was too late; the fire trucks were there. I just drove home. You asked me if I was religious. Well, I even prayed to God that night and told him how sorry I was that I didn't want this to happen; it just did happen. I can't even understand myself. This was not me.

INVESTIGATOR: Roxie, we also spoke to your husband, Keith, you know. We were going to interview all of Jeff's employees anyway, but Keith came to the station on his own and told us that he suspected that you started the fire at Jeff's and that you also started a fire at a restaurant where your friends were hosting a party, and then at a nursing home where you worked and were fired the next day.

ROXIE: Keith's a goddamn liar. That son of a bitch would say anything to screw me. I had nothing to do with those fires. That's ridiculous. You guys are setting me up. This is some sort of conspiracy to get me, to make me into some kind of monster. I should have never talked to you. You didn't have anything on me. Confederate flags? They're all over the place. I want a lawyer. I'm done with this interview. You're not going to set me up like this.

Roxie was arrested and charged with arson for the fire at Jeff's Tire Warehouse. Keith hired a lawyer who tried to get Roxie out on bail, but the judge rejected it because of her risk to the community. She was kept at the county jail awaiting trial. Roxie's lawyer retained Dr. Richard Kingsbury, a psychiatrist who has done extensive research on complex nerve circuitry in the brain, which explains why people act the way they do. Dr. Kingsbury published a journal article about his research:

People set destructive fires for many reasons. Sometimes it is to get insurance money, or out of anger and revenge, or because they are mentally deficient and like to watch the flame but do not understand the danger it creates. Fire setting can also be associated with mental disorders, like depression, anxiety, posttraumatic stress, alcohol and drug abuse, or even serious psychotic conditions in which the person is not in touch with reality. Fire setting sometimes becomes a pattern of behavior all by itself. Then it is called an impulse control disorder, more specifically pyromania.[1] Other impulse control disorders include kleptomania, or failure to stop stealing objects that are not needed; intermittent explosive disorder, or out-of-proportion outbursts of verbal or physical aggression; and gambling disorder, or persistent gambling behavior despite personal ruin. People with impulse control disorders have problems with self-control and continue their behaviors even if it is destructive to themselves or others. Those with pyromania set fires because they like to, not just because they might benefit from it monetarily or because of anger. Men are more often fire setters (i.e., pyromaniacs) than women are, but a small number of women are too. Before they set a fire, pyromaniacs feel tense and emotionally upset and are relieved once the fire is set. They like watching the fire and the damage that the fire causes; sometimes, they get sexually aroused with it. As children, they may have already started playing with matches or started fires. They like risky behaviors. Many women fire setters were sexually promiscuous in their teenage years, and some were victims of sexual assault as children. Women fire setters often come from an unstable home, with a family history of alcohol or drug abuse. Women who continue setting fires, even after they've been criminally convicted, typically have a history of other crimes such as fraud or theft. Women fire setters are not easily treated psychiatrically.

After hours of talking with her, Roxie's lawyer was finally able to get her to admit that she set the previous fires along with the one at Jeff's Tire Warehouse. He suspected that neither of the stories she told the Grafton police was the whole story. He also knew that a jury would not find much sympathy for her pattern of fire setting, unless he could show that her fire setting over many years was irrational and must be due to a mental disorder. This led him to Dr. Kingsbury. Roxie's best defense was insanity, and Dr. Kingsbury could prove it.

The jurisdiction in which Roxie lives and will face trial defines insanity using both of the typical categories—namely, that the person was unable to think rationally or was unable to control herself.[2] The specific language in that jurisdiction says that Roxie may be found insane if she was unable to appreciate the criminality of the conduct for which she is charged or unable to conform that conduct to the requirements of the law. There is not much doubt that Roxie knew, understood, and appreciated that setting a fire at Jeff's Tire Warehouse was criminal. She was hiding her actions from the police for a reason. But could she "conform" her conduct and not do something against the law? This really comes down to whether Roxie could have controlled herself to not set the fire. If pyromania is an impulse control disorder, and she has a problem with self-control, maybe she couldn't.

Dr. Kingsbury interviewed Roxie three times, for a total of fourteen hours. He also arranged for her to have an MRI of her brain to see if any brain structures were abnormal. No abnormalities were found, but Dr. Kingsbury explained in his report that is not unusual, since the brain condition that is responsible for impulse control disorders is one of abnormal functioning of the brain and not necessarily abnormal structures:

"The pathology lies in the neurotransmitter system where impulses travel across brain cells by chemicals, and depending on which parts of the brain are involved, there can be too little or too much of those chemicals.[3] Our research is still experimental, so our methods are not used on patients yet, but in the laboratory, we can see these changes in a brain that is not functioning well, compared to one that is," he wrote.

In his direct testimony during Roxie's trial, Dr. Kingsbury explained his findings further to the jury, turning to look at them as he might have to students in the classroom at the university where he teaches.

"Roxie's family history dramatically shows how various family members suffer from impulse control disorders. Her mother, brothers, and sister have been addicted to drugs, and her older brother, Robert, has a long history of antisocial criminal behavior for which he has spent most of his adult life in jail. They clearly have problems with self-control, which is the hallmark of impulse control disorders. The real question is why so many of them in the family have this problem and how the brain is involved. Well, we know that people with impulse control disorders have a deficiency in the ability to produce or use chemical transmitters, one of them being dopamine, which results in a 'reward deficiency syndrome.'[4] What this means is they have an insufficiency of usual feelings of satisfaction that we all need. They may be born with this deficiency, or they may have a greater likelihood of developing it, particularly when they've been exposed to prolonged periods of stress. Sometimes prolonged alcohol or drug abuse can also lead to reward deficiency syndrome, but that mechanism was not how Roxie developed hers. Yes, she does like a little wine here or there, but she is not an alcoholic or drug abuser.

"More importantly, however, in spending fourteen hours evaluating Roxie, I was able to determine that her family history and home life exposed her to prolonged periods of stress. Her mother was unavailable because of drug addiction. Her father escaped the family by becoming a workaholic. Roxie became the mother substitute for her younger brother and sister and essentially took care of the household. This is not what a young girl should be doing.[5] Also, I learned about Roxie's brother Robert sexually abusing her but also teaching her from an early age the types of behaviors that she copied and that became part of her. Fire setting was her reward. It drove up her dopamine levels to give her enormous feelings of satisfaction, when most of the time she was anxious, depressed, and lonely. She cut herself as a teenager and later burned herself to trigger dopamine and find satisfaction. She set fires for the same reason. Roxie's father being a firefighter is no coincidence here. She was looking for something to hold on to for comfort. She couldn't get that from her mother or her siblings, although she did unfortunately get close to Robert. But she really wanted her father. She wanted to be like him. She wanted to be around fires.

"The way to understand impulse control disorders, including pyromania, is that reward deficiency syndrome is a hole that needs to be filled. We all need that type of satisfaction, but most of us get it in a normal way and not through these kinds of extremes. For Roxie, these impulses for satisfaction are like an instinct. She can't define it for herself, but it's there pushing her forward, forcing her to fill the hole…In my opinion, Roxie lacked substantial capacity to conform her conduct to the requirements of the law. She may have understood that it was criminal, but she did not have the capacity to stop it," he said.

Roxie's lawyer was very pleased with Dr. Kingsbury's direct testimony and saw how the jury was taken by the scholarly witness. This was cutting-edge science. Her lawyer wasn't going to let Roxie testify because she already had three different stories, and he didn't want to take the chance that she might come up with something new on the witness stand that would contradict Dr. Kingsbury's scientific account of her behavior. Her lawyer was also pleased when the prosecutor only briefly cross-examined Dr. Kingsbury.

PROSECUTOR: Doctor, would you agree that it is often difficult for psychiatrists to determine if someone couldn't control their conduct or if they just didn't control it?

DR. KINGSBURY: Yes, that is the traditional view, but we are now in a much better position to make the determination due to our understanding of brain functioning, dopamine chemical transmitters, and reward deficiency syndrome. So in select cases, it is possible to conclude as to the capacity certain individuals have or don't have to control their conduct.

The prosecutor knew that his own expert witness would offset Dr. Kingsbury, so he didn't want to get into a scientific debate with him. The doctor obviously knew his science well.

Dr. Noel Harris was a soft-spoken psychiatrist who looked and dressed more like a country doctor than a city psychiatrist, but Dr. Harris was the favorite of this prosecutor as an expert witness because of his plain speech. Sometimes, after a day of trial, the prosecutor and Dr. Harris would go to the Holiday Inn lounge for a martini. The prosecutor was so confident in Dr. Harris that he decided not to challenge Dr. Kingsbury's right to discuss reward deficiency syndrome, even though it may not yet have been generally accepted by the scientific community.[6] Dr. Kingsbury had done enough research in the field that the judge would probably let him testify about it anyway. Dr. Harris spent only half the time that Dr. Kingsbury did interviewing Roxie, and he conducted no neurological or psychological tests. His report was brief, which was the way he liked it, so he would have more wiggle room on the witness stand. The prosecutor knew that he didn't have to prepare Dr. Harris very much. He would give Dr. Harris a few brief opening questions, and then let him run with it.

> PROSECUTOR: Dr. Harris, following your evaluation of Roxie Marsh, were you able to arrive at a diagnosis?
>
> DR. HARRIS: Yes, I was.
>
> PROSECUTOR: And what is that diagnosis?
>
> DR. HARRIS: Well, she has a longstanding mood disorder, primarily depression, but the diagnosis that best fits her behavior is pyromania, an impulse control disorder.
>
> PROSECUTOR: So it sounds like you and Dr. Kingsbury are essentially in agreement on the diagnosis. Is that correct?
>
> DR. HARRIS: Yes, I think we do agree on that.
>
> PROSECUTOR: Have you also arrived at an opinion on whether or not Roxie Marsh, in setting Jeff's Tire Warehouse on fire, was unable to conform her conduct to the requirements of the law?
>
> DR. HARRIS: Yes, I have.
>
> PROSECUTOR: And what is that?

Dr. Harris: My opinion is that there is insufficient basis to conclude that she could not control herself.

Prosecutor: So are you saying that she was not insane at the time?

Dr. Harris: That's correct. She was not insane.

Prosecutor: Dr. Harris, would you please give the jury the basis for your opinion?

Dr. Harris did not look at the jury when he explained his opinion, having read years earlier that the jury doesn't always like an expert invading "their space." He also felt like he didn't want to look like he was playing to them. Instead, he looked at and spoke to the prosecutor, who was cleverly standing next to the jury box, so that Dr. Harris was in effect speaking to the jury.

"In the first place, I still believe that psychiatrists are not very good at knowing who couldn't control their behavior and who just didn't control their behavior. Dr. Kingsbury's opinion that Roxie has reward deficiency syndrome is pure speculation. He has no brain imaging or other diagnostic study that shows she has reward deficiency syndrome. There is no laboratory test that shows she has a deficiency in dopamine. He also can't show that Roxie was going to be a pyromaniac from birth because of her family's genes. She just as easily developed this habit of setting fires because she found it aroused her when she was young, so it became a way of being aroused again when she was older.

"Since there is no way to prove that Roxie has reward deficiency syndrome, we have to look at her history and what her history tells us about whether she can control or can't control her behavior. She might have liked watching matches burn when she was young, but she only set two fires in her youth, even though she was anxious and depressed a lot of the time. Therefore, sometimes when she was anxious and depressed, she didn't set a fire, and sometimes—those two times in her youth—she did. That shows that if she didn't want to set a fire, she didn't have to do it. In the years that followed, there were two other fires that she set prior to Jeff's Tire Warehouse: One was at a restaurant where her friends were celebrating their son's bar mitzvah. She had bad feelings about those friends for several years before that. She didn't rush to their house to set a fire. She waited for when the opportunity presented itself. If you wait for an opportunity, that means you're controlling your behavior. She also set a fire at the nursing home where she worked because the nursing supervisor screamed at her. Well, she had been having problems with that nursing supervisor for some time before that, and she hated that job for eight years. Even when she was feeling bad about the work and about her nursing supervisor, she did not resort to her old habit until that one day when she left work early and was furious at the supervisor. So this fire was not because she was just trying to arouse herself, even if she liked it. It was because she was angry. There's no way to conclude that setting the fire was from some type of chemical imbalance or that she couldn't have walked past the cleaning-supply closet if she wanted to, instead of lighting it on fire.

"Now with Jeff's Tire Warehouse, it's important to look at all that happened in order to see if Roxie couldn't control herself or she just didn't control herself. She was mad at Jeff already for a while but didn't set the warehouse on fire. She hated his alleged sexual innuendos, but she didn't set the fire every time he made her feel bad. Even on the night when she set the fire, she didn't do it when she was still at Jeff's and everyone else had gone home. She went home too, and only then did she return. She waited for it to be dark. She made a point of driving behind the warehouse where she wouldn't be seen so she could control the manner in which she was going to set this fire. She then drove away a short distance so she could watch it burn. This wasn't sudden, impulsive, or instinctive behavior. It was a plan. You can't have a plan and yet not be able to control your behavior. That's the whole point of a plan. You're going to control your behavior in the best way that you can and in the way that is least likely to end up badly for you. That's what Roxie did. She planned the fire. She didn't just go into a sudden frenzy, lighting everything in sight…Look, she has some significant mental problems. That's not my point. My point is that you can have a mental disorder but not be insane."

Roxie's lawyer had a lengthy cross-examination of Dr. Harris, and Dr. Harris knew enough not to fight him on points that he could make for his case. But he stuck to his opinion that Roxie was not insane. On his way out of the courtroom, Dr. Harris spoke to George, one of his medical students who had observed his testimony, and proudly asked, "Roxie's lawyer couldn't touch me. Don't you agree?"

Dr. Harris and George went back to his office to discuss the testimony further. George was a philosophy major before going on to medical school and liked to engage in provocative debates. Then Dr. Harris began explaining again the difference between instinctive behavior, which is not controllable, and planned behavior.

"You know, when a hungry wolf is stalking caribou in the Yukon, he doesn't just jump in the middle of the herd to ease his instinctive hunger. He hides and waits and slowly tracks their progress until he sees a calf or a sickly animal falling behind. It's then that he strikes. So even if it's instinctive and does not involve human reasoning, it can also be planned, can't it?" George said.

Just then, the phone rang. It was the prosecutor informing Dr. Harris that the jury came back with their decision. Roxie was guilty of arson. They did not find her insane. Dr. Harris ended his discussion with George early so he could meet the prosecutor for a martini.

Is Dr. Harris right that if you plan something, your behavior is not instinctive, and you must be in control? How much planning is needed to make the point? Dr. Kingsbury's opinion was a scientific story, and he did not consider Roxie's planning at all. But Dr. Harris only picked out the facts that showed how Roxie planned or delayed her behavior. That wasn't the whole story either. Doesn't her personal story of childhood trauma, lack of parenting, and familial addiction say something too? Wouldn't it be easier for someone without Roxie's personal story to control his or her behavior? Shouldn't Roxie's personal story at least impact her sentence?

The Good Night Motel

Figure 9. *Western Motel*, by Edward Hopper, Corbis Historical, photo: Fine Art, Getty Images #544172742.

Jill Madison came out of room eleven of the Good Night Motel and closed the door behind her. As she walked by room ten, she stopped, quietly drew her ear to the door, and listened for a few seconds. She then pulled away, whispering to herself, That's just like him. He's gone.

Jill walked down the length of the one-story motel to the office, where the male receptionist was sitting, drinking coffee and eating a donut. Before he could get up to greet her, Jill placed the room key and a pair of scissors on the counter. Both the scissors and Jill's hands were stained with a substance that looked like blood, but the receptionist was not sure. Jill said to him, "Don't go back to room eleven; just call the police. Something awful happened. You've got to take over from here."

The receptionist didn't know what to do. He stood up and took the key, but when he looked as if he might go to the room, her eyes grew larger. He picked up the phone instead and called the police.

Thornton police came to the motel within fifteen minutes or so and weren't in any hurry. The receptionist had given them Jill's name, which they recognized from her strange calls the previous day. The receptionist walked one of the police officers down to room eleven, while the other one stayed with Jill in the office. The receptionist then opened the door, and they went in. The lights were on, but it took a few seconds for them to orient themselves to what they saw. The receptionist then quickly turned away and rushed out the door, holding back from vomiting. The officer went straight to the bed, where two young children were covered with blood, their inner organs spilling out of their bodies. One of the children couldn't have been more than a year old. After the officer confirmed they were dead, he stood up unsteadily and looked around the room. In the disarray, every article in the room, every surface, seemed spattered with blood. He closed the door behind him as he left and told the receptionist that no one was to go into the room. It was a crime scene. He went back to the motel office, where the other officer had called for an ambulance to take Jill to Lincoln Hospital. Jill's arms were cut and needed stitches, and she had to be medically examined. At the emergency department, Jill admitted that she killed her children. A police officer stayed with her. Once treated, she would be placed under arrest. As she lay on the examining table, Jill thought she heard a plane buzzing overhead. Her eyes darted up to the ceiling. Then she turned to the nurse standing next to her and said, "He may try to blow up the hospital, you know."

Jill and Paul Madison were sweethearts from high school. Paul was popular and played sports, and the girls loved him. Jill was shy but very pretty and liked well enough, except that the girls were jealous of her for landing Paul. Their jealousy made her feel special, although she never completely trusted Paul. After they finished high school, Paul worked for his uncle Rob's construction company. Jill worked at a convenience store. They continued to date each other and were married within a couple of years. A year and a half into their marriage, their first daughter Samantha was born. Paul was making good money by then, so Jill quit her job. Jill's life was pretty good.

After Samantha's birth, Jill began to get moody, irritable, and more withdrawn. If Paul asked her what was wrong, she would say, "Nothing," or she would blame him for being at work all the time and not helping with the baby. Jill was not sleeping well. Paul talked to Jill's parents about it, and they were concerned because they had not seen her like this before. Paul didn't tell them what he was really thinking.

"Jill's parents were always nice to me and loved Jill very much. But her mom is kind of crazy. She's a nice person and all that but very nervous and afraid. She hardly left the house for years. Even at our wedding, she stayed for just a short time, and Jill's dad drove her home. She didn't go to the rehearsal dinner. I didn't know the mother's sister, Aunt Lucy, but I heard that she killed herself. I was sure worried that Jill might be going down that road."

Paul tried to be more understanding of Jill. He helped with the baby when he could and even encouraged her to go bowling with her friend Kayla, which Jill liked to do. He told her that in the next couple of years, he would build a house for them. Samantha had been colicky and was up all night in the first several months but then began sleeping through the night, so Jill got more rest. Gradually, Jill's irritability and moodiness improved. She also became very attached to Samantha. Paul thought she was overly attached, but at least his relationship with Jill was better. The three of them frequently went out together to dinner, shopping, or just for a ride. Jill was apprehensive about leaving Samantha with anyone. Once, when Jill did agree to leave Samantha with a neighbor so she and Paul could go out to dinner, she began having difficulty breathing at the table and became so frightened that Paul took her home.

When Samantha was two years old, Jill became pregnant again. The one-bedroom apartment in which they lived was too small for a second child, so Paul decided that this was the time to build their house. They gave up the apartment and moved into a finished basement area in Jill's parents' home. They thought that Jill's mother could help with the new baby while Paul was completing construction on their house. Jill seemed delighted with this plan. She was quite close to her mother. After their second daughter, Hannah, was born, the arrangement couldn't have been better. Six months later, construction was done, and the Madisons moved into their new home.

The house was in a wooded area about five miles from Thornton, on a three-acre parcel of land. Jill could barely see her neighbors from the house, and even if she shouted, they wouldn't hear her. Most of the time, Jill, Samantha, and Hannah were alone in the house. Paul was busier than ever on new construction projects, taking on as much work as he could since their expenses had increased substantially with the new baby and the new house.

Very gradually, Jill became irritable and moody again and more fearful. It didn't help that Paul often worked into the late evening hours. She was afraid to be alone with the children. She would not let them out of her sight and became even more attached to the two of them than she had been with Samantha alone. Jill talked to her mother by telephone several times a day. That helped briefly. Jill did find that by staying busy with projects at the house, she could distract herself. She started making lists of things to do every day—decorating the girls' room, painting furniture, planting flowers and bushes—in between taking care of Samantha and the new baby. Jill was always in motion. By the time the girls went to bed in the evening, she was so revved up that only a couple of glasses of wine could help her wind down. Paul became concerned again.

"I'd come home from work and could tell she'd been drinking. It's not as if I thought she was an alcoholic, but I knew she was using wine to try to relax after rushing around like a madwoman all day. I tried to tell her she was doing too much. She needed to slow down. She'd get angry with me. She'd blame me for building this house in the woods so far from her parents or for leaving her alone all day with no one around. She'd say I wasn't concerned about her safety or the kids' safety. I know I was working more hours, but it was all for them. After a few weeks of this kind of talk, Jill got worse. She withdrew completely from me and seemed to be afraid of me. I'd catch her looking at me from the corner of her eye, like I was her enemy or something. It wasn't much fun coming home.

"After drinking wine, Jill would fall asleep but then get up a few hours later—wide awake—and pace around the house. I'd wake up and tell her to go back to bed. She might snap at me, but more often she would just glare and say nothing."

Jill and her friend Kayla went bowling once a week. They were best friends. They brought their children along, taking turns watching them while the other bowled. Kayla's son Trevor was Samantha's age, so they got along well, and Hannah was an easy baby. Jill and Kayla had bowled together since high school when they were on the same intramural team. Kayla knew Jill as well as anyone else did. Kayla also became concerned about her.

"Jill was bad-mouthing Paul all the time about how he was more interested in his work than in her and the kids and how she didn't believe he was always working when he said he was. One Saturday, when Paul told her he was at his uncle's office, she went by with the kids, and no one was there. She later confronted him, and he admitted that he and his uncle had left the office a little early and went for a beer at Benny's Bar and Grill. She didn't believe him. She thought he was having an affair. I tried to tell her she had no proof, but she said she just knew.

"Then she started saying that Paul has people watching her. Like one time at the bowling alley, she said this guy was staring at her but would turn away if she looked at him. Another time, when the pin changer in our lane didn't work, she said Paul had someone behind the pins doing it on purpose. The last time we bowled, when we first came down to our lane, there was Coke spilled on the floor, and Jill said Paul had someone do that. She said he wanted to make her crazy so he could go off with his whore and take the kids with them. She said she could see it in his eyes and in how he acted and that there was something different about him."

Jill complained to her mother about Paul, too, and told her she believed Paul was having an affair. Her mother didn't know what to think and asked her if she was unhappy in the marriage. Had she considered a separation? Her mother said Jill and the girls could move back into the house with them if that would make it easier. She also wondered if they needed marriage counseling. Jill said she'd consider moving back to her parents' home but was afraid of what Paul would do if she and the girls moved out. No, he hadn't been violent yet, but this would give him the excuse. Or maybe he didn't need an excuse. Maybe that was his plan all along. The more Jill thought about it, the more she convinced herself of the worst: "He's not just trying to make me go crazy. He wants to kill me."

Jill's suspicions about Paul were confirmed in her mind a week later when she saw a news story on television that an unidentified woman's body had been found on Meadowlark Road near the gravel pit just outside of Thornton. Jill knew that was close to where Paul and Uncle Rob were building houses in a new development. They probably used gravel from that same pit. When Paul returned home that evening, she cautiously asked him if he had heard about the body. He said he did, but there was no evidence of foul play so far. Someone said it might be a suicide. He went on to tell Jill of another woman's body that was found near that gravel pit years ago. That one had a scar on her cheek, and Hells Angels were suspected because that was their punishment for someone who has a "big mouth." No one was ever caught for the crime. It was the way Paul said "big mouth" that seemed directed at her.

Jill couldn't sleep all night, convinced that next to her was the killer of two women and that her fate was set. The following morning, when Paul left for work, he said to her, "Have a good day," which meant that this was to be her last day. Jill called the Thornton Police Department.

"This is Jill Madison, and I have information about the crime at Meadowlark Road. My husband, Paul Madison, is responsible. He admitted it to me last night. And you should look into the death of a woman who was found in the same place a few years ago. That's the woman with a scar on her cheek.

"I'm afraid that he's going to kill me next and take my children away to California with someone who he's having an affair with. He always wanted to go to California.

"You can find Paul Madison at his uncle's office at Bridgewood Construction. Well, he may be at the construction site; I don't know where he is half the time. He likes to hang out at Benny's. Yeah, he'll probably be at Benny's this afternoon. I want you to know I'm in great danger. I wouldn't be surprised if he killed more people. Please hurry."

The dispatcher at the Thornton Police Department listened and tried to calm Jill down to elicit more information, but her speech was too pressured and disjointed, and she sounded hysterical. The dispatcher later said that Jill seemed genuinely afraid and convinced of what she was reporting but that she didn't make much sense.

Later that same afternoon, Jill called the Thornton Police Department again.

"This is Jill Madison. I don't know if you found him yet, but I can't stay at this house. The children are with me, and we're all scared. You probably should check on Brad Desmond too; he's the manager at Strikes and Spares bowling alley. That's the one on Crestview Avenue. He may be dead. I told my husband how nice Brad is to us and the kids, and I could tell he didn't like it.

"Do you think I should take the kids somewhere, where he can't find us? But he has his ways. He thinks I don't know what he's doing. I know what he's doing. I'm afraid of going to my mother's—he never liked her; he told me she was crazy. She's a very nervous person. She'll just be upset if I go there.

"Paul plays mind games with me. He tries to convince me that I'm crazy. Look, I'm not making this up. My daughter Samantha asked me if Daddy was going to kill us. I told her no and that I would protect her. You see, she knows too. You don't believe me, do you? He's dangerous. You have to do something."

After Jill hung up, the dispatcher called Bridgewood Construction and spoke to Uncle Rob. Paul wasn't there. Uncle Rob knew that Jill was acting strangely from what Paul had told him. He said Paul told her parents that Jill needed help, but Jill wouldn't listen to them when they suggested it. Maybe the family could convince her to go to the hospital. Uncle Rob said he'd call Jill's parents himself and would talk to Paul when he returned to the office.

Jill rushed around the house gathering clothes for Samantha and diapers for Hannah and packed them in a duffel bag. She was afraid that she might forget something. As they were leaving through the kitchen door into the garage, Jill also grabbed a pair of scissors from the counter—for protection. She then drove with the girls down to the convenience store where she previously worked and bought a premade pizza, along with a half gallon of milk and a bottle of pink zinfandel wine. Before leaving the store, she asked if she could use their telephone and called home. When Paul answered, she didn't say anything and hung up. She drove to the other side of Thornton to the Good Night Motel. She checked into room eleven and parked her car behind the motel so it wouldn't be seen from the road.

After Jill was sutured and bandaged at Lincoln Hospital, she provided the following account to Thornton police about the events of the previous night.

"Once I heard his voice on the phone when I called from the convenience store, I knew that you guys had not arrested Paul and that the girls and I would be in danger no matter where we went. He'd always be able to find us. He has connections; he knows everybody. I couldn't go far because I had no money. Paul handles all that. He'd find me even if I was at my parents' home. I had to go somewhere just to think of what I should do next.

"I didn't think he would kill the girls, but I knew he'd kill me as long as I was out there somewhere. He'd kill me even if he had to pay someone off. Then what? What would happen to the girls? Oh yeah, they might be in sunny California, but the whore wouldn't be good to them. What kind of lies would he tell the girls about my death? Sooner or later they would discover the truth—that their father had killed me.

"I thought we might be safe for the night in the motel room, but then I heard a tapping in the wall coming from the next room. I told the children to stay still and listened. It was not loud but steady. There would be like three or four taps and then nothing, then three or four again, sometimes a few more, and then nothing. It was too coincidental to be nothing. I put my ear to the wall, and in between the taps, I heard a whisper. Someone was talking softly so I wouldn't hear them. It was Paul. He found us already. When would he make his move?

"I turned on the television set, thinking he'll probably wait until we fell asleep. I was scared to death and afraid to leave our room. The panic was so bad that I thought my chest would burst open. I could hardly breathe. Then I decided. I had no choice but to kill the girls and then myself.

"After the girls fell asleep, I went to Samantha first and put a pillow on her face, holding it down with my left hand while I stabbed her with the scissors in my right hand. I needed the full force of my arm to do it—I remember that—but I don't remember how many times I stabbed her. All of it is just a big blur. I think I must have done the same thing to Hannah, but I don't remember that at all.

"I had to make sure they were dead before I killed myself. I first tried to stab myself in the stomach, but I didn't have the force to do it. The scissors weren't sharp enough to go through. I tried cutting my arms. I even tried to electrocute myself with the light fixture. Nothing worked. I laid down next to Samantha and Hannah and cried. The television was on all night. I didn't sleep at all. I didn't hear the tapping anymore.

"I drank a glass of the pink zinfandel earlier that evening, but after I heard the tapping, I knew I had to have my wits about me so I could protect the children. I didn't drink after that. In the morning, I couldn't bear looking at the girls' bodies anymore, so I went to the motel office."

Jill was not discharged to the police from the emergency department but transferred to the psychiatric unit at Lincoln Hospital. Her formal arrest was postponed, although she was still under police detention. On the psychiatric unit, she gave a similar description of the previous day's events and her fear of her husband. Her mood was described as alternating between detached and uncontrollable sobbing. When she did speak, her thought processes were hard to follow. She would jump from one topic to another without finishing what she was saying. It was all about Paul and her paranoia toward him. Jill was diagnosed as having a paranoid psychotic disorder[1] and prescribed antipsychotic medication. She was out of contact with reality with irrational fears. The intensity of her paranoia diminished over the first week she was on the psychiatric unit, but she did not completely give up her belief that Paul had wanted to kill her and to take the children away. Nothing that her treatment providers could say changed her mind. Most important was that her psychotic disorder appeared after the birth of her second daughter, Hannah. Jill had mental changes after Samantha's birth also but not to the same degree. She may have been moody, irritable, and withdrawn then, but she was not psychotic or paranoid. Her mental condition after Hannah's birth was, most likely, a postpartum psychosis.[2]

Jill's parents hired a lawyer to represent her, knowing she would be facing criminal charges. The lawyer met her on the psychiatric unit at

Lincoln Hospital and, with Jill's permission, spoke to her treating psychiatrist, Dr. Helen Graves.

"Many women experience postpartum blues, some have postpartum depression, and a smaller number have the severe symptoms of postpartum psychosis. Most psychiatrists use the term *postpartum*, but it's not an official psychiatric diagnosis. However, it is a very useful description. Postpartum mental states can be related to hormonal changes occurring in the new mother but can also be linked to life changes, in particular the new responsibilities of motherhood, which can be frightening, and the confinement that a new child brings with no end in sight. In the vast majority of cases, women will work through these feelings and, in bonding with the new baby, will take on their new identity as a mother. Postpartum depression and postpartum psychosis are also linked to the development of other mental illnesses later in the life of the mother, such as depressive disorder, bipolar disorder, and delusional disorder.[3] Postpartum depression and postpartum psychosis are serious mental disorders that can lead to suicidal thinking and at times to homicidal thinking. Like with other serious mental disorders, there is often a family history of similar conditions even if the disorders are not identical. This was the case in Jill's family. Fortunately, most women with postpartum depression or postpartum psychosis can be successfully treated and respond to psychiatric medications. Jill recovered from her postpartum symptoms after Samantha was born on her own without any treatment. She has recovered partially with psychiatric treatment from her postpartum psychosis that started after Hannah, but she hasn't fully lost her suspicions about Paul," Dr. Graves explained.

Jill was discharged after two weeks on the psychiatric unit and transferred to the county jail, facing charges of second-degree murder for the deaths of Samantha and Hannah. Jill's lawyer filed a notice of insanity. He asked Dr. Graves if she would be an expert witness in Jill's case, but Dr. Graves said that would be a conflict for her and could hurt her therapeutic relationship with Jill.[4] Dr. Graves also explained that she consults at the county jail and will continue treating Jill there. She recommended that a forensic psychiatrist from the larger city of Richmond be an expert witness, Dr. Robert Gleason, who is familiar with the insanity defense and has performed many evaluations of this kind. Jill's lawyer contacted Dr. Gleason, who agreed to evaluate Jill. First, Dr. Gleason asked to review all the police records, as well as medical and psychiatric records from Lincoln Hospital. This included witness statements from her husband, Paul; her parents; her friend Kayla; and others. After Dr. Gleason reviewed those records, he gave his initial impressions to Jill's lawyer.

"Many of us may have suspicions about our partner or spouse at times, but it doesn't get to the level of what Jill suspected. Jill's thinking was so unusual that it is likely a 'delusion,' a fixed false belief without proof as a result of a mental disorder. In many cases, it's not easy to determine if a person's thinking is delusional or is just distorted by a story the person believes about herself or about others. Since no two people ever think exactly alike, the story may seem distorted from our perspective—not from hers—but that would not be a delusion. It's easy to see distortions in court when witnesses testify about what they saw or heard, when it is completely at odds with what someone else saw or heard at the same time and at the same place. We may just have a different way of viewing things, we may incorrectly remember what we viewed, someone may have suggested incorrect information to us, we remembered not what happened but what we believe must have happened, or our memory changed with time and interfering sources. Just think. If we can easily distort what we saw or heard, imagine how easy it is to distort our explanation of what was going on when we saw or heard it!"

Jill's lawyer then asked Dr. Gleason, "How do we really know that Paul wasn't trying to make Jill go crazy or that he wasn't trying to kill her?"

"We don't," said Dr. Gleason. "But that's the wrong question. It isn't whether we can show that Paul wasn't trying to kill Jill; it's whether Jill can show that he was. Unfortunately, Jill's initial belief came from her distorted feelings more than Paul's behavior, which she misinterpreted and for which he had reasonable explanations. Jill's suspicion that Paul wasn't where he said he was, and so could be having an affair, may not have been entirely unreasonable. But those suspicions grew to an extreme such that they became more fantasy than reality. No doubt there are killers who very successfully hide their motives and also give reasonable explanations for their behavior. Psychiatrists are not necessarily any better at knowing which explanations are true and which are not. That's why for us forensic psychiatrists, at least, it is important to have corroboration before we accept someone's explanations, and we should not assume that we can decide which facts are correct if there is a reasonable dispute. Otherwise, we would be doing the job of the jury. Keeping that in mind, however, Jill's beliefs were so unusual, and there were numerous instances where she ignored reasonable explanations, that her suspicions about Paul appear to have come from her disturbed mental state. Jill's narrative was not reliable; it was not a story that made sense—unless she was mentally ill."

Dr. Gleason's analysis of the issues was helpful to Jill's lawyer, and he was the right person to evaluate Jill. As in all cases where insanity is a defense, the lawyer will have to show that Jill was suffering from a mental illness at the time of the criminal behavior. Dr. Gleason had said that most psychiatrists, and most jurisdictions that allow the insanity defense, would consider a psychotic disorder or postpartum psychosis such as Jill's to be a mental illness. In addition, not only does Jill's own account sound delusional but her delusions were also recognized by family members, by her friend Kayla, and by the Thornton police whom she called in fear for her life on the day that she later killed her children. Her delusions were also documented at Lincoln Hospital's psychiatric unit. Therefore, it was likely that she was mentally ill on the night she killed her children, since she was mentally ill just before and just after the killing. The only thing left to determine was whether Jill's mental illness was sufficient to make her insane that night.

In the jurisdiction where the crime occurred, the definition of insanity falls into the category in which the defendant was unable to think rationally.[5] More specifically, this jurisdiction says that, in order for her to have been insane, Jill did not know what she was doing or did not know that it was wrong.[6] It's pretty clear that Jill knew what she was doing. She knew that she was killing her children and that she had killed them. She reports that she doesn't remember everything about the killing, but even if she forgot some of it, that doesn't mean she did not know what she was doing. She knew it and remembered it well enough the next morning when she could no longer look at the bodies and went to the motel office to ask the receptionist to call the police. From that, it sounds like she may have known it was criminal. But did she know it was wrong?

Jill's lawyer asked Dr. Gleason how he would deal with that issue in his evaluation.

"One of the problems in considering if a person knew right from wrong is that a person may know only as much as her story, her personal narrative, tells her," Dr. Gleason said. "That narrative includes values and viewpoints that are different from one person to another. What's wrong for me may not be wrong for you. That makes the word 'wrong' unclear. Now, if the word was 'criminal,' it would not be so unclear. Jill might have thought killing her children was the right thing to do for whatever reason, but she still could have known it was criminal and against the law.

"As in many insanity cases, notwithstanding which definition is used, the underlying question is, Why did Jill really do it? Is there a better explanation than insanity? Is there a better or more compelling story than her mental illness? Jill's actions in killing her children were violent in the extreme, but there is no indication that she was angry at her children. In fact, she was overly attached and protective of them, so that killing them out of anger doesn't quite fit. It could be argued that she wanted to kill them to punish Paul so he couldn't have them. However, she was running away from Paul in fear for her life, and in her own mind, if she died, her children would suffer from being raised by him and an imaginary woman who did not care for them. The truth that he had killed their mother would eventually come out. These were hardships they shouldn't face. Therefore, by ending their lives now, she was saving them from greater hardships to come.

"It may not have been logical or rational for Jill to think this way, but it made sense to someone who was suffering from a psychotic mental illness. Jill knew others might perceive her actions as wrong, but in her own delusional state of mind, it was right. It may also be hard to understand why she couldn't kill herself if she could kill her children. Was her own attempt at suicide half-hearted? Perhaps, but once again, Jill's mental illness appears to overshadow more ordinary reasoning. Jill had no prior history of violence or aggressiveness, and even if this was a very violent act, she thought it was for the love of her children, and they would all be at peace together."

Dr. Gleason evaluated Jill over three days. He did find that Jill was insane at the time she killed her children—that she suffered from a paranoid psychotic disorder in which she falsely believed her husband Paul was trying to kill her, and that she killed her children to protect them from hardships they would face once she was dead. Dr. Gleason believed that her mental illness was triggered by neurohormonal factors in the postpartum time period, along with a familial, biological predisposition to mental illness. Because of Dr. Gleason's reputation and the overwhelming police records showing Jill's unusual thinking and behavior, Jill's lawyer was able to enter into a plea agreement with the prosecutor to accept Dr. Gleason's findings that they provided a sufficient basis for an insanity defense.[7] His findings were presented in court along with the plea agreement between the defense and prosecution, and the court found Jill not guilty by reason of insanity without a jury trial. She was committed to the psychiatric unit at the state prison for a minimum of five years and was to have periodic psychiatric evaluations to determine whether or not she was still dangerous to the community.

Jill adjusted well to the psychiatric unit at the state prison and continued to be prescribed antipsychotic medication for her delusional thinking. As the intensity of her suspicions diminished, she had to deal with overwhelming guilt and sorrow for what she had done. She wrote Paul many letters, expressing her deep regrets and begging for his forgiveness. She said that she didn't expect him to reconcile with her but just wanted him to know that she was suffering as much as he was. Paul didn't answer her letters for the first couple of years but, eventually, decided he would visit her at the psychiatric unit. Jill was overjoyed, and for most of the two-hour visit, they held each other and cried. Paul continued to see her regularly after that, and his love for her returned. It would never be the same, but they were able to understand the devastating effects of mental illness, and with that, they had consolation. The psychiatric reevaluation at the end of five years was favorable for Jill. She did not show any symptoms of paranoia or psychosis, and she had good insight into her mental illness. Paul testified at a court hearing held to determine her dangerousness and said that Jill would return to live with him in his apartment. He felt she was no longer a danger to herself or others. Paul had sold their house in the woods, and they would start a new life. Dr. Gleason and the psychiatrist from the psychiatric unit at the state prison also testified and concluded that she no longer posed a danger to herself or others. The court found that Jill could be released with psychiatric monitoring and continuing psychiatric medication. Within a year of her release, Jill became pregnant again. She and Paul were apprehensive but thrilled. With the permission of her psychiatrist, she stopped her psychiatric medication so that it would not impact the pregnancy or harm the baby. Paul told her he could support their family without Jill having to go to work. Jill's life was pretty good.

Really? Isn't this like the story we heard before? Is it possible to accurately predict that someone will not be a danger in the future after such an unpredictable act? How can dangerousness be assessed when someone has been confined to a psychiatric unit for five years? Weren't Jill's actions unusually violent, as the crime scene showed? Does her risk of violence increase without psychiatric medication? Or with a third pregnancy? How much can we trust a psychiatric opinion on future dangerousness without regard for a prior story of extreme dangerousness?

Pops

Figure 10. Unnamed—Portrait of Suffering Man, DigitalVision Vectors, photo: lupashchenkoiryna, Getty Images #1133575224.

In one of the four patient rooms on the low-stimulus wing of Emerson Hospital's Behavioral Health Unit, George Murphy, a psychiatric nurse, was taking a clinical history from Ronald Aubrey, a patient who was brought to the hospital by Cloverdale police the night before. Ronald, now in a hospital gown, sat quietly on his bed, staring blankly at the wall. His hair was disheveled, and the stubble of his gray beard protruded randomly across his cheeks and chin. George tried taking notes of his interview with Ronald but gave up when Ronald's responses were too incoherent. He put the chart down and just let Ronald ramble.

"I looked for Pops all through the apartment…Where did he go? It's Sunday; he wouldn't be working in the store. I went downstairs to see anyway. He wasn't…he wasn't there. The doors were locked…He's always there…but not on Sunday, not on Sunday…I know that; don't think I don't. Don't look at me like that…Where is he?"

George could see the tension build in Ronald as he spoke and knew enough not to challenge him. Ronald was a big man. You wouldn't want him for an enemy. From experience, George knew how to converse with potentially dangerous patients: show concern and interest without trying to take control of the conversation. Allowing yourself to fall into the patient's thoughts, even if they are disorganized and incoherent, helps generate more information: "So, Ronald, who's Pops?"

"My father…You know that. He wouldn't like it that they brought me here. What is this place? I'm not letting you people cut me up. Pops will get me out. Is he here already? Did you see him? He wasn't at the store. He's always at the store…not Sunday. I thought they came to look for him…They were all over the place…I kept calling, 'Pops, Pops'…Then they grabbed me…three or four of them…'What are you doing?…We have to find Pops.' They dragged me out, five or six of them…I'll sue them…Wait 'til I find Pops."

George had reviewed Ronald's hospital records before meeting with him, including his two prior admissions to the behavioral health unit. The last one seven years ago was again for alcohol detoxification and depression. The social worker had taken an extensive history from Ronald at that time, as well as history provided by Ronald's older brother, Martin. She learned that both brothers worked at Aubrey Shoes, a store that was in the family for over fifty years. It was founded by Ronald's grandfather Joseph Aubrey, then passed to his father, Joseph Jr., also known as Pops, and then to the brothers. Martin was the one who ran the store, and after their father's death fifteen years ago, it was only natural that he became Pops.

George asked Ronald, "When did you last see Pops?"

Everyone in the small community of Cloverdale knew Martin and Ronald Aubrey. Aubrey Shoes was Martin's life, just as it had been their father's. Their grandfather nearly lost the store because of alcoholism. Pops, who was only nineteen years old, took over the store and kept it running. Their mother, Ellen, also worked at the store and helped expand it to include outer apparel, hats and scarves, and a collection of umbrellas imprinted with Paris street scenes. She and Pops hoped their sons would eventually take over the store. They no longer lived in the apartment above the store, having bought a ranch home outside of town. But Martin lived there, as did Ronald at times.

Martin and Ronald couldn't be more different. Martin was five years older than Ronald, soft spoken, industrious, frugal, and some would say too organized. He never married, did not drink much, and had few outside interests except for collecting vintage maps. The apartment was decorated with the largest of them, and the others he kept in file folders under his bed to show the few visitors who came to their apartment. Martin worked part time at the store while still in high school and after graduation worked there full time. Ronald hated the store and rebelled against his father. Ronald was loud, boisterous, and impulsive. He drank a lot and dropped out of high school to travel the country in a dune buggy with his friend Moe, who had built the vehicle in Moe's father's garage. Somewhere in Arizona, three or four months into their travels, they were arrested for drunkenness and disorderly conduct at a Mexican restaurant. Martin wired them money to get out of jail. By then, the dune buggy wouldn't have made the trip home, so they sold it for parts and bought airfare.

Ronald was married twice. His first marriage to Charlotte lasted only three years. Charlotte wouldn't put up with his drinking and not working. Ronald was a salesman, a good salesman when sober, but he couldn't keep a job for long. He didn't do well with authority figures, a pattern that was left over from his relationship with his father and his older brother. Inevitably, Ronald would have heated confrontations with his supervisors, followed by verbal or written warnings, and then termination. This gave Ronald another excuse to drink. Ronald's marriage to his second wife, Susan, lasted for eight years, and by then his drinking had increased to the point that he was becoming physically abusive. She obtained restraining orders against him twice but took him back each time after he completed rehab at Emerson Hospital and promised to attend Alcoholics Anonymous meetings. His sobriety was short lived.

Whenever Ronald was kicked out of the house by either of his wives, and sometimes by his girlfriends, he returned to the apartment over the store to stay with Martin. Martin would let Ronald stay without voicing criticism but would sigh condescendingly or smirk, looking up and down at Ronald's pitiful condition. Ronald was in no position to confront Martin. After their father died, Martin became Pops both in name and authority. Even their mother, Ellen, began to call Martin Pops and relied on him to manage her finances and take care of her house. By then she had stopped working at the store.

Martin expected Ronald to work at the store when he lived with him, which Ronald despised. He had no choice. Martin was his safety net. He didn't envy Martin for running the store; he didn't want to and couldn't do it even if he tried.

Ronald did not stop drinking when he lived with Martin, and Martin didn't try to stop him. Martin felt that it was better for Ronald to drink at home where he was safe. By then, Ronald had lost his driver's license for being a habitual offender, so he couldn't go out with friends to bars easily. He had lost most of his friends anyway. Even Moe was living respectably with a wife and children. From the apartment, Ronald could walk to the liquor store and bring home his Jack Daniel's and sometimes a six-pack of Heineken for Martin. Martin's Heineken would last a week; the Jack Daniel's no more than two days. Ronald drank into the night while watching sports on television until he passed out in his recliner. He didn't work more than twenty hours a week at the store and would sleep until noon before going downstairs to work. The brothers eventually settled into this strange harmony, and Ronald no longer wanted to move out of the apartment. After Ellen died, it was just him and Pops and the store.

Affidavit in Support of Arrest Warrant
By Sergeant Eric Kearns
Cloverdale Police Department

1. On Sunday, March 3, Officer Jack Wilkins and I responded to Aubrey Shoes on 142 Union Avenue after a neighbor, Catherine Lewis, reported hearing shouts coming from the upstairs apartment, which is owned and occupied by Martin and Ronald Aubrey. The store was closed, so we proceeded to the back of the premises, where there was a door that appeared to be an access to the

upstairs apartment. I rang the doorbell and then knocked loudly, but there was no response. The door was unlocked, so we went in.

2. Once inside, we were in a square corridor where we saw a door that appeared to be an entrance to the back of the store and a stairway leading up to the apartment. The door at the top of the stairs was open. I called out to see if anyone was there. There was no response. We went in and found ourselves in the living area of the apartment, which was neat and orderly and with a number of old maps hanging in frames on the walls. Nothing seemed out of place.

3. From the living area, there was a small hallway that led to two bedrooms. We entered the first of these, which was to the right of the hallway and saw a disheveled bed, clothes strewn about on the floor, and a recliner that faced a small-screen television. On an end table next to the recliner was a bottle of Jack Daniel's whiskey, three-fourths empty, and a glass with the residue of what appeared to be the same whiskey. We left the room and proceeded into the second bedroom to the left of the hallway. Upon entering, we immediately saw the body of an elderly man in his pajamas on the floor next to the bed. There was a pool of a dark substance that appeared to be blood next to the head and a large bloody gash on the man's forehead. We immediately examined the body and determined that the individual was deceased. We also noted bruising on both sides of the face, bloodstains from the right ear, and numerous bloodstains on the pajama top. We then cordoned off the area as a crime scene and notified the investigation unit at the police station, as well as the coroner.

4. Officer Wilkins and I continued searching the apartment but found no evidence of anyone else there. Officer Wilkins stayed in the apartment with the body, while I went downstairs to see if I could gain access to the back of the store. That door was also unlocked, so I entered with my service weapon drawn. At first

glance, it appeared there was no one in the store, but then I heard scuffling coming from an office behind the store counter. I called out to ask if anyone was there and indicated that I was a police officer. I instructed that anyone there should come out with their hands raised. I also radioed to Officer Wilkins to come down as backup. I heard someone mumbling unintelligibly in the office, and Officer Wilkins and I entered slowly. I saw an elderly man sitting behind a desk sorting through papers. He looked up, asked what I wanted, and said it's Sunday so the store was closed. I tried to engage him in conversation, but it was apparent that he was becoming agitated. He demanded that we leave the store. I then told him we were police officers and that we found someone upstairs in the apartment who was hurt. He began shouting that it was his apartment and that we had no right to go up there. I told him that we did have a right since someone was hurt, and we needed to find out what happened. The man kept arguing and would not move from his chair behind the desk. I could see both of his hands, and there was no sign of a weapon, so I signaled to Officer Wilkins that we needed to take the man into custody. I went around one side of the desk, and Officer Wilkins went around the other. As we tried to apprehend the man, he became belligerent, swinging at us with his arms. He was shouting gibberish and saying something about "Pops." The man was good sized, and it became clear that he would not let us take him into custody. Officer Wilkins then backed off and pulled out his Taser with which he shot the man. The Taser slowed the man down sufficiently that we were able to apply handcuffs. By then, other police officers had arrived, and we took the man, still thrashing about, to our police cruiser. Because the man appeared frightened and confused, we decided to bring him to Emerson Hospital to be medically evaluated. In his pocket, we found a wallet from which we were able to identify him as Ronald Aubrey.

5. A major crime unit investigation identified the deceased as Martin Aubrey, sixty-six years old, owner of Aubrey's Shoes, and brother

of Ronald Aubrey, sixty-one years old. Autopsy findings determined that Martin Aubrey's death was by blunt force trauma to the head from multiple blows. A hammer under the bed next to where the body was discovered showed bloodstains, which laboratory analysis confirmed matched the deceased's blood.

Although Ronald remained at Emerson Hospital on the behavioral health unit, an arrest warrant was issued against him for the murder of his brother Martin. The arrest was to be effected upon his discharge from the hospital. The court ordered the hospital to report when the discharge was to take place. After news of Martin's death was publicized in the newspaper, the Aubrey family lawyer came to Emerson Hospital to see Ronald. He was shocked not only by Martin's death but also by how confused Ronald was. Although Ronald was being treated by a psychiatrist at the behavioral health unit, the lawyer wanted a forensic psychiatrist to evaluate him as soon as possible in order to document his mental state close to the time of the incident for which he was being charged. There were no forensic psychiatrists in their community, but the lawyer knew of Dr. Robert Gleason, a forensic psychiatrist from Richmond, and contacted him. Dr. Gleason understood the urgency. He agreed to come to Emerson Hospital to evaluate Ronald.

When Dr. Gleason arrived at the behavioral health unit of Emerson Hospital, Ronald was in the dayroom finishing his lunch. He sat alone at a table in the corner of the room. Dr. Gleason introduced himself and told Ronald that their lawyer had sent him. He asked if Ronald would mind talking to him in one of the interview rooms. He stressed the need for privacy, suspecting that Ronald might be fearful of going with him otherwise. He tried to project an informal manner. Ronald nodded and got up from the table. Dr. Gleason noticed that one of Ronald's eyelids was drooping and that his eyes appeared to dart from side to side. As they walked down the hallway to the interview room, Dr. Gleason saw that Ronald was unsteady on his feet. After entering the interview room, Dr. Gleason motioned for Ronald to have a seat on the couch, and he sat next to him in an easy chair, careful not to encroach on Ronald's space. He did not take notes but simply tried to establish a dialogue.

Dr. Gleason: Ronald, why are you here?

Ronald: I've been here. I don't like it. I don't like it. I'm trying to call the police, but they won't give me the phone.

Dr. Gleason: But what's the name of this place?

Ronald: They cut people up here. They want to cut me up. Pops is coming. They're all crazy.

Dr. Gleason: Just for the record, Ronald, what is Pops's full name?

Ronald: It's Pops. It's Pops. Don't be stupid.

Dr. Gleason: Oh, I see. Wasn't that you and Pops in the gift shop downstairs yesterday?

Ronald: We were just getting some things I needed. He helps me out.

Dr. Gleason: Well, it must have cost a lot of money because you had a bag full of stuff.

Ronald: Pops has money; it wasn't that much, but I've got to get out of here before they cut me up.

Dr. Gleason: Where is your brother, Martin?

Ronald: He's been sick, too sick. They cut him up. He can't work the store no more. I can't do it.

Dr. Gleason: Is Martin still alive?

RONALD: Just barely, just barely. He doesn't need to work in the store anymore. It's too much for him. I can't do it.

DR. GLEASON: The nurses told me that Martin is coming to visit you today. Is that right?

RONALD: Yeah, they said sometime around two o'clock, if he can make it; he's in a bad way. I thought he was never going to get out of the hospital. I was glad to bring him home, but that was just the start of it.

DR. GLEASON: What hospital was he at, Ronald?

RONALD: I don't know anymore; I don't keep track of them. There are so many of them anyway. They're all the same.

DR. GLEASON: So what are the two of you going to do about the store?

RONALD: There's nothing we can do. No one wants it. I should have left there years ago. No one wants it now. I can't do it…(*angrily*) Don't you know I can't do it?

DR. GLEASON: But Martin brought you here. Why did he do that?

RONALD: He said it wouldn't be for long, but I don't need to be here. I need to help him.

DR. GLEASON: Who is "him," Ronald?

RONALD: Pops, it's Pops. We can't do it anymore. If Pops was going to die, then I was going to die. I had a dream to kill myself…several times. He just kept calling doctors all the time. They wouldn't call back. I can't take care of him.

That nurse who brought him out in a wheelchair looked at me real funny and said, "You take good care of him now." What is she saying? Doesn't she know I can't take care of him? What did she want me to do?

Dr. Gleason: What was Pops sick with?

Ronald: All kinds of stuff. I can't even pronounce some of it.

Dr. Gleason: You mean like tuberculosis?

Ronald: Yeah, yeah, that too. That was the worst one.

Dr. Gleason: And meningitis?

Ronald: There were too many of those; I couldn't even pronounce it.

Dr. Gleason: And diverticulosis?

Ronald: How many can one person have? It was just too much. I couldn't take care of him.

Dr. Gleason: Ronald, are you in trouble with the law now?

Ronald: There must have been five or six of them trying to hold me down. Where were the police? I'll get Pops to sue them. That shouldn't happen to a person, dumping me here so they can cut me up. Pops won't let that happen.

Dr. Gleason: Ronald, what happened Sunday in your apartment?

RONALD: You know what happened, don't you? I won't go through it again. He had to have another operation…I didn't sleep all night.

DR. GLEASON: Are you talking about Martin?

RONALD: (*Appears perplexed and mumbles to himself.*)

DR. GLEASON: Were you and Martin together at the apartment on Sunday?

RONALD: It was a mercy killing…Everyone, everyone said it…You got to commit suicide…The doctors wouldn't call back. When he went to bed, he said, "Good night, Ronald." I knew what he meant.

DR. GLEASON: You must have thought what you did was right?

RONALD: That's what they wanted. They can kill people if they want to.

Dr. Gleason then administered Ronald a cognitive screening test that consisted mostly of simple memory tasks and mental calculations. Ronald's score was in the range of severe cognitive impairment, such as dementia.[1] Dr. Gleason realized that Ronald was an unreliable historian, so he would have to fill in the blanks about Ronald's personal history from other sources. He learned from the nurses that when Ronald was first admitted, he went through alcohol withdrawal and was confused, agitated, and physically sick. After a few days, and with medication, the withdrawal symptoms abated, but Ronald continued to show defects in his memory and could not provide coherent answers to their questions. When Dr. Gleason looked at Ronald's prior hospital records, it appeared that he had deteriorated in his mental capacity compared to how he was described then. Catherine Lewis, the neighbor who had called the Cloverdale police when she heard shouting in the Aubrey apartment, had come to visit Ronald at the behavioral health unit. Ronald didn't recognize her. Catherine provided the nurses with information that Martin had been having stomach pain for several months, which eventually was diagnosed as gallstones. Martin went into the hospital for gallbladder surgery without complications. However, Martin told Catherine that Ronald believed Martin was hiding something from him—that Martin would need more surgery and was probably going to die. Martin could not convince him otherwise. He believed that Ronald's drinking over many years took its toll on him and made it difficult to talk to him rationally. Martin was also worried that Ronald was becoming depressed because he made comments suggesting he was suicidal, and Ronald implied that if anything happened to Martin, he would have to kill himself. Martin was sufficiently concerned that he kept all his medications, including painkillers, hidden from Ronald in his office desk downstairs in the store where Ronald would not be able to find them. Ronald was deathly afraid of being left alone, not knowing how he could survive without Martin. Martin knew that Ronald would never be able to run the store, but his own health was better than Ronald's, so he hoped to take care of Ronald for a long time. Martin never gave any indication to Catherine that he was afraid of Ronald.

The Cloverdale police investigation concluded that Martin was killed by multiple hammer blows to the head in his bed and additional blows after he rolled off the bed, apparently trying to get away. The hammer found under the bed was the suspected implement of the assault, and smeared blood on the hammer's handle had a partial thumbprint that matched Ronald's. Bloodstains on Ronald's shoes and on his shirt were Martin's blood, and further stains were found on the steps leading downstairs into the store's office. Drawers had been pulled out from the desk where Ronald was seated when he was first seen by police. Several bottles of painkillers with their tops removed were on the ground with medication having spilled out on the floor, probably during Ronald's scuffle with police. Ronald was charged with second-degree murder of his brother Martin.

The Aubrey family lawyer contacted a colleague in the community who was a criminal defense lawyer, and both met with Dr. Gleason to review his findings from the psychiatric evaluation. Dr. Gleason said that Ronald was suffering from dementia, a chronic disease of the brain, as a result of alcoholism. Specifically, he diagnosed Ronald as having Wernicke-Korsakoff syndrome,[2] which is frequently seen in alcoholics, due to depletion of vitamin B1, either from poor nutrition or by some yet unexplained mechanism. Patients have nervous system damage that can impair eye movement, balance and coordination, and memory. Only 25 percent recover when given high-dose administration of vitamin B1. There are no current diagnostic studies that specifically show pathology of the nervous system. The diagnosis is made from the characteristic features of the disorder. Based on Ronald's present condition, Dr. Gleason said Ronald would not be able to rationally work with his lawyer or rationally follow the criminal proceedings against him. Therefore, it was Dr. Gleason's opinion that Ronald was incompetent to stand trial, and it was unlikely that his competency could be restored.[3] The criminal defense lawyer then prepared a motion to the court seeking a determination that Ronald was in fact incompetent to stand trial. In the motion, he cited Dr. Gleason's opinion. The court, in turn, scheduled a hearing on the matter, at which Dr. Gleason testified about Ronald's diagnosis and how he arrived at it.

"In my evaluation of Ronald Aubrey, I was able to show classic signs of 'confabulation,' which basically means that a person makes up stories to fill in gaps in his memory. This happens in one degree or another with most of us, either intentionally or unintentionally, when we need to fill in gaps in our own memory. But with disorders like Korsakoff's, the memory gap is due to brain damage, not just that we can't remember everything. In Korsakoff's, the confabulation is dramatic and can be elicited by feeding the patient erroneous information to see how willing he is to incorporate that information and accept it as true. Confabulation also occurs in other types of dementia, where there is a progressive deterioration of brain function and memory, yet patients will deny that they have a memory impairment at all.[4] In cases where there is damage to the parts of the brain responsible for vision, patients who are blind may actually deny that they are blind even though they cannot see.[5] Confabulation can also occur in serious mental disorders, such as psychosis, where patients spin wild tales and fables to explain what's going on around them because they are out of contact with reality. Ronald's confabulation is not due to psychosis but dementia. He has not only serious cognitive impairment and memory loss but also Wernicke's criteria, which frequently accompanies Korsakoff's. On physical observation, for example, a drooping eyelid, eyes darting back and forth, and difficulty maintaining balance when walking further demonstrate the damage to Ronald's nervous system."[6]

Dr. Gleason then discussed his reasons for concluding that Ronald was incompetent to stand trial.

"Many criminal defendants will say that they do not remember parts or all of the alleged crime, so in and of itself, that does not make someone incompetent to stand trial. But with Ronald, he will have difficulty understanding what the court proceeding is about and what he has been charged with and why, and he can't provide any help to his lawyer to defend him. If Ronald was to go on the witness stand, for example, his testimony would be incoherent, inconsistent, and contradictory because of his brain disease. On cross-examination, he could easily be led to accept things that are not true, just as he accepted my erroneous suggestions that Martin had been to the hospital gift shop with him, that Martin was still alive and suffering from tuberculosis and meningitis, and other untruths. When we have memory gaps, sometimes they can be filled by others with correct or incorrect information, and sometimes we can fill them ourselves with things that we have imagined happened even if in reality they had not. Once a confabulation is formed, a person may stubbornly stick to it regardless of what true information is presented. There are also reports from Ronald and Martin's neighbor Catherine Lewis that suggest Ronald became delusional about his brother Martin, erroneously thinking that Martin was dying and that he would be left alone, and Ronald himself incoherently discussed mercy killing and suicide. What Ronald was thinking may never be completely understood because he cannot provide reliable information to a lawyer or to a psychiatrist, and he would be unable to do so in a court proceeding."

In addition to Dr. Gleason, the attending psychiatrist from the behavioral health unit at Emerson Hospital also testified and concurred with the diagnosis of Wernicke-Korsakoff syndrome. The attending psychiatrist did not form an opinion on whether Ronald was competent to stand trial or not because he correctly did not believe that was his role. But the confirmation of the diagnosis persuaded the prosecutor to accept Dr. Gleason's findings and the court to affirm that Ronald was incompetent to stand trial.

Ronald was placed in a state psychiatric facility where he was treated with high doses of vitamin B1, without any appreciable improvement. In fact, when a hearing was held six months later, Ronald's mental condition had deteriorated further, although he was no longer drinking. Because of the violent behavior that led to the charges against him, his talk of suicide, and his deteriorating condition, Ronald was determined to be a danger to himself and others and placed permanently in a state-operated nursing facility.

Did Ronald actually engage in mercy killing of Martin, when the description of his assault could easily suggest rage? If it was rage, who was it toward? Which Pops? Were his actions the result of longstanding resentment toward his brother? Toward his father? Or was it, as suggested by Dr. Gleason, that he believed Martin was dying, and he was so dependent and afraid that without his brother, he could not survive? Ronald's brain disease is so well established by signs and symptoms that it would be almost impossible to fake, so the answer to these questions may not matter. But couldn't both stories be true, rage and fear, released by a sick brain?

Nice Shoes

Figure 11. *Portrait of Madame Soustras*, Hulton Archive, photo: Heritage Images, Getty Images #961440804.

"I want you to know that I'm not going to hurt you," Kenny said. "That was never my intention. I know you think this is weird, but you're going to be fine. I've never hurt anyone in my life. I just want you to know that. You don't have to look at me if it's going to gross you out, but that's as far as this goes. I'm almost done…Oh, oh, oh.

"I know I brought my pistol along, but I'd never use it on you. I've never used it on anyone. Can we just talk for a few minutes? I'll let you go; I promise. You're the first person I've done this with. From the first day I saw you coming out of the travel agency and going to your car… those maroon ankle boots…you looked so good in them. What is it about a four-inch heel? It doesn't matter; it was pretty cool. I like stiletto heels and peep-toe shoes too. The heel is important…The heel is important. I've also seen some really exciting caged block heels.

"I've gotten to know a little bit about shoes. I even have a small collection that I bought at secondhand clothing stores. I wouldn't have wanted new shoes because no one had put their feet into them yet. That would spoil the whole thing. It's knowing that the feet have been in them or are still in them that's most important. Just like you are right now in those ankle boots. I could see why you might have thought I was going to rape you, but I would never do that. Having you undress down to your underwear was good enough, but you had to…you had to keep those boots on. I wish I could ask you out sometime after all this…after all this is over. You know what I mean?"

Veronica Talbot was curled up between her bed and the nightstand, in her underwear and nylons, and still wearing her maroon ankle boots. She was about six feet away from Kenny Cooper, who was wearing a nylon stocking mask over his head. His hands were still inside the front of his sweatpants, and a pistol was on the ground next to him. Veronica's eyes were red from crying, but now they were only distant. When she returned from work that afternoon and walked into the kitchen from the garage where she parked her car, a figure wearing a nylon stocking mask, black sweatshirt, and black sweatpants was seated at the table, pointing a pistol at her. At first, she did not know if it was a man or a woman since his voice was squeaky, but then she saw his hands and knew it was a man. He told her not to be afraid, he was not going to hurt her, but he had a personal request. He led Veronica at gunpoint from the kitchen through the living room into her bedroom, obviously knowing where it was. He then reassured her that he was not going to hurt her, and would not even touch her, but wanted her to do what he said.

"Maybe you think I'm stupid thinking that we could go out together," Kenny said, "but you'd always be safe with me. I could see us meeting at a restaurant, you coming through the door with those boots, or maybe the black suede wedges from your closet? I did look through your closet already. I apologize for that. You'd never have to do it with me, you know what I mean? I'm not asking for sex, but maybe after dinner we could go someplace where I could just watch you like this. I'd pay for everything, of course. I have a business, you know.

"You must have some great stories. Have you traveled around the world? I figure working at a travel agency, you'd have that opportunity. I haven't been out of Woodsville much. In high school we went on a school trip to Washington, DC; that was pretty cool. And when I joined the marines, I was in boot camp in San Diego, but I never finished. I don't know what got into me, thinking that I could be a marine. I didn't do anything so bad. I just didn't fit in. So they gave me a general discharge under honorable conditions. They knew I did not want to be there anymore. Bet you're wondering how I got into your house, with the double-bolt lock and all? Well, let's just say I've been doing this for a long time.

"You know, I feel like I've known you a long time too; isn't that crazy? Here now, I've been doing all the talking though. You're not saying anything. I don't think you're afraid anymore. I hope you don't call the police when I leave. I promise I will never come back here again. But maybe you'd consider going out with me. You don't have to commit to it now or anything like that. Just consider it. Then maybe—I'm just saying maybe—if we ran into each other…I promise I won't approach you first. I'll let you make the first move. If you just walk on by, that's fine.

"You know, what I'd really like to do is take off this nylon stocking. It's hot under here. If you promise not to call the police, I'll take it off. Maybe that sounds stupid, but I think it's worth the chance."

Kenny took off the nylon stocking mask, stood up, and said, "See, I'm not a monster. You had nothing to be afraid of."

Kenny then took a picture of Veronica's legs with his cell phone, but only from the knees down, the maroon ankle boots on display. He wanted to have something to remember her by. He asked her if she needed anything more, and she shook her head. He waved shyly and left. Veronica took off her boots and threw them across the room. She put on a robe and with shaky hands dialed 911. She was breathing so rapidly that she could hardly get the words out. The dispatcher gleaned enough information to notify the Woodsville police. They were at Veronica's house in less than ten minutes. Kenny Cooper was easy to find. Less than forty-eight hours later, two squad cars pulled up to the three-decker house on Water Street where he had an apartment. Kenny's van was out in front of the house with an inscription on the side that read:

COOPER'S LOCKSMITH SERVICES
Quick and Affordable

Woodsville was once a thriving mill town, but with cheap labor from developing countries, the mill closed down just as so many did throughout New England. Kenny's father and mother were both deceased. Kenny's father had worked at the mill and met Kenny's mother there. She stopped working at the mill once the first of her three daughters was born. Kenny was the fourth child, a much later surprise, and stayed under the domination of his mother and sisters throughout his childhood and adolescence. The father was under their domination too, but he learned how to hide out in his woodworking shop in the garage. He was quiet and unassertive—a kind man. Kenny was an odd little boy who appeared content in his fantasies and seemed not to care that he had few friends. He liked being alone. He was just a fair student and nice enough that he was liked by his teachers and not bullied by his peers. The Coopers were churchgoers and went to Sunday mass as a family at St. Agnes Catholic Church every week. Kenny was an altar boy for a few years, but once he grew taller than the newer group of altar boys, he quit. His peers had quit earlier. Kenny's family connection to St. Agnes was a benefit for him when he started his locksmith business. The parishioners already knew him, and he only advertised in the weekly church bulletin, which was enough to keep the business going. He was never going to be rich, and he did not need much. Kenny had to repeat the sixth grade but eventually did finish high school. At the suggestion of his father, he enlisted in the US Marine Corps. His father wanted to toughen him up so he would not be as unassertive as his father saw himself. When Kenny returned from boot camp, he could see his father's disappointment. Kenny was just glad to be home.

When Kenny entered his adolescent years, and his hormonal juices began flowing, he found himself curious about his sisters' underwear. If they were not home, he would search the bureaus in their bedrooms, fondling bras, panties, and nylon stockings and physically relieving himself. He had no interest in putting on their underwear, only touching it. At an eighth-grade birthday party for Chrissy Steiner, Chrissy pulled Kenny into the bathroom and began making out with him. She guided his hand down the front of her pants, but when he felt her soft wetness, Kenny panicked, ran out of the bathroom, and left the party. Near the Steiner home was an empty children's playground. Kenny sat shaking and crying on one of the swings for over half an hour before he returned home. When he thought about that day later, he became unbearably anxious, so he didn't let himself think about it. He still had sexual urges, but he wanted no part of what Chrissy wanted. He continued going into his sisters' bedrooms. He also went into their closets and played with their shoes—there were a lot of shoes. One summer, Kenny's friend Barry Nelson showed him a peephole between the men's and women's changing rooms at the Woodsville town pool. He liked watching women undress but had difficulty looking up higher than their knees. He was disappointed at the shoes they wore, which for the most part were sneakers or sandals.

Kenny did not date in high school, except for going to the prom with his cousin Margaret. Margaret was the last person in the world to whom he could be attracted, and she never wore nice shoes. Kenny did not marry. His sexual life slowly compartmentalized. He satisfied himself with internet images of women wearing exciting shoes, which he downloaded and cropped, along with a small collection of worn shoes he acquired. If he had the opportunity, sometimes he stole a pair of shoes from a closet at a residence where he was changing locks, but only if there were many pairs left so they would not be missed. Over time, he looked for new ways to satisfy his passion—by pretending to browse at shoe stores where he could watch women trying on shoes or by positioning his car by the curb of a pedestrian walkway where he could watch fancy-dressed women approaching his car from a distance and time his pleasure. The closer the ones with nice shoes came, the more excited he became. He even toyed with the idea of calling a woman to his car where he could expose himself to her. That was very exciting but too dangerous. What if she freaked out and called the police? Kenny started identifying attractive women with nice shoes who went home from work or out for lunch at a predictable time. He positioned his car with a clear view. He experimented at different streets in town. One late afternoon, he was parked at a strip mall and spotted a very attractive woman coming out of a travel agency with gorgeous maroon ankle boots. He watched her going toward her car, which was only two cars away from his. Once he identified her car, he knew exactly where she would be walking the next day when she came out of the travel agency. If he was lucky and could position his car just right, he could watch her opening her driver's side door, sitting down in the car, and swinging her exposed legs and boots after her. It was a view worth waiting for.

After a few successful encounters of this kind, Kenny began wondering where the woman with the maroon ankle boots lived. One day he followed her home. He learned her name was Veronica by looking in her mailbox and that she lived alone. He knew when she would be away from her house. He then drove to her house, parked about a block away, snuck into her backyard, and easily unlocked the back door. He hoped that maybe this was the day she had worn another pair of shoes to work so he could find the maroon ankle boots in her closet. They weren't there, but he was able to fondle her other shoes, including a pair of black suede high heels he found; their texture was terrific. Being in Veronica's bedroom was much more exciting than watching her from his car. Before he left her home, he made sure that all the shoes were exactly as he had found them and that the back door was locked.

But Kenny was torn. On the one hand, watching Veronica walking to her car and seeing her legs and her shoes from such a short distance away was exciting, but on the other hand, being in her bedroom and touching her shoes was exciting too. If only he could combine both. He was thrilled by these thoughts but also frightened. For weeks, he pictured Veronica coming home to find him waiting for her. He would never want to hurt Veronica. He pictured how he could persuade her to fulfill his fantasy, how she would understand that he was not a danger, and how this innocent encounter would be satisfying to both of them.

When Woodsville police came to Kenny's apartment to question him, he politely invited them in.

"I know why you're here," he said. "To tell you the truth, I've been waiting for you. I thought I had a deal with her, and maybe she and I could meet soon, but then I realized she would never want to be with someone like me. Look how she dresses. How cool she is. I'm not cool at all. I can't be angry at her. I should have known better. What's going to happen to me now?"

The police asked Kenny if he had any firearms in his apartment, to which he said he did. Accompanied by one of the police officers, he went to his bedroom and pulled out his 9 mm Sig Sauer pistol from the top drawer of his nightstand. The police officer removed the magazine from the pistol and ejected a live shell from the chamber.

"I would never have shot her, you know," Kenny said. "I'm not that kind of person. I like target practice, and in my work, you never know what you'll run into when you go out on a call. You may not believe it, but sometimes people who want to break into a house will call a locksmith."

Kenny's pistol and shells were confiscated. Kenny agreed to go to the police station, where he signed a full confession without asking for a lawyer. He didn't think he needed a lawyer because he knew he was guilty. Kenny was charged with sexual assault, criminal threatening, burglary, false imprisonment, and lewd and lascivious conduct. At his arraignment, a public defense lawyer was appointed to represent him. The lawyer was concerned that Kenny confessed too soon. This made his defense much harder, if he should want to go to trial. Later, after reading the police reports and Veronica's statement, the lawyer knew he must have Kenny evaluated by a psychiatrist. His alleged behavior was so odd that it suggested a mental disorder.

Dr. Phyllis Webber, a well-known forensic psychiatrist in the region, met with Kenny at the county jail, since the judge had determined that he was potentially dangerous and denied him bail. Dr. Webber interviewed Kenny for about four hours. She also administered a lengthy psychological test to help assess Kenny's personality makeup and whether or not he suffered from a mental disorder. Based on her evaluation, she concluded that Kenny did suffer from a mental disorder, but not one that made him psychotic—that is, out of contact with reality. Kenny was aware of his actions, knew that they were wrong, and knew that they were illegal. He also planned his actions carefully and disguised himself with a nylon stocking mask so he would not be identified, so he knew his actions were criminal. He appeared to be in control of his actions, although taking off the mask and asking Veronica out to dinner was strange. Dr. Webber advised Kenny's lawyer that she could not conclude that he was insane when he broke into Veronica's house.

Kenny's lawyer discussed Dr. Webber's conclusions with Kenny and told him that going to trial would be risky since he had confessed to everything already and that a jury would not be sympathetic to him. His best alternative was to plead guilty to reduced charges, if the prosecutor would agree, and his lawyer would argue for a reduced sentence. Specifically, the lawyer had concerns that if Kenny was sentenced to more than a year, he would automatically be required to register as a sex offender.[1] This meant that for an indefinite period of time, and no matter where he lived, his personal identifying information and the fact he was a sex offender would be made public. It would all be posted on the internet. The lawyer also thought that, at a sentencing hearing, Dr. Webber could testify to Kenny's mental disorder, how it impacted his behavior, and how it could be treated. Moreover, Dr. Webber could show a human side of Kenny and his personal struggles, so he didn't appear like a monster. Kenny agreed, and because he had no prior criminal history, the prosecutor agreed to reduce the charges to criminal threatening, lewd and lascivious conduct, and false imprisonment if Kenny pled guilty. The lewd and lascivious conduct charge could still be an offense qualifying for the sex offender registry, and the prosecutor would argue at the sentencing hearing for a two- to five-year prison term. Kenny's lawyer would be allowed, as part of the agreement, to argue for a lesser sentence—no more than one year—which would keep him off the sex offender registry. The judge accepted the plea agreement and scheduled a sentencing hearing in sixty days. Dr. Webber was the only witness, but Veronica was allowed to make a victim statement at the end of the hearing.

At the sentencing hearing, Kenny's lawyer introduced Dr. Webber's report of her psychiatric evaluation to the judge, which also included her professional credentials. Dr. Webber then took the witness stand, where she underwent direct examination by Kenny's lawyer.

> Lawyer: Dr. Webber, having psychiatrically evaluated Kenny Cooper, you prepared an evaluation report as to your findings and opinions. That report is already introduced as evidence and speaks for itself. However, I would like to highlight some of your opinions today by asking first, did you find that Mr. Cooper suffered from a mental disorder?
>
> Dr. Webber: Yes, I did.
>
> Lawyer: What is your diagnosis?
>
> Dr. Webber: In my opinion, Mr. Cooper suffers from a fetishistic disorder.
>
> Lawyer: OK, Doctor. Now you're going to have to help us with that one. Can you tell the court in simple words what a fetishistic disorder is?
>
> Dr. Webber: Fetishistic disorders are part of a larger group of conditions we call paraphilias,[2] which mean an intense and persistent sexual interest in something other than direct genital stimulation or foreplay prior to genital stimulation between consenting partners. More simply, sexual things that consenting partners normally do, even if kinky, do not necessarily represent a disorder. But if you're distressed about it, or if it can result in criminal charges because the partner is not consenting, then we think of it as abnormal. Fetishistic disorder[3] is an intense and persistent sexual attraction to objects or body parts that may not traditionally be viewed as sexual. For example, some people have an overly intense sexual interest in

bras, diapers, gloves, spandex or rubber materials, and, not infrequently, shoes. Or, they may have a persistent sexual interest in body parts such as hair, navels, or feet. We call this a fetish.

Lawyer: How does something like this get started, Doctor?

Dr. Webber: It's hard to say what the precise cause is, but fetishistic disorders typically develop in adolescence when an individual may not have or has difficulty establishing normal sexual relationships. They may have experienced rejection or humiliation in their attempts at sexual contact, so the fetish allows them to find sexual satisfaction in less socially acceptable ways that don't expose them to rejection or humiliation. As human beings, we need sexual contact, so if one way does not work for us, we may look for it in other ways, even deviant ones. What makes it a disorder is that the other ways create problems for the person with the disorder, but they can't stop it.

Lawyer: Doctor, what can you tell us about Kenny Cooper and how this disorder got started in him?

Dr. Webber: Well, once again, the precise cause is not known, but looking at his history, we see that he was a developmentally awkward child and adolescent who had social anxiety problems from an early age. He tended to stay by himself most of the time and in his own fantasy world. He was passive and unassertive, like his father, and in a household with strong females, meaning his mother and his three older sisters. It is speculative to say that he was dominated and afraid of women because of this, but it may not be coincidental. Then, in the eighth grade, he had a particularly traumatic incident when an aggressive girl his own age made a sexual advance toward him at a birthday party, and he experienced an intense panic attack and left in a hurry. If he had difficulty in social relations already, exploring sexual relations now became even harder. He felt powerless and out of control in sexual matters, but this did not stop his sexual desire. First feet, and then shoes, became safer for him, and the fetish was born.

Lawyer: So, Doctor, how do we get from liking shoes to doing what Kenny is charged with?

Dr. Webber: Well, you're right—initially it was all about looking at shoes, touching his sisters' shoes, and browsing in shoe departments where women were trying on shoes. Then he started collecting shoe images on the internet and worn shoes that he built into a small collection. But he's still looking for human contact. That's why new shoes, which had never been worn, were not attractive to him. He really wanted the woman in the shoe. He wanted to see women wearing shoes while they were walking down the street to where he was watching in his car. He was tempted to expose himself to those women but fought that back because he was afraid that they might call the police. Then Veronica Talbot came along and became the ideal combination of shoes and woman, so he became obsessed with her.

Lawyer: But, Doctor, that's still far away from breaking into someone's home, isn't it?

Dr. Webber: Yes, it is, but he had a coincidental opportunity, being a locksmith. Knowing her pattern of being away from home, he used his locksmith skills to gain access to Ms. Talbot's home and to the shoes in her bedroom closet. He could now picture her in her shoes, which he fondled in her bedroom, and built his fantasy around that. This was a whole other level of excitement and danger, but in his mind, it was a manageable danger. Safe danger. Safe at least from not having to have actual sexual relations. The last step was to encounter her there in her bedroom, wearing the shoes that he loved. Breaking into her house became almost inevitable.

Lawyer: Was he seeking sexual relations with Ms. Talbot?

Dr. Webber: No, I don't think he was, at least at that time, even when he talked to her about going out to dinner together. Sexual relations were not yet part of his thinking.

Lawyer: Isn't it really abnormal for him to have talked to Ms. Talbot about having dinner together after putting her in this horrible situation?

Dr. Webber: Yes, but this is not an uncommon feature with individuals who have a paraphilia. They often believe, even if the victim is frightened and protests, that the victim is also enjoying the experience as much as they are. This distortion comes, at times, from not recognizing facial and emotional cues from the victim, which should show that enjoyment is far from what the victim is experiencing and could not experience.[4] Or it can be that the perpetrator is so sexually aroused that he believes or wants to believe that the victim must be aroused too. So it's not surprising to me that he would be distorting her feelings that way. Kenny also probably thought he could encourage her feelings of enjoyment by being polite to her, not forcing physical contact with her, and sharing things about himself. He distorted the situation so much that he believed taking off his mask would bring them closer together.

LAWYER: He is a very disturbed individual, isn't he?

DR. WEBBER: Yes, he is.

LAWYER: What type of treatment would you recommend for Kenny?

DR. WEBBER: There's a number of things that can be done for individuals who have paraphilias and want to be treated. Sometimes hormonal treatment to lower testosterone, if the perpetrator is a man, can reduce the intensity of sexual urges. There are antidepressants that also reduce sexual urges and have been helpful. Group therapy with other individuals who have a paraphilia can help them see the distortions in their thinking, so they can recognize those distortions for what they are and not rationalize their behavior.

LAWYER: Dr. Webber, would you recommend that Kenny undergo such treatment?

DR. WEBBER: Yes, I certainly would. I think it could help him greatly.

On cross-examination, the prosecutor asked only a few questions.

PROSECUTOR: Dr. Webber, in your direct examination, you said at one point that once the sexual urge becomes so strong, Mr. Cooper "can't stop it." Does that mean he could not control his behavior?

DR. WEBBER: No, I can't say that, but it was much harder for him to control it because of the mental disorder.

PROSECUTOR: Well, Doctor, if you really felt he couldn't control it, you would have recommended that he pursue an insanity defense. Isn't that right?

DR. WEBBER: Yes, I probably would have.

PROSECUTOR: As you talked about Mr. Cooper's intense focus on Ms. Talbot, it sounded to me as if he was a stalker. Isn't that what stalkers do?

DR. WEBBER: Yes, it is. There are similar features in stalking, particularly the distortions that stalkers may have. But in Mr. Cooper's case, he was not trying to rekindle a previous relationship by convincing himself that Ms. Talbot still wanted him. He was going for her shoes and her feet, and at least not until he was sitting with her in her bedroom did he consider a relationship.

PROSECUTOR: Whatever you call it, Doctor, he wasn't giving up, was he?

DR. WEBBER: No, he didn't give up, but it was a different psychodynamic.

PROSECUTOR: Well, even if a sexual relationship was not part of his thinking originally, wasn't this all going in that direction? Wasn't he getting bolder each step of the way?

DR. WEBBER: Yes, it appears that he was.

PROSECUTOR: And he finally got to the step where he was sitting in the bedroom with her, forcing her to be there in her underwear, and with a pistol at his side. Isn't it likely that the next step would have been an attempt at sexual contact?

Dr. Webber: That is possible, but it is less likely, knowing how passive he is.

Prosecutor: But you can't guarantee this court that at some point as he became more emboldened, Mr. Cooper wouldn't be sexually assaultive?

Dr. Webber: No, I can't.

Prosecutor: Isn't it true, Doctor, that you also can't say Mr. Cooper will not continue to engage in this fetish of women's shoes and feet to the point of another similar attack on someone, can you?

Dr. Webber: I don't think that's likely, but I can't say within reasonable medical certainty that it couldn't happen again.

Prosecutor: And you can't say within reasonable medical certainty that the treatments you propose will keep Mr. Cooper from behaving this way in the future, can you?

Dr. Webber: No, I can't.

Prosecutor: Finally, Doctor, I just want to explore another side of this. When you said that Mr. Cooper had a distorted view that Veronica was perhaps enjoying or could enjoy what he was doing with her, don't you think that he might have seen the fear in her face and liked it?

Dr. Webber: I don't think he did, because he is not very good at reading facial expressions.

Prosecutor: But you are aware, Doctor, that sociopaths[5] don't always distort what their victim is feeling, and in fact, they relish seeing the fear in their victim's face. Isn't that right?

D‍r. W‍ebber: That is true, but I don't think that Mr. Cooper is a sociopath.

Prosecutor: But this was sociopathic behavior, wasn't it?

Dr. Webber: Yes, it was.

Prosecutor: And sociopaths like to exert power and control over their victims, don't they?

Dr. Webber: Yes, they do.

Prosecutor: And you have to admit that Mr. Cooper was exerting extreme control over Ms. Talbot.

Dr. Webber: Yes, he was.

Prosecutor: And there is no way that you can say he won't do it to her or some other person again, is there?

Dr. Webber: I can't guarantee it, but I don't think it's likely.

Veronica Talbot made a very brief victim statement, not from the witness stand, but from the first row of the gallery where she had been seated behind the prosecutor's desk.

"All this talk about mental disorders to me is just nonsense," she said, her voice trembling. "I found myself with the most fear I have ever felt in my life. There is no way that this animal did not know that I was afraid or could think that I would go out with him to dinner. I thought he was going to kill me. I was concerned about who would look after my aging mother. I wondered what I could have done to prevent this. Should I have had a burglar alarm? I don't care if he didn't need me to be naked; I felt naked and violated and trashed. I thought this was all foreplay for his next move. Even after he left the room, I wondered when he would be back. Even the next day. Even now with him in jail. I am telling you right now that if he isn't confined for a long time, he is going to do this again. There is no way that he shouldn't be on a sex offender registry. No way at all. I can't look at him now in this courtroom to tell him what he has done to me. I don't have to. He knows it, and don't let him fool anybody that he doesn't."

Kenny was sentenced to two to five years in state prison. Automatically, he would be placed on the sex offender registry when released. His potential for dangerousness may also have needed reevaluation after his sentence was completed.[6] While still awaiting transfer to the state prison, Kenny hung himself using strips of cloth from his jail garb.

Which is the true story—that Kenny was a passive, unassertive person with a mental disorder not of his choosing, and there is no reason to think that he could ever become a rapist, or that he was a sociopath who did not have the capacity to feel what another is feeling and found Veronica's fear, as well as her shoes, sexually exciting? If someone simply finds kinky sexual excitement from shoes and doesn't bother anybody, it would not be considered a mental disorder. Does that mean a crime makes it a disorder?

Does Kenny's suicide confirm that he was suffering from a mental disorder? Does Veronica's horror of what she experienced tell the true story of what was going on, and not Dr. Webber's psychiatric analysis?

Out of Africa

Figure 12. Nubian chiefs bring gifts to Pharaoh, Thebes, circa 1380 BC, DigitalVision Vectors, photo: ZU_09, Getty Images #924995688.

EMAIL

March 4, 2007:

Honorable Bruce Hamilton, Hamilton Design Corp, United States America

On information from international contract list, we inquire your firm's availability to assist in conducting transfer of larger overinvoice funds to United States America, from Republic of Senegal on completed bridge project, at substantial commission to your firm. Please respond as soon as convenience.

Truly yours,

Omar Moustapha

Bruce Hamilton smiled after reading the email, which sounded as if it was written by a foreigner. He thought it was probably one of those scams going around. However, it was nice to see himself being addressed in the name of his former company, Hamilton Design Corp., as if it were still in business—not closed six years ago in bankruptcy. Those were heady days. He was the architect who everyone wanted and had more work than he needed. They had made it: a ten-room house in Oakwood that was his pride, membership in the Oakwood Country Club—by invitation only—and the ability to mingle in the best of circles. His wife, Linda, played more golf than he did and spent much more. In matches with her girlfriends, the winner might get a trip to Cancún or Bermuda. Bruce and Linda both liked being seen at the country club lounge among wealthy and influential couples, some of whom would become clients of Hamilton Design. Then came the real estate bust, and it was hard to keep up with the country club membership fees, employee salaries, and finally the mortgage. Bruce and Linda had no children and didn't have much to keep them together during this crisis. He was seeing less and less of Linda. Linda finally announced that she and Nathan, her friend Margaret's husband, were having an affair, and Linda wanted a divorce. The two couples had been the best of friends. Nathan was a practicing surgeon and more or less immune to the real estate bust.

Bruce remembered how dead he felt inside and how unmoored he had become from the human connections of his past. Linda pulled him away from his parents, whom she called simple minded and unsophisticated. Bruce's father owned a car dealership, which had been passed down to him from his father. Linda said car dealers were crooks. Bruce couldn't entirely blame Linda because his father was a nasty and critical man. Bruce had learned how to deal with his father by keeping quiet and accepting abusive language. This is how Bruce dealt with Linda too. Perhaps it wasn't his father's or Linda's fault; as a child he did not argue or voice displeasure, even to peers. He didn't like to cause trouble.

After declaring bankruptcy and closing Hamilton Design, Bruce found a job as a draftsman for an engineering firm. There was nothing creative about this work, but he had no choice. Now and then he would stop at Charlie's Tavern, no longer at the country club lounge, for a beer or two. One Friday afternoon at happy hour, he met Gail, who had just escaped from an abusive marriage. She was sad and lonely but easy to talk to. Charlie was her cousin, so she could go to the tavern and sit at the bar without feeling out of place. Bruce would sit at the bar and watch sports on the big-screen television that hovered over the liquor bottles. From their chats, both of them realized how much they had in common. Bruce liked that Gail had no pretensions or fancy tastes. Gail admired Bruce for his intelligence and that he had a steady job. Bruce did not tell her about Hamilton Design and his bankruptcy. Gail did not tell Bruce about her teenage boys, Mark and Travis, whom she had difficulty controlling—particularly Travis, who was a lot like her ex-husband. Eventually, these nondisclosures came out into the open, but by then Bruce and Gail were emotionally involved with each other, and none of it mattered. Their relationship did not matter to Mark and Travis. They stayed cool toward Bruce. After Bruce and Gail married, the boys became openly hostile. Bruce did not admonish them, and they took advantage of it. Gail saw all this, and while she still loved Bruce, she started losing respect for him. Well, at least he paid the bills.

EMAIL

March 6, 2007:

Mr. Moustapha, I would need much more information before my company could consider your offer. Please supply.

Bruce Hamilton

Bruce just responded on a whim, without any thought that this could lead to a serious business arrangement. He also made a point of not sounding overly eager in his response, a tactic left over from Hamilton Design to give him an edge in contract negotiations. He remembered how he could pick and choose clients then. They really had been heady days.

EMAIL

March 7, 2007:

Thank you for response. Delighted you have interest. Northern Senegal engaged in a bridge project in recent wave of development. One bridge was completed by a contractor from France who was already paid 20.7 billion West African francs (37.05 million U.S. dollars), but with an overinvoice of the same amount from the Senegalese government which cannot be returned because corrupt officials within the government could have sanctions. I am Assistant Chief of Development asked to reroute the overinvoice, but cannot accept myself as citizen of Senegal and still living here.

If Hamilton Design Corp can assist in bringing the funds to United States bank account, I could then take possession of 12.04 billion West African francs (22.2 million U.S. dollars), and commission to Hamilton Design Corp of 8.3 billion West African francs (14.8 million U.S. dollars). Please know not illegal, only accounting correction. If can be effected this transfer, I may also be able to come to U.S. with my wife and daughters.

Truly yours,

Omar

    Bruce had to admit that he was intrigued. He remembered how Linda urged him to put Hamilton Design on an international contractor list for services offered, and he thought this must be how Moustapha found him. The sums of money being discussed were incredible. Could this deal be true? Bruce looked up on the internet and discovered that Senegal was engaged in a major infrastructure expansion in the northern part of the country, including the construction of bridges. They had a rising economy and were flush with money from venture capitalists who anticipated Senegal drilling for offshore oil, which would take it out of its third-world status. What did he have to lose?

EMAIL

March 14, 2007:

Omar, please provide details on how this would work from my end.

Bruce

Bruce heard nothing back for the next six days, which worried him. On the morning of the seventh day, he did receive a message.

EMAIL

March 14, 2007:

I just learned from our partners in London Westminster Bank Group, that they will send you a contract after reviewing your credit score. Please send account information so we can proceed. I also advise for you to create a bank account separate from your company so not to jeopardize your own assets.

Truly yours,

Omar

Now Bruce became concerned. Since his bankruptcy, he had not maintained good credit. However, after Bruce's mother's death a few years ago, his father sold the car dealership and their family home and moved into an assisted-living apartment. He contacted Bruce, their only child, and gave him power of lawyer over financial matters, which his father no longer felt comfortable managing. Now with power of lawyer, Bruce went to his father's bank and added himself on one of his father's checking accounts, putting money into it from a brokerage account his father had maintained. In this way he could "piggyback" onto his father's good credit. He also procured a credit card in his and his father's names, again piggybacking onto his father's good credit. He sent that information on to Omar, hoping that his poor credit history would not be discovered. Several days after that, Omar contacted him.

EMAIL

March 20, 2007:

Good news, Bruce. Your credit is satisfactory, and I learned that the overinvoice money has already left Senegal first to one of Senegal's banks in Paris, and soon on to Westminster Bank Group. The money should be available within seven days in London. Attached is your contract to sign and return. I will keep in touch as I learn more.

Please also see attached picture of my wife Khady, and daughters Aminata and Coumba.

Truly yours,

Omar

Bruce was cautiously optimistic now. He felt he knew Omar personally. He would have liked to send a picture of Gail with Mark and Travis, but the boys weren't his children. They hated him. It would have been disingenuous to send such a picture. He didn't hear anything from Omar for over a week.

EMAIL

March 29, 2007:

Bruce, money is still in Paris. They won't transfer it to the Westminster Bank Group until a British surtax of .01% is paid which, in U.S. dollars, is $3430 and a transfer fee of $1250, for a total of $4680. It needs to be paid from the U.S. and not from my account in Senegal. I talked to the bank in Paris twice, surprised by development. They assured all is okay once taxes and transfer fee are paid. Good news also, Bruce. Just heard of a building project in Ghana with same overinvoice situation. My colleague in Ghana says the overinvoice is 50.4 million U.S. dollars, and if you could help like with us, your commission would be 50% or 25.2 million U.S. dollars. Don't know all details yet but very promising.

Can you send taxes and fee?

Truly yours,

Omar

Bruce was irritated with this development but felt bad for Omar, who was trying his best to make the deal happen. He sent the money by check from his and his father's account, adding extra funds from the brokerage account.

EMAIL

April 12, 2007:

Bruce, so excited. I brought my wife Khady and daughters to London, so when money released we can come to

United States America and meet you. Westminster Bank Group said no problems when I first came, then told me that the bank in Paris has still not sent the money. They say amount higher than the intermediary's limits set for first time users. They say this is technicality but that we need a Paris lawyer to help resolve.

They recommend Bisson and Lambert Associates. Frederic Lambert has experience and can take care of but needs a retainer of 10,000 Euros ($11,806). I said too much money, but they say other firms higher.

So there is. Can you do? Will do differently with Ghana, and not use Paris bank.

Truly yours,

Omar

Reluctantly, Bruce took the money straight from the brokerage account and wired it to Bisson and Lambert Associates—they insisted on wire transfers—while his head was still swimming with the incredible amounts of money from two transfer contracts that he was to control.

During the next two weeks, Bruce and Omar were in frequent contact, more on personal than financial matters. Bruce learned how Omar's parents were killed when their car hit a landmine during a separatist movement in the 1980s in the southern part of Senegal and how he was raised by his poor but loving aunt. He learned how Omar finished high school and college and eventually became a bureaucrat for the government of Senegal but always dreamed of living in the United States. His wife, Khady, had the same dream, and now, having moved their family to London, they were just one step away from reaching it. Bruce also shared a bit about his background, the ambivalent relationship he had with his father, and his work as an architect. He stopped short of telling Omar about his failed marriage with Linda and the collapse of his firm. He thought he may be able to share those things soon, since he was beginning to consider Omar his friend. The next communication from Omar, however, was a bit of a setback.

EMAIL

April 29, 2007:

Bruce, I just heard from Lawyer Lambert who said that the Paris bank was being stubborn and not releasing money yet, so he would have to file suit. This requires an additional retainer of $7500, and a filing fee of $2200. He asking that $9700 be wired right away so the suit would not be delayed until next court cycle.

But Bruce I have spoken with the Deputy Finance Minister of Ghana, Kofi Addo, who wants to enter into a contract with you for the overinvoice payment of 210 million cedi (50.4 million U.S. dollars) that we discussed, for which Bruce you receive commission of 25.2 million U.S. dollars. They will not need to go through a Europe bank first, so it will be smooth. The money will go straight to the World Credit Group in New York City. Only a transfer fee of $20,000 would be needed by you, but they would send $42,000 to you directly from which take it. Do not do anything until you receive the check for $42,000.

Truly yours,

Omar

Bruce did not know where he would get the $9,700 to pay Bisson and Lambert to file for the lawsuit since his father's brokerage account did not have that much in it. However, his father had a retirement account that was well over $2 million, so $9,700 would not be missed. He would pay it all back anyway once he received his commission. He transferred $10,000 from the retirement account to the checking account and wired Bisson and Lambert the additional retainer and filing fee. He also followed Omar's advice in waiting for a check from Ghana for any transfer fees that were needed by the World Credit Group. Several days later, as Omar had told him, a check in his name from the deputy finance minister of Ghana for $42,000 arrived, with a deadline of just twenty-four hours for Bruce to send the $20,000 to the World Credit Group in New York City. Bruce wrote out a $20,000 check from that same account and sent it on to New York City. The bank, knowing of his father's substantial assets, covered the check. A week later, Bruce was called to come to the Thornton Police Department about a counterfeit check that he had deposited and a check that he wrote that was not covered by sufficient funds. When Bruce came to the police department, he was told that he was being charged with theft by deception for trying to deposit a $42,000 counterfeit check and for writing a $20,000 check not fully covered by his account, which was cashed by a foreign national in New York City whose true identity was not known. It appeared to the police that both of these charges were part of a failed scheme to defraud the bank. When Bruce appeared in court at a preliminary hearing without a lawyer, he reported how he had been swindled and was the victim, not the perpetrator, of fraud. He agreed to a plea of guilty with a suspended sentence of one year, to be dropped after a year if he could show good behavior and that he had paid the bank's losses.

Bruce paid the bank's losses by taking more money from his father's retirement account. He also wrote to Omar to tell him about these developments. Omar was shocked and said he would look into it. He later contacted Bruce and said he had spoken with the deputy finance minister, who was not aware of the counterfeit check but said that the $50.4 million had already been transferred to the World Credit Group anyway and was ready to be released to a US bank. The minister suspected that his emails with Omar had been intercepted by hackers who perpetrated the fraud. The minister said he would take personal responsibility for any further requirements to ensure that the funds were properly released. Omar also told Bruce that Bisson and Lambert had contacted him and said that the case was moving well for him; the Paris bank might agree to a settlement. Omar told Bruce, "I keep you posted."

EMAIL

May 17, 2007:

Bruce, very excited, everything good is happening. Deputy Finance Minister confirmed that the 50.4 million U.S. dollars was ready to be released from the World Credit Group in New York City. However, the Minister does not want to take any chances because of the fraud that happened so he wants me to personally come to New York City to assure that it all goes correctly. I am so thrilled that I can now start a new life with my family and both you and me will be comfortable with money. All I have to do is come to New York City Bruce but unfortunately I need to borrow some money from you for travel to New York City from London and an apartment when we get there. I will pay you back immediately. Total cost $8200.

My wife Khady and I can't wait to meet you, if you can lend the money.

Truly yours,

Omar

Of course Bruce would lend Omar the money. He sent him the $8,200, which he took from his father's retirement account, but Omar did not arrive as expected and was stuck in London. Omar's daughter Coumba was sick with a fever and needed hospitalization immediately; the wait for a hospital bed through the UK National Health Service was dangerously long, so a private hospital was needed. Hospital costs amounted to more than $15,000, which Omar did not have but borrowed from Bruce. Bisson and Lambert also needed additional funds of $23,000 for an appeal on an adverse decision by the judge in their case, which Bruce paid. Meanwhile, Bruce's contractual business as mediator in the transfer of funds out of Africa was growing through Omar and other sources with substantial sums when converted to US currency: an abandoned bank account with $40 million in Mali; $62 million of family funds from a deceased former president of Uganda; an elderly widow from Nigeria without heirs with a fortune of $29 million; overpayments on construction projects of $31 million in Botswana, $72 million in the Democratic Republic of the Congo, and $45 million in Namibia; a lost family treasure worth $110 million in Angola; and others, all of which were ready to be released through Hamilton Design but for miscellaneous transfer fees, taxes, and costs. Bruce was spending all his free time and a good amount of work time handling these multiple transactions and using his father's retirement account when needed; costs mounted to over $650,000. When the principals in Mali who had contracted with Bruce for the transfer of $40 million sent him a preliminary commission check of $120,000, he deposited it into his account and, according to their instructions, sent on $60,000 from the account to a fraudulent financial institution in Delaware, which was to complete the transaction. Bruce's bank notified federal authorities. Bruce was indicted in federal court for bank fraud.

Bruce's court-appointed lawyer questioned him about his actions and asked him how he could have been taken in by all these scams.

"They weren't all scams, you know—just some of them," Bruce said. "The trick is to recognize which ones are and which ones aren't. I actually got pretty good at this. If the feds ever wanted a consultant, I would probably be a good resource for them. This last deal from Mali, Omar told me, was solid, but somebody hacked into the emails and ripped me off. You have to be careful with those foreigners, but this $120,000 is small change compared to what's going on in my business. I'll be able to pay full restitution for any bank losses, so I'm not that worried."

The lawyer was shocked to hear this and tried to tell Bruce that these so-called contracts with him were just a network of scammers using him because they recognized an easy target. As for Omar, he was probably the ringleader.

"No, no, no, no! Omar is not part of a scam. I know him," Bruce said. "He's my friend; I helped him get to the United States. He calls me regularly from Albany, where he lives with his family. He wanted to be close to New York City so that he could have contact with the financial institutions there, particularly the World Credit Group. You just don't understand how big this is."

The lawyer tried to explain to Bruce that if he were to go to trial with this story, he would be crushed, and this time it would not just be a matter of restitution. He was facing ten to fifteen years in federal prison.

"Look, by the time I go to trial, there will be millions of dollars in my bank account as evidence that these contracts are real. Besides, Omar will come and testify, I'm sure," said Bruce.

The lawyer was frustrated but also concerned because Bruce appeared to genuinely believe this nonsense. He wondered if Bruce was even competent to stand trial.[1] Maybe he suffered from a mental illness. Maybe he was insane. Cautiously, the lawyer asked Bruce if he ever had a mental illness and whether he might consider mental illness as a defense of his actions, especially because he didn't think he did anything wrong.

"Oh, I get it; now I'm crazy? You don't know what you're talking about. You haven't worked with these people like I have and seen all the official documents and bank records—all kinds of stuff. No way am I going to say that I am mentally ill, because I'm not!" Bruce said.

Bruce's lawyer, not seeing any other option, petitioned the court for a competency evaluation. He explained that he did not think that Bruce could rationally work with him or rationally follow the proceedings because he had no insight into his irrational beliefs. In addition, Bruce wanted him to gather all the evidence that Bruce had in his possession to show how most of the contracts in which he had entered with these scammers were legitimate and that he still rightly expected to amass a fortune once the transfers were made. The prosecutor was skeptical and believed that Bruce's so-called mental illness was as phony as his fraudulent financial dealings. However, he did not oppose the competency evaluation. The judge appointed a respected forensic psychiatrist, Dr. Phyllis Webber, to conduct the evaluation, after which a competency hearing would be held to address Dr. Webber's opinions.

Dr. Webber did conduct a competency evaluation of Bruce. She reviewed all the criminal investigation reports and met with Bruce on two occasions for a total of seven hours. Dr. Webber was mild mannered and nonjudgmental during the interviews, so Bruce did not resist the evaluation. In fact, he supplied Dr. Webber with a banker's box of financial records from his various transactions to show how they were legitimate and that he was not mentally ill. He wanted Dr. Webber to also speak with Omar, but for some reason, Bruce was having difficulty contacting him. He was sure that Omar would help out and corroborate that none of this was because of a mental illness.

After completing her evaluation, Dr. Webber wrote a report in which she concluded that Bruce suffered from a mental illness known as *delusional disorder*,[2] which made him not competent to stand trial because he did not recognize his mental illness and therefore could not work rationally with his lawyer in his defense. She also concluded that because of his mental illness, he did not understand that what he was doing was wrong and that this could qualify him for an insanity defense if he were to go to trial.[3] But he couldn't go to trial using an insanity defense because he did not accept that he was insane, and no other rational defense was possible.[4]

On direct examination by Bruce's lawyer at the competency hearing, Dr. Webber explained her opinions.

"Mr. Hamilton is suffering from a delusional disorder. This is a psychotic delusion in which a person has fixed false beliefs that are patently absurd, yet the person cannot give them up. When he was first contacted by a man named Omar from Senegal, he was skeptical of the scam in which he was purportedly to make millions of dollars by helping transfer funds to the United States. But the suggestion was so strong that Mr. Hamilton began to immerse himself in it. All of us are potentially suggestible for different reasons and under different circumstances. Suggestibility is seen in its most dramatic form in cult behavior, such as the Jonestown massacre in 1978 when over nine hundred people committed mass suicide under the influence of a deviant psychopath. Suggestibility may also be internal based on our own beliefs or things that we want to believe. The belief itself is a fantasy, but fantasy is important in the way our minds normally work.[5] We start with fantasies, daydreams, and things we might hope for, and then we may in fact go on to make the fantasies a reality. Delusions are a step beyond a fantasy and are based on deeper mental pathology. They are not just a different way of viewing things but in fact a totally irrational belief without basis.

"Why Mr. Hamilton progressed from a suggestion to a fantasy to a delusion is difficult to completely understand. He once had a successful design company, which was an outlet for his creativity and intelligence and brought him a high-end way of life without concern for money. Then he lost his business, his wife, and his way of life. He was no longer creative and felt like he was in a mindless job. His second marriage was also troubled for different reasons and did not give him personal satisfaction. No doubt there are genetic and biological factors that also play a role, as they do in most psychotic illnesses, meaning those in which a person is out of contact with reality.

"In any case, his delusions were inspired by a windfall of money that should have been hard to believe, but what was more important than the money was that he felt alive again, creative, and the delusion was too important to his newfound identity to give up.

"Although competency to stand trial and insanity are two different issues, Mr. Hamilton's lawyer could not go to court, as Mr. Hamilton wants to prove that all these fantastical contracts were legitimate. Without the insanity defense, based on Mr. Hamilton's delusional disorder, which he does not recognize, there is no defense. Therefore, this makes Mr. Hamilton unable to rationally work with his lawyer or rationally follow the court proceedings against him. And so, in my opinion, he is not competent to stand trial."

The prosecutor's cross-examination of Dr. Webber was tough because the prosecutor wasn't buying into the mental illness.

> PROSECUTOR: Would you agree, Doctor, that these scams out of Africa are common knowledge on the internet and

in the press and that people are always being warned about them?

Dr. Webber: Yes, that's true, and that is why Mr. Hamilton was skeptical at the beginning as well. However, his suggestibility was far greater because of his discouraged mental state and the losses in his life that he suffered.

Prosecutor: You are not saying that everyone who is foolish enough to go along with these scams has a delusional disorder?

Dr. Webber: No, I am not. Some people, as you say, are just foolish, but Mr. Hamilton's situation is different.

Prosecutor: Well, Doctor, does he have a history of mental illness or mental health treatment?

Dr. Webber: No, he does not.

Prosecutor: And if one were to sit down with him over coffee, could one tell that he had a delusional disorder?

Dr. Webber: Probably not, because delusional disorder is one of those mental illnesses in which, outside of the narrow range of false beliefs, a person can look normal and function normally. But those delusions invade the person's life, and if he was to start talking about his delusions, it wouldn't be long before you'd recognize that something is wrong with him.

Prosecutor: You said that he was vulnerable because of his discouraged mental state, but you have to admit that all the money that he was going to get was the most exciting thing to him, wasn't it?

Dr. Webber: Yes, that was part of it but not necessarily the most important part.

Prosecutor: Doctor, aren't we really just talking about greed and wanting to get something for nothing?

Dr. Webber: I don't think it's that simple with Mr. Hamilton, although it may be for others, because the vast majority of people who are swindled would never continue to allow themselves to be drawn into something like this again. That's the difference. It isn't just one scheme that went bad. It's his total investment in scheme after scheme that did not bring him any money and for which he was previously arrested. If money was the most important reason, he would not have thrown so much money away.

Prosecutor: You say that Mr. Hamilton was insane and did not think what he was doing was wrong, but he basically stole more than $650,000 from his father's retirement account. Didn't he know that was wrong?

Dr. Webber: He believed that he was just borrowing the money and that it would all be paid back.

Prosecutor: Doctor, he did not get permission from his father to, as he says, *borrow* this money. His elderly father didn't even know it was being taken. How isn't that wrong?

Dr. Webber: Well, that's a possible argument about how the insanity defense doesn't fit him, but in trial this would all be fleshed out, so that the insanity defense may or may not be successful. But with his delusional disorder, the insanity defense can't even be introduced because he has to plead insanity, and he can't reject this defense rationally since he does not recognize his mental illness. He has no other rational defense.

Prosecutor: So isn't that just an easy way to get out of trial: to not plead an insanity defense when your lawyer wants you to?

Dr. Webber: He's not gaming the system here; he wants to bring all his financial records into trial. He wants to call a fictional man named Omar as his witness who, for some strange reason, now is not available. You can't even talk to him about alternatives because his delusions are so entrenched and so vast.

Prosecutor: Well, if he's not competent to stand trial now, will he ever be competent?

Dr. Webber: It is possible that with treatment, the intensity of his delusions may be reduced, or the delusions could even be eliminated. To be accurate, I must say that delusional disorder is typically very hard to treat, but if Mr. Hamilton could get to the point that he would at least partially recognize that there might be a mental illness and that an insanity defense is to his benefit, he might rationally accept it even if the delusions are not all gone.

Prosecutor: And do you think that this is likely to happen when he knows what he is facing if found guilty otherwise?

Dr. Webber: I think it's a reasonable possibility, and he should have that opportunity.

The judge found Bruce not competent to stand trial and ordered that he be sent to a federal medical hospital for observation and treatment to restore his competency to stand trial. Bruce was not pleased with this and was determined to bring his financial records so that he could convince the psychiatrists at the hospital that he was not mentally ill. For the first few months, he continued to press his mental-health treatment providers into believing what he believed. He did accept that he was depressed and felt guilty about losing his father's money. Curiously, his father did not have animosity toward him, and for the first time in their lives, he communicated tenderly with Bruce, both in writing and when he visited the hospital. His father did believe that Bruce was mentally ill, or this would never have happened. Bruce's wife, Gail, also visited him and was loving toward him again. She, too, believed he was mentally ill. Bruce's psychiatrists at the hospital became convinced that he did have a delusional disorder, and one very understanding psychotherapist urged him to consider the insanity defense even if he did not completely agree with it.

Six months later, a second competency hearing was held, at which Dr. Webber, having reevaluated Bruce, reported that while he still suffered from a delusional disorder, his symptoms were not as intense, and he was willing to accept the insanity defense. The prosecutor, having received records and reports from the hospital in which they, too, found him to be suffering from delusional disorder, was forced to stipulate to the plea of insanity, and Bruce did not have to go to trial. The judge found him not guilty by reason of insanity and not a danger to anyone, but a guardian was appointed over all his financial matters. All bank accounts were taken away from him. He was required to continue in mental health treatment with close monitoring of all his activities. He was also required to continue taking small doses of an antipsychotic medication, which Dr. Webber and the psychiatrists at the hospital believed helped him. Bruce applied for Social Security disability benefits, which were granted on the basis of the psychiatric reports. Bruce's relationship with his wife and his father continued to be good, and he spent most of his days doing chores around the house, cooking meals, and playing video games on the computer, often late into the night. Gail thought he was becoming addicted to video games, but at least it was a safe addiction.

Late one evening after Gail and the boys had gone to bed, Bruce checked his email.

EMAIL

November 22, 2008:

Dear Bruce, I was so glad to hear from you again. We are doing fine in Albany, and would love to have a chance to meet with you. I am glad things are going well for you, and you fixed those legal things. This may not be good time, and no pressure from me, but I've heard from my contacts about substantial overinvoice in Uganda building project. Really could use your help.

Truly yours,

Omar

Our fantasies are all imaginary narratives. They are stories of what we believe or want to believe. And if our narratives are never completely true, how many of them are fantasies? Are the narratives of what we have accomplished, who we are, where we are going in life, who we love, and who loves us really fantasies? We certainly rely on narratives for our identity. How fragile are they if fantasies are included? How suggestible can we be to a competing narrative for better or for worse? How easy is it to stick to our story? If we stick to a story, regardless of the proof against it, is that necessarily delusional? Did Bruce need the new narrative of an international financier because he lost the one of a successful architect? Was Bruce delusional or just greedy? If he had gone to trial, would a jury have found him insane? Will Bruce write Omar back?

Little Saints

Figure 13. *Miracle of Crucifix Speaking to St. Francis*, DeAgostini, photo: DEA/G, Gnemmi, Getty Images #944639278.

Welcome Home Little Saints said the sign outside of the Town and Country Motel. Inside, in the Cabot conference room, Dougie Stengler was at the podium looking at faces from his childhood. Some were very familiar, and he knew them by name; others just by sight; and still others not at all. The boys came and went regularly in those days, and if you made it to the eighth-grade graduation, you couldn't remember them all. Dougie knew he looked young even at thirty-four and hoped some would remember him. His name was on the letter inviting them to the reunion, but if they came, it wasn't for him; it was for the "unresolved issues" from the home that the letter suggested. Purposely, Dougie did not greet people when he arrived, timing his arrival for when he was introduced at the podium. He didn't want to be questioned too soon.

"Welcome home, Little Saints," he said. "I know many of you came a long way to be here, and since you did, I know you need to be here. Here, as you know, is less than three miles away from Governor's Hill, where many of us met each other. We all have different memories, and I wonder how you feel when you think about those years. I know how I feel, and it doesn't feel good. You'd think that after all these years, there's nothing left, but there is—there is. None of us wanted to be at the home, and we came from crap, or we wouldn't have been there. From one crap to a bigger crap, I'd say. I'm sure the good reverend Spence didn't think so, and certainly not the Church of Good Grace, but it was what it was."

Reverend Victor Spence was the pastor and spiritual leader of the local ministry for the National Church of Good Grace, which, almost one hundred years ago, founded the Little Saints Home for Boys as a refuge for orphans and the feeble minded. Over time, it began accepting boys who had become, behaviorally, problems for their parents and teachers and who required a residential school. Invariably, the families of these boys were dysfunctional, and their parents often abusive. The staff knew that the parents did not provide much of a childhood foundation, so the behavioral problems of the boys carried on at the home.

Little Saints Home accommodated up to sixty-five residents and provided schooling from kindergarten to eighth grade. In Dougie's years, Mr. Brandon Maclure was the principal and also taught science. The other teachers were Miss Dorothy Turner, Miss Charlotte Peters, and Mr. Eugene Burke. Mr. Burke was also the residential supervisor and lived in Gabriel House, where boys six to eight years old resided. There were teachers' aides and several male residential assistants who provided round-the-clock supervision. Boys nine to eleven years old resided in Michael House, and boys twelve to fourteen years old resided in Raphael House. Little Saints Home was known for its harsh discipline, but those were the days when this was more or less accepted as necessary for the boys' social and religious development. Dougie Stengler talked about the methods of discipline that were used and that the audience acknowledged by cynical laughter or murmuring among one another. In recalling specific incidents, he referred to their spiritual leader as "Reverend" Spence and to their principal as "Mister" Maclure. The teachers were also "Miss" Turner and

"Miss" Peters. However, when he talked about Eugene Burke, he used no title.

"And don't forget Eu-geeene! How many remember him? Show your hands. Most of you, I guess. I remember when me and Larry Giorgio climbed the fire escape and flew a kite from the roof of Gabriel House. Eugene was mad as a hornet when he saw it and tried to get us to fess up. Of course, we didn't. I also remember how in math class, Larry, me, and Nick Patterson would shift our chairs around whenever Eugene was using the blackboard. Each time he turned around, we'd be in a different place. Everyone laughed but Eugene. Those are the funny things, but some of the stuff was not so funny—not funny at all. Do you ever find yourself feeling the creeps when you think of Eugene? I do, and now I know why. I didn't for a long time. It's funny how you can forget things, you know? In some part of your head though…they're not gone. I have a fifteen-year-old son now; his name is Alex. He's a great kid. His mother and I never married, but after I got clean from drugs—I had to lick my demons first—she began letting me see him on weekends. He was three years old then. I loved taking him places, playing with him, and going to the movies. I loved it when he put his arms around my neck, and I loved hugging him too. But one thing I couldn't figure out: I didn't want him on my lap. I could carry him, have him sleep next to me in the bed, sit close to me on the chair…but not sit on my lap. Once, Alex and I were at McDonald's having a cheeseburger when an older guy came in by himself with a long coat and wearing rubber shoe covers. We called them 'rubbers' then, but not the kind you're thinking of. It was snowing outside, but I hadn't seen men wearing rubber shoe covers for I don't know how long. Something about the guy creeped me out, but I couldn't figure out what. The guy walked right past the table where Alex and I were sitting, and I had this instinct or whatever to get up from my seat and go and sit next to Alex, like I had to protect him. Then, out of nowhere, I remembered Eugene. Eugene wore rubbers on his shoes, and he had a long coat. This guy wasn't Eugene, but he creeped me out anyway, but why should I protect Alex? That's what I thought to myself: why should I protect Alex? It didn't make sense until years later when I brought it up to my counselor as we were exploring my childhood. Then I knew. I knew a lot of stuff then."

There was no laughter or murmuring in the audience now. In fact, the men were completely still. Were they just taken back to that time by what Dougie remembered and how it bothered him, or something else? Did they anticipate what Dougie would talk about next? Did they know because Dougie was stirring up their own memories? Perhaps they were embarrassed. Some may have been glad their wives weren't with them. The invitation specifically asked family members not come since the topics that might be discussed surrounded personal "unresolved issues."

"I don't know if this ever happened to you," Dougie said. "I know five or six of you were my age and in Eugene's class with me. Some of you may have been older or younger than me, but Eugene was there for a long time. I bet most of you had him as a teacher, especially those that lived in Gabriel House when they were young. One of the things I remembered after seeing the guy at McDonald's is how Eugene would call me into his office if I screwed up somehow and then would tell me I had a choice. I could have time-out in the broom closet with the door closed, or we could have a 'heart-to-heart.' That meant we would talk about what I did, and how it was wrong, and how I would try to be better, and how I would pray not to follow the path of the devil. We would have this heart-to-heart while I sat on Eugene's lap. I always remembered the broom closet and how dark it was, and you never knew when you're getting out. I didn't remember the heart-to-heart talks until after that day at McDonald's with Alex and needing to protect him from something. Soon after that, I figured out why I didn't want Alex on my lap. I never—I mean really never—thought of touching Alex in the wrong way if he sat on my lap; that wasn't it at all. It was just that it seemed so creepy, it scared me. Gradually, I began to remember more and more. How Eugene would touch me first over my pants and later put his hand inside my pants. He had this holy book with pictures we would sometimes look at together, which was big enough to cover what he was doing underneath it. I remember sometimes he would start breathing really heavy, like he was hurting or something, and then my pants would be all wet."

Dougie stopped talking at this point. His voice started to crack, and almost silently he began to cry. Dougie was clearly having difficulty continuing, so the man who had introduced him at the podium came forward and assisted him to a table on the right side of the room where another man and a woman were sitting. The man then came back to the podium and addressed the audience.

"Gentlemen, my name is Bob Anderson. I am from the law firm of Anderson and Parker. My partner, Molly Parker, is seated next to Dougie, as is our associate Jack Schwartz. Let me tell you how I am involved here. About a year and a half ago, following the day at McDonald's that Dougie has described to you, and after he had started counseling, he came to our office. Dougie heard about our office successfully litigating a case against a church whose pastors had engaged in sexual abuse of children in their congregation, which had been covered up by church officials. Dougie told us that he was not interested in litigation, but only justice. Eugene Burke, who engaged in sexual abuse, as well as others who should have prevented it, needed to be brought to justice for their actions. After listening to Dougie's account, we were moved and outraged that this had taken place and wondered how many others may have been victims of this type of abuse. Frankly, that's why this reunion has been arranged. Dougie said that since the abuse had affected him so much, he was sure there were others from the Little Saints Home for Boys who were also abused, and affected, and may have buried in their minds what had occurred. We advised Dougie that whether or not he wants to pursue litigation is not our concern. We as officers of the court want to see justice too. The first step in this would be to hold the perpetrators of abuse criminally accountable and to establish beyond a reasonable doubt that the abuse occurred. Whether or not civil litigation should be pursued subsequently is entirely up to each victim. We also arranged for Dougie to be evaluated by Dr. Glen Marshall, a forensic psychologist and expert on 'posttraumatic stress disorder,' sometimes referred to as PTSD,[1] which is a common effect of sexual abuse on a person and causes lasting symptoms and even functional impairment. Dr. Marshall and his colleague, Dr. Brenda Kendall, are with us today seated at the table on the left side of the room and will be providing a lecture tomorrow morning on PTSD. You can see how Dougie has suffered from the effects of sexual abuse and how difficult it was for him to come to the realization that he was abused. He had buried it for so many years. It had affected his relationship with his son in subtle but real ways.

Just as it wasn't easy for Dougie to remember what happened and put it in its correct context, it would be hard for anyone to come forward today and openly acknowledge similar experiences at the Little Saints Home for Boys. However, let me put it another way, and feel free to acknowledge this much or not: did any of you feel that Dougie's account of what he experienced made sense with what you remember about your residential experience at the Little Saints Home?"

After a moment's hesitation, one by one, a number of men in the audience began to raise their hands, fifteen of them, almost half of the audience. But the others appeared just as riveted to the question and perhaps not yet willing to acknowledge what they remembered. Dougie, having composed himself, jumped up from his seat, came back to the podium, and took the microphone from Bob Anderson.

"Thank you, guys. Thank you so much. You can't know what that means to me. You have helped me so much. If I can help you, too, in any way, I will be glad to do so. I look forward to our mingling and talking together and remembering some of the good times. You know they don't all have to be bad times."

Bob Anderson then took some questions from the audience. One man asked how someone like Eugene could face criminal prosecution when the incidents occurred so long ago. Bob told him it was a very good question, and the man clearly understood a little about the statute of limitations. However, Bob explained that the statute of limitations in many jurisdictions, including this one, did not apply to childhood sexual abuse, so an individual like Eugene Burke could still be prosecuted criminally.[2] Another man asked, if Eugene was criminally convicted, what the sense of civil litigation would be since he was unlikely to have any significant assets. The man added that he was not posing the question because he would necessarily want to sue Eugene, but only that he wanted to know what the point of it was. Bob again acknowledged it as a good question and explained how even if Eugene did not have assets, those who should have protected the boys might, and that would include Mr. Maclure, Reverend Spence, and the National Church of Good Grace, which has a supervisory relationship to local ministries and promotes and enforces ethical practices.[3]

The reunion was a success. Old friendships were rekindled, and new friendships were made. The presentation by the two psychologists also went well. Some of the men had private sessions with one or the other psychologist, who helped them process their memories. Several of the men wanted to first engage in psychotherapy with a trauma expert in their own community before going forward with a criminal or civil claim. However, counting Dougie, six of the men were prepared to give their account to the county prosecutor's office. With the help of Bob Anderson, who wrote up the particulars of each account, these six formally claimed that they were sexually assaulted by Eugene Burke when they were residents of the Little Saints Home for Boys. The six were Dougie Stengler, Nick Patterson, Dean Riley, and Ned Belanger, all from the same class, and Mark Kellogg and Darrel Metz, from the class behind theirs. Eugene Burke was charged with having committed felonious sexual assault on six children over twenty-five years ago.

Eugene Burke, in his seventies and never married, was suffering from the early stages of dementia, a chronic degenerative brain disease.[4] He denied the allegations against him and had only vague recollections of the boys. He admitted that he might have let the boys sit on his lap occasionally since they had no father or mother in their lives and needed a parent figure. He thought he remembered Dougie Stengler as one of several boys who made fun of him, disrupted the classroom, and was almost impossible to teach. Eugene Burke was found marginally competent to stand trial because of his dementia and on the witness stand appeared frail and impaired, frequently answering that he had no memory of what was asked.[5] Dougie did not make a very good witness because of several angry outbursts against Burke's lawyer, and the jury could not reach a unanimous verdict. The prosecution decided not to seek a new trial, anticipating that this time, Burke would likely be found incompetent to stand trial. Nonetheless, Dougie Stengler and the other five wanted to pursue a civil suit against Eugene Burke, as well as the principal Brandon Maclure, the pastor and spiritual leader Victor Spence, and elders from the National Church of Good Grace for, among other things, their negligence in hiring Eugene Burke and not protecting the boys from his sexual assaults. Bob Anderson and his firm represented each of the boys in separate suits.

The lawyers chose to litigate Dougie's suit first, rather than all the boys at once, so they could keep the focus on his personal history and how he was damaged rather than the group experience. However, in support of his claim, they would use two of the other boys, Mark Kellogg and Darrel Metz, to corroborate a pattern of behavior by Eugene Burke. Mark and Darrel did not know Dougie because they were both younger and not in the same class. Not having a personal relationship with Dougie until now would make them more credible. The suit was filed in federal court because all the parties were not from the same jurisdiction:[6]

<u>COMPLAINT</u>
DOUGLAS STENGLER
v.
EUGENE BURKE
BRANDON MACLURE
VICTOR SPENCE
NATIONAL CHURCH OF GOOD GRACE

Like many of the boys at the Little Saints Home, Dougie came from a troubled background. His parents were never married, and his father was incarcerated for drug dealing when Dougie was born. His mother, only nineteen years old, was already addicted to heroin and cocaine; the one brought her down, and the other picked her back up. Dougie was slow to talk, restless, hyperactive, and too much for his mother to handle, even though she said she wanted to keep him. Her own mother took care of Dougie for a while, but as he began to show problems with defiance and aggression, he was also too much for her. She put him in a nursery school, which was more of a day care than a school. He did not fit in well. He was aggressive with his classmates, once stabbing a little girl in the neck with a pencil and kicking his teacher in the shins if he was reprimanded. He had kicked his mother and grandmother too. Dougie was isolated from the other children, so he learned to play by himself. Someone had given him an eight-inch action figure doll that had the head of a mouse with two antennas protruding and a muscular human body draped with a protective shield from the shoulders to the waist. Dougie called the doll Vinny. He was often seen engaging in fantasy conversations with Vinny, sometimes using violent language. When he was placed in the Little Saints Home, Dougie was six years old, and Vinny was the only thing he insisted on taking with him. You couldn't have pried Vinny out of Dougie's hands. At night, the boys would hear him talking to Vinny in bed, and they started to make fun of him. Dougie learned to keep it quiet. At times he would walk around with his shoulders back and his arms dropped in a battle pose, as if he were Vinny. He later reported that Vinny's voice talked to him and told him what to do when he was not playing with the doll.

Dougie was still defiant and aggressive, but the structure and strict discipline at Little Saints Home made him learn to keep his defiance relatively hidden and to be sneaky. He did make friends with a few of the boys who were socially more immature and looked up to him. He made them act out his aggression on others and would praise them when they were defiant to teachers and staff. A couple of times he was placed in a foster home on a trial basis, but his violence increased dramatically, or he ran away. Before long he was returned to the Little Saints Home. By the time he was in the seventh grade, Dougie and several other boys were beginning to use alcohol and marijuana, which they procured through their residential assistants as payoff for not revealing that the resident assistants were going off grounds at night. Since the Little Saints Home did not keep boys after the eighth grade, Dougie eventually had to live with a foster family. He attended a public high school. Now the opportunities to procure alcohol and drugs were much greater. He could also make money by selling a little marijuana. Dougie began experimenting with acid, mushrooms, and cocaine. When he was seventeen years old, he was arrested for possession with intent to distribute cocaine and was placed in a residential alcohol and drug treatment program for a month. He received intense individual and group treatment and was assigned a mental health counselor. He didn't trust the counselor and did not reveal much about himself. He didn't tell the counselor that he was still hearing Vinny's voice. After completing the treatment program, which he told his friends was a joke, Dougie did not return to school and gave into his addictions. Selling drugs paid a lot more than the landscaping or construction jobs in which his friends worked. Predictably, he experimented with narcotic analgesics, which were sold on the street, and found that they made him feel "normal."[7] Eventually this led to heroin, and he became a full-fledged addict. Like his mother, he found the combination of heroin and cocaine to work the best for him.

Dougie's adult life was chaotic. He was arrested a number of times for distributing controlled substances. He was placed in three or four more alcohol and drug treatment programs—unsuccessfully—and was convicted on a burglary charge for which he spent two years in prison. He could not hold down a job when released, and inevitably he returned to dealing drugs. Dougie had several long-term relationships with women. The longest was eight years with Jade, who also was an addict but successfully went through an alcohol and drug treatment program in Florida paid for by her grandfather. She stayed clean after that. She kept trying to get Dougie back into a treatment program and to take him to her Narcotics Anonymous meetings. He went along with her at times but was not fully engaged. Worse yet, when he got high, all his aggression came out on Jade. Out of desperation and fear, she called the police, and Dougie accumulated a number of assault charges. He was known as a "regular" at the county jail. Jade had a child by Dougie, Alex, whom Dougie loved. She thought the boy would help him get clean, and he did cut down on his drinking and drugs, but there were still frightening relapses. Jade also took out restraining orders against Dougie, which he violated without much thought. He would spend the night in jail and then come back crying to Jade, who always took him back.

After one relapse in which he severely beat Jade and had no memory of it, Dougie was shown police pictures of Jade's injuries to her face, trunk, and arms. One of her eyes was swollen shut, and her cheeks were too puffy to smile, a smile that Dougie always thought was so beautiful. For the first time in his life, Dougie decided he needed mental health treatment. He needed to understand what was wrong with him and how he could do something like that.

"I had a chance to think about this at the county jail," he said. "I couldn't get those pictures of how Jade looked out of my mind. It was awful. I wrote a letter to her telling her how sorry I was, but she didn't write back. I found out she had another restraining order against me, so I couldn't even write her if I wanted to without violating it. These jail counselors are just quacks, but one of them, Christine, told me I had a fatal disease, and I was in the terminal stages. I busted out crying in front of her. I'd never done anything like that before. She was right. This might be my last chance. Christine knew a counselor who was a straight shooter and had been an addict himself. When I got out of jail, I went to see him."

Dougie saw the counselor and, as usual, did not trust him at first, even with Christine's recommendation. But the counselor took the time to go through Dougie's life and learn all about him. He wasn't judgmental or condescending. He told Dougie to call him Wayne, and they set up a series of meetings to explore Dougie's life in detail. Dougie told Wayne how much he loved Alex and also confided about how it had bothered him to have Alex sit on his lap. He spoke of the incident at McDonald's. Wayne began exploring whether Dougie had a history of abuse. Dougie said, "No, I was the abuser, if anything."

Then Wayne talked about how children who have been abused try to forget it because it is so puzzling and painful at the time and about how the truth about childhood abuse is coming out more and more. People are finally confronting it even if it occurred many years ago. Some of these abusers are being sent to jail, and the people who protected them are being sued—rightfully so. Dougie began to consider the possibility that he was abused and strained his memory for clues. Once it became clear, he found the lawyer.

"I started thinking to myself, Could that have happened to me?" he told the lawyer. "I mean, how did I get so screwed up? I don't remember much about my mom, and I only met my dad once when I was a teenager. He didn't seem very interested. Mom died when I was at the Little Saints Home. But what about the home? Was there something there? Whenever I thought about the home, my stomach would bother me. It wasn't something I wanted to think about. But I didn't really know why. Yeah, all that religious stuff was not for me, and they were pretty strict. But why would my stomach bother me?

"I hadn't been back to the home for many years—didn't really want to go back. The buildings were still there, but no more kids. Wayne asked me if I had anything from the home that might help my memory. At first, I said I didn't, but then I remembered some drawings that I saved from when I was really a little kid and a couple of English reports I had to do. There was also some kind of pamphlet or magazine that would come out every year about what was going on at the home, and I saved two or three of them; I don't know why. After the meeting with Wayne, I went home and found in some boxes of my old stuff two issues of that school publication, which was called *Marching On: A Year of Progress*. I had one for 1986, when I was seven years old, and a couple more from later on, 1990 and 1991. I started looking at the 1986 one. It was divided up into three parts for each of the houses where we lived. The part that was mine, Gabriel House, talked about student life, activities, what community service was done—things like that. It also had a picture of all of us from Gabriel House, outside in front with a couple of the residential assistants and Eugene Burke, our residential supervisor. Well, he was the residential supervisor of all three houses but lived with us in ours. I was looking at the picture and remembered how we called him Eu-geeene, and I started to not feel right. My stomach started hurting. I kept looking at Eugene—at his face and his weird expression. That moment, for some reason, I hated him. I mean really hated him. And then I remembered how I didn't want my son Alex to sit on my lap, and I kept thinking about Eugene and remembered sitting on his lap and looking through a holy book with pictures. I didn't know what was going on then with Eugene, but now it was all coming back: the broom closet, how dark and awful it was if you were locked inside, and it didn't matter how you felt; sitting on Eugene's lap was better. I went back to Wayne and took the *Marching On* publication. I showed him the picture of us standing in front of Gabriel House, and I told him, 'Wayne, I know what happened to me.'"

At trial, Dougie's lawyer, Bob Anderson, chose to put him on the stand as his first witness. Dougie gave his account of his life and struggles, including the anxieties that plagued him and for which he finally went to counseling with Wayne. He then was asked how he came to remember the sexual abuse by Eugene Burke and what specifically Burke did to him and how often. By this time in his testimony, Dougie was weeping and had to stop several times to compose himself before he could go on. Each of the defendants had their own lawyer, but as a group they decided to allow the more experienced lawyer, William Ross, retained by the National Church of Good Grace, to cross-examine the plaintiff's witnesses. William Ross knew that coming down hard on Dougie could appear as if he were revictimizing him, so he saved the hard cross-examination for the plaintiff's expert witness, Dr. Glen Marshall. He asked Dougie only a couple of questions.

> Lawyer Ross: Mr. Stengler, I just want to be clear that you did not remember the alleged abuse by Mr. Burke for over twenty-five years until you began counseling. Is that right?
>
> Dougie: It is not alleged; it happened, and I know it happened.
>
> Lawyer Ross: Pardon me. I was not trying to insult you, but that's what this trial is all about—whether the abuse occurred—and this has not been determined yet.
>
> Dougie: You know what you're trying to do—protect this sex abuser and somehow make me look bad. Well, you're the people that did this to me, and you are now trying to get out of it.

At this point the judge admonished the lawyer to simply ask the question and Dougie to simply answer it and not argue.

> Lawyer Ross: My apologies, your honor. Isn't it true, Mr. Stengler, that you did not remember being sexually abused by Mr. Burke until over twenty-five years later when you were in counseling?

DOUGIE: Yes, and I'm glad I did because it explains a lot about my life. I finally feel the freedom of knowing what occurred, even if it is painful.

Lawyer Ross told the court he had no further questions, and Dougie left the witness stand. Lawyer Anderson then called Mark Kellogg to the stand. Mark and Darrel Metz were the two boys a year behind Dougie who remembered the sexual abuse of Eugene Burke at the Little Saints reunion and were asked in this trial to help corroborate Dougie's account. Lawyer Anderson did not question Mark on his life's story or what he had suffered because of the sexual abuse; he simply asked about the specifics of what Burke did to him, how he did it, and how often. Mark testified that he could not remember how many times it was but that he knew that it happened at least monthly over the course of that entire school year, that he was asked to sit on Burke's lap, and that Burke fondled him each time. Mark was also tearful during his testimony but knew that his day in court was still to come. Lawyer Ross was then allowed to cross-examine Mark.

LAWYER ROSS: Mr. Kellogg, you testified that Eugene Burke sexually abused you at least monthly during the year that you were residing at Gabriel House, but you could not provide the exact number of times. Is that correct?

MARK: That's right, but it was at least monthly.

LAWYER ROSS: And you were seven years old when that happened?

MARK: I was going on eight.

LAWYER ROSS: And I believe you also indicated that you had no memory of this abuse until over twenty-five years later. Is that correct?

Mark: That's right. But when we came to the reunion and began talking with each other, the memories came flooding back. It was unbelievable what had happened to me and the other guys. Something had to be done about this.

Lawyer Ross: Now you didn't know Dougie at that time, did you?

Mark: No, I didn't; he was a year ahead of me and had already moved out of Gabriel House.

Lawyer Ross: I have some records here from Little Saints Home for Boys, which were already introduced as evidence, and they include a roster of all the residents, what years they were there, and in which of the three houses. The roster shows that you arrived at Little Saints in the summer of 1987 when you were seven years old and resided at Gabriel House for one year. Do you recall that, or can you confirm it?

Mark: That sounds right because in 1987, my parents were divorced, and neither one wanted to keep me, and I was at Gabriel House only for one year, so, yeah, that sounds right.

Lawyer Ross: The records also show, with regard to faculty attendance, that Mr. Burke was the residential supervisor of all three houses and resided at Gabriel House. However, the records show that in September 1987, Mr. Burke was involved in a motor vehicle accident with severe injuries to his pelvis and left hip and was out of work on a medical leave of absence for the remainder of the 1987–1988 school year. He lived with his parents and not at Gabriel House during his recovery.

After objections by Lawyer Anderson that this wasn't a question and should not be allowed as evidence, Lawyer Ross explained that he was about to ask the question but needed to establish a foundation with Mark. Since the records had already been accepted as evidence, he was allowed to continue.

> Lawyer Ross: If Mr. Burke was on a medical leave of absence from September 1987 for the rest of the 1987–1988 school year and no longer at Gabriel House, doesn't that mean there was no way he could have been sexually abusing you at least monthly?
>
> Mark: You son of a bitch. Don't call me a liar. I know what happened. This is some kind of trick to get you people out of taking the blame. I know what happened. It happened at least monthly. It was awful. Nobody should have to put up with that.

The judge admonished Mark for his outburst and allowed the cross-examination to continue.

> Lawyer Ross: But Mr. Kellogg, you didn't know what happened for twenty-five years, and if these records are correct, it couldn't have happened as you said. Isn't that right?

Mark burst into tears and was allowed to leave the witness stand. He glared at Lawyer Ross as he passed by. After conferring with his assistant, Lawyer Anderson decided not to call Darrel Metz, the boy that was in Mark's class, as the second corroborating witness.

Lawyer Anderson next called his psychology expert, Dr. Glen Marshall, to the stand. On direct examination, he brought out Dr. Marshall's qualifications as a forensic psychologist, his years of experience, and his intensive evaluation of Dougie, from which he was able to form a diagnosis and opinions about the cause of Dougie's severe anxiety problems.

Dr. Marshall: As a result of my psychological evaluation, I have concluded that Mr. Stengler suffers from post-traumatic stress disorder—that is, PTSD—a condition in which a person who has been traumatized experiences intrusive recollections of the trauma, sometimes nightmares, and develops a fear of situations that are reminders of the trauma. He tries to avoid such situations. There is also a physiological—by that I mean bodily—reaction that becomes a part of the person. They have a heightened startle response, they keep vigil waiting for another trauma to occur, they lose concentration and can become irritable, and they have difficulty sleeping.

My second diagnosis is dissociative disorder. This frequently arises because when individuals are being traumatized and have no control over the situation, their mind can separate away from the body and what is going on, like a protective mechanism. This is especially true in childhood when what was going on can't even be understood by the child. And, I should add, there is a significant body of literature that shows that children who have been sexually abused develop not only these diagnoses but also aggressive behaviors, poor impulse control, alcohol and drug abuse, and troubled interpersonal relationships, all of which Dougie Stengler has demonstrated during his life.

The results of my psychological evaluation show that Dougie Stengler was sexually abused on multiple occasions over a one- to two-year period by Eugene Burke and that these abusive experiences severely affected his social and emotional development and his psychological functioning in a number of ways. In short, he is a damaged person because of the sexual abuse, and it will stay with him for the rest of his life.

LAWYER ANDERSON: Dr. Marshall, you said that individuals who have been traumatized and develop posttraumatic stress disorder have intrusive recollections of the trauma that they can't get rid of, but in Dougie's case, he had no memory of it for over twenty-five years. Isn't that inconsistent?

DR. MARSHALL: Not at all. We know that posttraumatic stress disorder does not have to show up immediately and is sometimes in a delayed form, emerging weeks, months, or even years later. After being triggered with some event or events that remind the person of the old trauma, the memory now comes back to the surface. This is not much different from a psychoanalytical concept called *repression*, in which painful or unacceptable memories are buried but still do their damage on the person's emotions and behavior and are later recovered. Sometimes they are recovered on their own, and sometimes with the help of counselors or psychotherapists. Here, the good work by Dougie's counselor, Wayne, allowed a repressed memory to become recovered.

Lawyer Anderson ended his questioning with Dr. Marshall, and Lawyer Ross began his cross-examination. First, Dr. Marshall was asked about the scientific literature that he discussed that shows how sexual abuse is associated with emotional and behavioral problems, and Dr. Marshall agreed that an "association" is not necessarily the cause, but he emphasized how the association here was quite strong. Lawyer Ross then went on to ask about Dougie's former corroborating witness, Mark Kellogg.

LAWYER ROSS: Dr. Marshall, you are aware that Mark Kellogg was introduced as a corroborating witness for Mr. Stengler. Is that right?

DR. MARSHALL: Yes, it is.

LAWYER ROSS: And you are aware, that during cross-examination, records from Little Saints Home for Boys were produced to show that Eugene Burke could not have frequently abused Mr. Kellogg, because Mr. Burke was out on a long-term medical leave of absence?

At this point Lawyer Anderson objected, saying that this was not about Mr. Kellogg but about Mr. Stengler, and the records do not show that Mr. Burke was on a medical leave of absence when Mr. Stengler was residing at Gabriel House and that this whole line of questioning should be excluded. Lawyer Ross disagreed but was willing to show the relevance by asking Dr. Marshall one more question. The judge granted a limited inquiry.

LAWYER ROSS: Dr. Marshall, isn't it true that you also conducted a psychological evaluation of Mr. Kellogg?

DR. MARSHALL: Yes, I did.

LAWYER ROSS: And didn't you also diagnose him as having posttraumatic stress disorder?

DR. MARSHALL: Yes, I did.

LAWYER ROSS: And didn't you attribute Mr. Kellogg's posttraumatic stress disorder to multiple occasions of sexual abuse over a one-year period of time when Mr. Kellogg resided in Gabriel House?

DR. MARSHALL: Yes, I did, but there may be extenuating circumstances here. I would need to reevaluate Mr. Kellogg on these issues. It is possible that he expanded the number of times that he was abused beyond what is objectively possible, but that does not take away from my diagnosis and the relationship of the diagnosis to sexual abuse.

LAWYER ROSS: But you would agree that Mr. Kellogg's condition could not have been due to multiple occasions of sexual abuse by Mr. Burke, if Mr. Burke was not there?

DR. MARSHALL: That's possible, but I don't know that yet.

Lawyer Anderson called a number of other witnesses, including the principal Brandon Maclure, and the pastor and spiritual leader Reverend Victor Spence. Both were in their eighties and had limited memory of the events in question. They denied having any knowledge of Eugene Burke's sexual abuse and claimed that the children were well protected from such things. Burke was not called by Lawyer Anderson to testify because his dementia could help draw sympathy toward him. After Lawyer Anderson rested his case, Lawyer Ross called his first and most important witness, a forensic psychiatrist well known outside of that jurisdiction, Dr. Phyllis Webber. Dr. Webber also evaluated Dougie Stengler. After being asked about her credentials and how she conducted her evaluation, she, too, was asked about her conclusions.

DR. WEBBER: My psychiatric evaluation shows that Mr. Stengler has serious mental and emotional problems. Some of these were evident in early childhood before he was placed in the Little Saints Home. They included attention deficit hyperactivity disorder, learning disorder, and what would best be described as oppositional defiant disorder, which showed up as disregard for authority and physical acting-out behaviors.[8] His family history shows a strong predisposition to alcohol and drug abuse, which became one of Mr. Stengler's problems later in his teenage years and into early adulthood. In my opinion, Mr. Stengler also has an anxiety disorder with features of posttraumatic stress and dissociation.[9] What this means, essentially, is that he has significant anxiety problems, similar to what one might have if he suffered a major trauma in life, but the source of that trauma is not clear. It could well be the abuse and neglect by his family and by foster parents before he was placed in Little Saints, or it could have included sexual abuse by Eugene Burke if that actually took place. As for his dissociation, that simply means he has a rich fantasy life and likes to escape from reality. In fact, at times he has been psychotic, hearing and communicating with an action figure named Vinny. He is not, therefore, a reliable historian.[10]

Lawyer Ross: Why didn't you diagnose Mr. Stengler with posttraumatic stress disorder?

Dr. Webber: It's because we can't psychiatrically determine if the trauma he claims was inflicted or not. No psychological tests or evaluation methods can do it.[11]

Lawyer Ross: But, Doctor, you know that a number of the boys from Little Saints have claimed similar abuse by Eugene Burke?

Dr. Webber: Yes, I do, and if that establishes the abuse factually for the purpose of this trial, that's fine. But I can't independently determine that. I have great concerns about how the memories of the alleged sexual abuse came to light twenty-five years later when there was no memory during that whole period of time, and in a very suggestible atmosphere, at a reunion that was arranged with the assumption that sexual abuse occurred and with the purpose of looking for victims. Some of the boys who then claimed to remember the abuse were shown that it couldn't have occurred since Burke was not there.

Lawyer Ross: But you heard Dr. Marshall in his testimony say that there can be delayed posttraumatic stress disorder, a recognized form of the condition similar to repressed memories. Is that right?

Dr. Webber: Yes, that is true in some instances, but the concept of repressed memories is very controversial. Some authorities don't believe it at all. I happen to believe it, because we don't remember everything that happened in our lives all the time; some memories, including painful memories, are put away, and we can be reminded of them later. But any memories from over twenty-five years ago should be suspect because they decay over time, they are harder to corroborate, and they can be distorted by all sorts of factors. That's why there is the legal principle of the statute of limitations—

Immediately, Lawyer Anderson stood up and objected, saying that Dr. Webber was not allowed to testify on legal principles and that the legal principle here is one that, for public policy reasons, has been modified so that victims of sexual abuse in their childhood, who are so helpless and vulnerable, still have an opportunity for justice even if it is long after the abuse. The judge sustained the objection, and Lawyer Ross went on.

Lawyer Ross: Don't reference the statute of limitations here, Doctor, but tell us just from a psychiatric standpoint what happens with memories over time.

Dr. Webber: They are greatly distorted by both external and internal factors, and most importantly, all of us tend to remember what we want to remember and how an event took place even if, remarkably, it was not so. There have been countless studies to show how fragile our memories are and how we alter them to create a narrative that we want to believe. Here, Mr. Stengler's memories, which reportedly were repressed, were recovered at a time when childhood sexual abuse by teachers, counselors, and religious authorities was at the forefront in society, and there was an opportunity for a monetary windfall if such a memory were true. Psychotherapists and counselors began exploring more intensively the possibility of childhood sexual abuse in their patients' histories, in some ways steering them to a memory that can help their patients make sense of their lives even if it did not occur or was not responsible for their psychological problems. Mr. Stengler became heavily involved in this quest and sought legal assistance, which led to a reunion, and a number of the men in this atmosphere began remembering things when they were boys that they had either forgotten or that had never happened. The presence of lawyers and psychologists implied that these memories existed and were not searched for in vain. That is what happened, in my opinion, with Mark Kellogg and Darrel Metz, both of whom recovered memories of abuse by Eugene Burke that could not have happened because he was on a medical leave of absence.

Lawyer Anderson again stood up and objected, but Lawyer Ross argued that since Dr. Marshall had evaluated those two men and had expressed opinions about them, Dr. Webber should have the opportunity to consider the reliability of Dr. Marshall's conclusions. The objection was overruled by the judge.

>Lawyer Ross: Were there other aspects of your evaluation that led you to believe Mr. Stengler's memories were not reliable?

>Dr. Webber: Please understand that I cannot make a factual determination whether those things occurred or did not occur, but the reliability of a person's memory under the circumstances of a repressed and then recovered memory is important and needs to be looked at psychiatrically, at least if one is going to attribute a major mental disorder

to such recovered memories. Also, I can reasonably say that there is no psychological method for Dr. Marshall to determine that the events occurred. Dr. Marshall talked about a dissociative disorder with which I agree, but that does not have to be a result of something that occurred when Mr. Stengler was on Mr. Burke's lap. Dissociation is a common occurrence in individuals who have rich fantasy lives and sometimes leads to bizarre symptoms, including identification with another personality. Mr. Stengler's intense involvement with an action figure he named Vinny suggests that.

Lawyer Ross: So, Doctor, can you summarize the essence of your opinion in lay terms?

Dr. Webber: Mr. Stengler has evidence of an anxiety disorder with features of posttraumatic stress and dissociation. He does have significant mental disorders, but he had mental disorders before he came to the Little Saints Home, and he had a family history that predisposed him to mental disorders. The circumstance of his recovered memory—that he was abused over twenty-five years ago and did not remember it until now, including the circumstances of how it was recovered—makes him an unreliable historian. No psychiatrist or psychologist, in my opinion, can conclude that his mental disorders must be from the alleged sexual abuse of Eugene Burke.

Lawyer Anderson cross-examined Dr. Webber in some detail, and she gave him points that she needed to without arguing with him but stuck to her opinions anyway. After closing arguments, the jury was instructed and deliberated for about two days, then returned a verdict in favor of Mr. Stengler of $3.4 million due to the negligence of the National Church of Good Grace in its hiring practices, the lack of supervision of its associated members, and the inadequate protection of the boys over whom the organization was responsible.

How reliable were Dougie Stengler's memories? How about Mark Kellogg's and Darrel Metz's? Does the favorable outcome for Dougie suggest the effects of a current social narrative about the extent of childhood sexual abuse within our formerly respected and authoritative institutions? Does a social narrative like this help counselors look for abuse that may have been ignored—or to suggest abuse that might not have occurred?

People who make claims about memories that are later determined not to be true are not necessarily malingerers. They are typically convinced of those memories, even if the memories are grossly distorted or false. When confronted with evidence that is beyond dispute, scientific literature shows they may still argue that their memory is true.[12] Is it that hard to give up something we believe or have believed for a long time? Since memories are the building blocks of our narratives and can be easily distorted, can we be sure about any narratives from twenty-five years ago? Does Dougie's personal and criminal history suggest someone who is not a reliable informant? If so, could he be a malingerer?

Insanity

Figure 14. *Don Quixote Riding His Horse against Full Moon*,
E+, photo: aluxum, Getty Images #1007161400.

Jeffrey Forbes and his mother, Gloria, were driving home from Uncle Will's funeral. Gloria's sister Joan was too upset by her husband Will's unexpected death to have a reception after the funeral, so Gloria missed a chance to talk to people, to receive condolences, and to be the center of attention. She told Joan she'd be glad to make all the arrangements. Joan wouldn't have to do a thing. She offered to pay for the reception. Joan didn't listen.

"That's just not right. Everyone has a reception," Gloria said. "If my husband died, I'd want a reception no matter how bad I felt. You have to have closure on these things. I'm sure people were offended. Here they came to the funeral—some came to the wake too—and they missed work and had no reception. It's not right. If it were my husband…Well, who knows where he is. He may be dead for all we know, what with his drinking and fighting…You're lucky you never really knew your father—you're lucky. Oh, he could charm people all right, telling jokes, playing the guitar, singing…I thought if I heard him sing 'Midnight Special' one more time, I'd scream…and then he was gone…disappeared with his guitar and not much else…Not a call after that…Not one support check…Not one. I had to raise you myself. It was not easy, and you didn't make it easy. You still can't live on your own…"

Jeffrey heard all this before, and he wasn't listening. He just kept driving, occasionally grunting, "Hmm," and letting her talk. Uncle Will told him about his father too—how they all partied and drank together; his father drank more. He could really hold his liquor. He was quite the guy with the ladies too; one was not enough. Uncle Will said, "That's probably why he left the two of you and never returned." Jeffrey remembered seeing the photograph of his father and mother along with Uncle Will and Aunt Joan on the Virginia Beach boardwalk. Joan was laughing and had her arms around his father's neck, with his mother and Uncle Will standing next to them, barely smiling. Jeffrey always liked that photograph.

Jeffrey thought he would miss Uncle Will's stories. Uncle Will was also the only one who would rehire him no matter how much trouble he had been in. He was the only one who would praise him for his work. Jeffrey remembered Uncle Will saying, "Jeffrey, you can frame a house about as fast as anyone I've had work for me." The construction company would likely fold without Uncle Will.

Jeffrey drove into their driveway and then into the garage. He and his mother both got out of the car and went into the kitchen through the garage door.

"There's nothing to be done about it now. I can imagine the talk. Already, Mrs. Morrison came over and asked me if there was going to be a reception. I didn't say anything, but I did roll my eyes. She knew that I didn't think it was right; well, who would? Not even a cup of coffee and some pastries? Well, Jeffrey, we can have a reception right here, the two of us. I'll make some coffee, and we still have a little pound cake. You sit right down here, and I'll get it for us," his mother said.

The two of them sat at the kitchen table for about half an hour. Jeffrey drank his coffee but did not want any pound cake. He was waiting for an opportunity to go outside to have a cigarette. He thought about how strange it was that at thirty-six years old, he had to wait for a smoke. His mother, meanwhile, kept talking. He noticed when she finished a sentence that her mouth was still open preparing for the next sentence. There was no opportunity to interrupt her, not that he wanted to. He thought about Uncle Will's skiff and outboard motor and how they went fishing together. Maybe Aunt Joan will give him the skiff.

"Uncle Will was sure someone you could rely on," his mother continued. "He was very good to you. It's not easy to find someone to rely on. No, it's not easy. Who will be there when things need fixing? Look at the linoleum curling up by the range. It looks awful. Who will fix things like that?"

Jeffrey got the message. He stood up from the kitchen table and went to the pantry, opened it, and stooped over to retrieve the hammer from a large cardboard box on the pantry floor. He then went over to the range, bent down, and inspected the grimy curled edge of the linoleum. He looked up and said, "Do we have any tacks?"

Gloria put down the dish towel, smiled at Jeffrey, rolled her eyes a bit, and then went over and knelt down by the pantry. She began to rummage through the items on the floor of the pantry, looking for the box of tacks. Without turning around to face Jeffrey, she said, "Dear, I guess I will always have to take care of you."

Without saying a word or, for that matter, without uttering any sound, Jeffrey raised his arm high and struck his mother's head hard with the hammer. She slumped forward from the blow, and he struck her again, and again, and again. Blood was pulsing out through the spreading lacerations made by the hammer. There was as much blood on him as on his mother. Her body, still on contracted knees, leaned against the pantry doorway. Bone, skin, hair, and blood mixed together in a shape no longer recognizable as a skull. Jeffrey stood looking at what was left of his mother. He was breathing heavily. He then dropped the hammer, took off all his clothes, and threw them in a heap into the pantry next to his mother's body. It almost looked like two bodies. He cleaned his glasses of blood spatter, sat down at the kitchen table, and lit up a cigarette.

Once his breathing normalized, Jeffrey wrapped his mother's body and his clothes in a brown tarp that he brought from the garage. He tightened the tarp around its contents with bungee cords and dragged it to the car, where he stuffed it into the trunk. He cleaned up the kitchen only superficially, having no illusions that the bloodstains would not be detected. He didn't want Aunt Joan to freak out when she came over. He then drove to Bert's Donut Shop with his mother's body in the trunk. He had a couple cups of black coffee at the counter and chatted with Bert's daughter, who managed the shop. He had known the daughter from high school. He told her about Uncle Will's funeral. She asked how his mother was taking it, and he said, "As well as could be expected."

Jeffrey bought a couple of apple fritters and a large black coffee to go and drove to Wolf Creek Gorge, where he rolled the tarp and its contents over the edge into a thicket of brush. He knew it would be found eventually, but it bought him some time. Not three months later, two US Marshalls were flying Jeffrey back from Montana. He had not resisted his arrest. He chatted with them about fishing for brown trout on the Beaver Head River. He had always wanted to fish out west.

Jeffrey was charged with first-degree murder for killing his mother. She had modest assets, but they were enough to hire a well-known defense lawyer in their community. After meeting with Jeffrey for over four hours, the lawyer was struck by Jeffrey's inability to explain why he killed his mother and by his total lack of remorse. In fact, Jeffrey seemed to have no emotions at all. They could have been talking about the weather. Jeffrey did have a history of criminal assaults, which started when he was a juvenile. During an assembly in his high school auditorium, a student sitting behind Jeffrey kept pushing his glasses forward by the right temple, even after Jeffrey had told him to cut it out. Finally, Jeffrey spun around and struck the student in the nose, then jumped over the back of his own seat and continued thrashing the student with both fists until two teachers pulled him away. Sitting in the principal's office, he only said, "He kept pushing on my glasses." He gave no other explanation. Jeffrey was placed in a juvenile detention facility where he was a model detainee; he was usually quiet and kept to himself, but he was completely cooperative with staff. He was released on good behavior in four months. The assault on the other student appeared to have been out of character for him, an exception rather than a pattern of behavior. There was no indication that Jeffrey was a danger to others.

When Jeffrey was nineteen years old, he and his friend Chris Donahue stole a case of beer from a convenience store. On their way out of the store, an older, frail-looking clerk saw what they were doing and chased after them. Jeffrey slowed down, and when the old man was almost on top of him, Jeffrey stabbed him in the abdomen with a fish-scaling knife he had drawn from a sheath attached to his belt. The old man nearly bled to death. Jeffrey was charged with theft and assault with a deadly weapon. He pled guilty and was sentenced to seven and a half to fifteen years in the state prison. He was a model prisoner and was released on parole in only six years.

Jeffrey's only long-term relationship was with Diane, whom he met on Uncle Will's construction crew. She was a flagger. They began dating, and shortly thereafter, she invited him to live in her apartment. It was so good not living with his mother. But Diane was a free spirit and didn't always come home right after work. She liked getting together with "the girls." One day, Jeffrey prepared a fish dinner for the two of them and bought a bottle of her favorite chardonnay. When she finally returned close to midnight, he was waiting with cold fish and warm chardonnay still on the table. She sat down on an easy chair in the living room and began reading a magazine. Jeffrey stood in the doorway to the living room and asked her, "Where have you been?"

Diane didn't answer. He asked her again, and she still didn't answer, but several seconds later, she said, "Are you talking to me?"

He answered, "Well, who else is in the room?"

Diane looked down at her magazine, and in two strides Jeffrey leaped on her, both of them falling over with the easy chair. He grabbed Diane by the hair with his left hand and began pummeling her face with his right fist. She lost consciousness momentarily, but when she came to, she looked at him with terror in her eyes and begged him to stop. He stopped reluctantly, quietly gathered his belongings, and left the apartment. Diane called the police. Jeffrey pled guilty to first-degree assault and violation of parole. He served his sentence for the assault on Diane concurrently with the remaining nine years of his fifteen-year sentence for the earlier charges. Upon his release from prison, he returned home to live with his mother once again, only three years before Uncle Will's death.

Jeffrey's lawyer believed there was something mentally wrong with Jeffrey. He showed the same inability to explain the extent of his actions and lack of remorse in discussing his previous crimes as he did about killing his mother. He did tell the lawyer that when he was five years old, he was accidentally hit by a boy taking practice swings with a baseball bat and was kept in the hospital for three days. Perhaps there was something wrong with Jeffrey's brain. In this jurisdiction, insanity is defined based on the category of whether the person was unable to think rationally[1]—specifically was the person unable to know his behavior was wrong (even if he may have known it was criminal)?[2]

Jeffrey's lawyer was able to retrieve medical records from the three-day hospitalization, as well as Jeffrey's complete pediatric records. He then retained a neurologist, Dr. Victor Ruddick, to review the records and to personally examine Jeffrey. Dr. Ruddick liked doing court work and was frequently used by criminal defense lawyers. After reviewing the extensive records and personally examining Jeffrey, Dr. Ruddick produced a comprehensive neurological report. He concluded that Jeffrey suffered from the effects of a traumatic brain injury when he was five years old that kept him from forming emotional attachments with others, and the brain injury was responsible for subclinical seizures in which he would go into a violent rage and not remember what he had done.[3] At his deposition, which was requested by the prosecutor, Dr. Ruddick further elaborated on these opinions.

"My examination shows that Jeffrey Forbes sustained a traumatic brain injury when he was five years old. He had lost consciousness for over an hour and remained confused and disoriented, so he was hospitalized for observation and further testing. There was no sign of brain contusion or bleeding, but he clearly had a traumatic brain injury.[4] After three days in the hospital, he appeared to recover and was discharged.

"Two years later, when Jeffrey was seven years old and starting the second grade, teachers reported that he had problems maintaining attention in school. He was smart enough to pass from the first grade into the second grade but was not working up to his intelligence and potential. They thought he might suffer from an attention deficit disorder.[5] Jeffrey's pediatrician was contacted and, after obtaining a more detailed history from Jeffrey's mother, concurred with the diagnosis. He prescribed Jeffrey a stimulant medication for his attention problems, but it made him too nervous and disturbed his sleep, so it was discontinued. The issue of attention deficit disorder was never raised again, and Jeffrey somehow completed his studies and graduated from high school without medication. It is my opinion after reviewing his records that Jeffrey's attention deficits were due to the traumatic brain injury he suffered when he was five years old, which helps confirm that Jeffrey, in fact, has residual brain damage from the earlier injury.

"A traumatic brain injury would explain why Jeffrey has no explanation for his behavior, why he has a striking lack of remorse for his actions, and why he has an inability to display any emotions at all. These features are consistent with damage to the frontal lobes of the brain as a result of the traumatic brain injury.[6]

"On neurological examination, although Jeffrey did not have any major abnormalities, he did exhibit neurological soft signs,[7]- subtle coordination problems, and mild disturbances in his gait. In my opinion, these signs are further evidence of brain damage.

"Finally, when I discussed Jeffrey's history of violent, angry outbursts, particularly when he killed his mother, he reported no memory of his actions and was surprised when he learned what he did. This, in my opinion, is also consistent with a traumatic brain injury that causes subclinical seizures in which he does not fall to the ground and shake but rather suddenly explodes in anger. During his explosion, he is not aware of his actions, and that is why he does not remember them.

"In my opinion, Jeffrey was insane at the time he killed his mother because he was unaware of his actions due to the long-term effects of a traumatic brain injury. However, I would recommend that he undergo a comprehensive psychiatric evaluation to help identify other emotional and behavioral problems that could be a result of traumatic brain injury, taking into account my neurological findings."

The prosecutor then asked about Dr. Ruddick's background and experience in criminal cases, which was limited, since Dr. Ruddick mostly testified in accident cases. The prosecutor also tried to show how a neurologist's opinion was insufficient for final conclusions on insanity.

> PROSECUTOR: In your report, Doctor, you specifically suggested that Mr. Forbes be evaluated by a psychiatrist. Isn't that correct?
>
> DR. RUDDICK: Yes, I did.
>
> PROSECUTOR: And that's because you're not a psychiatrist?
>
> DR. RUDDICK: Yes, that is true.
>
> PROSECUTOR: You would agree that insanity requires that a person was suffering from a mental illness, correct?
>
> DR. RUDDICK: Yes, but modern neuroscience shows that mental illnesses have a neurological basis, and neurological illnesses have emotional and behavioral consequences. So the distinction is no longer as clear. In my opinion, Mr. Forbes's traumatic brain injury is both a neurological and mental illness.

Although Jeffrey's lawyer thought that the neurologist supported the insanity defense by himself, he had already agreed to retain a psychiatrist as suggested by Dr. Ruddick. The lawyer contacted Dr. Bertrand Wallace, a former superintendent of the state hospital and a well-regarded psychiatrist. Dr. Wallace reviewed the same medical records that Dr. Ruddick was provided and all available criminal records and conducted a personal examination of Jeffrey for over six hours. Dr. Wallace produced a comprehensive psychiatric report and concluded that Jeffrey suffered from schizophrenia, a mental illness that kept him from forming emotional attachments to other people and feeling remorse for his behavior. There were similarities between Jeffrey's schizophrenia and a traumatic brain injury, but the fundamental difference was that this was a brain disease, not a brain injury. At a deposition requested by the prosecutor, Dr. Wallace spoke about his findings.

"I have read Dr. Ruddick's neurological report, and I would defer to him on the question of traumatic brain injury. However, in my opinion, there is a disease process evident in Jeffrey Forbes. I believe he suffers from schizophrenia. Schizophrenia is a major mental illness, currently defined by problems with psychotic symptoms, such as hallucinations, delusions, and disorganized thinking and behaviors.[8] But after working as a psychiatrist for over forty years, I rely on core features of schizophrenia identified by early psychiatric thinkers who found that there is not only abnormal thinking but also abnormal emotional responsiveness and loss of empathy with others—an abnormal absence of emotions. In spending more than six hours with Jeffrey, I found him unable to show any emotion in almost any area, including in his description of the extremely violent behaviors of which he has been accused and previously convicted. It should be noted that research shows people with schizophrenia also have neurological soft signs, as Dr. Ruddick found with Jeffrey, but those signs are not necessarily from brain damage but can be from a brain disease such as schizophrenia. It is certainly possible that Jeffrey's angry outbursts are a subclinical seizure, but his main problem is that he is really unable to form an attachment with or regard for another human being. He lives in a fantasy world of his own and tends to be apathetic and indifferent toward other people. This keeps him from forming meaningful interpersonal relations. His disease is one in which other people do not exist for him and do not warrant attention, shame, or guilt. They are just an extension of himself to do with what he wants. In my opinion, Jeffrey was insane at the time he killed his mother because he was unable to know what he did was wrong. For him, it was perfectly right—a distortion caused by his schizophrenia."

Dr. Wallace's credentials and extensive experience were widely known, although some believed that he used outdated psychiatric concepts at times. The prosecutor focused during the deposition mainly on that potential weakness in his opinions.

> PROSECUTOR: Doctor, you indicated that individuals with schizophrenia are diagnosed commonly, and in the newest diagnostic manuals, as having hallucinations, delusions, or disorganized thinking and behaviors. Isn't that right?
>
> DR. WALLACE: Yes, that is right.
>
> PROSECUTOR: Did Mr. Forbes exhibit any hallucinations?
>
> DR. WALLACE: No.
>
> PROSECUTOR: Did Mr. Forbes exhibit any delusions?
>
> DR. WALLACE: No.
>
> PROSECUTOR: Did Mr. Forbes exhibit any disorganized thoughts or behaviors?
>
> DR. WALLACE: No, he did not, but those symptoms are not required for a diagnosis of simple schizophrenia.
>
> PROSECUTOR: But the diagnostic manuals that are in use today do not include the concept of "simple schizophrenia," do they?
>
> DR. WALLACE: No, they do not, but that does not mean simple schizophrenia does not exist. You have to understand that the newest diagnostic manuals are based on research criteria and do not confine psychiatrists to research terms. A clinical psychiatrist is allowed the latitude to make decisions based on his or her personal experience. In my experience, the core defect in all schizophrenias,

whether they have hallucinations or delusions, is a slow, gradual reduction of attachment to others, along with apathy and indifference. This is exactly what Mr. Forbes shows and what is most striking to anyone who speaks to him at length.

Prosecutor: But you agree that simple schizophrenia is not found in today's diagnostic manual, correct?

Dr. Wallace: That is correct.

With two qualified experts concluding that Jeffrey was insane, even with some differences between them, Jeffrey's lawyer felt confident in Jeffrey pleading not guilty by reason of insanity for killing his mother. Jeffrey was also in agreement, since he could not explain the killing otherwise.

After the depositions of Dr. Ruddick and Dr. Wallace, the prosecutor retained a forensic psychiatrist with a regional reputation, Dr. Robert Gleason. Dr. Gleason reviewed Jeffrey's criminal records, his hospitalization records from the head injury, and his extensive pediatric records, as well as the reports and depositions of Dr. Ruddick and Dr. Wallace. He then asked the prosecutor to obtain complete records from Jeffrey's prior conviction for theft and assault with a deadly weapon when he was nineteen years old. He learned that Jeffrey's friend Chris Donahue, who had been an accomplice, received a much lighter sentence. This was because Chris volunteered a great deal of information about Jeffrey that would have been damaging to Jeffrey in the trial, which led to Jeffrey's guilty plea. Some of the information that Chris provided included Jeffrey's prior thefts in convenience stores and other retail establishments from the time he was a teenager, vandalizing teachers' cars by throwing raw eggs on them, and setting fires in school or in garages of people he considered enemies. One exceptionally disturbing behavior, which Chris said he hated but didn't say about much because he did not want to lose Jeffrey's friendship, was capturing neighbors' cats and stuffing their rectums with firecrackers, then lighting the firecrackers and watching the cat explode. Chris said that Jeffrey laughed hysterically each time he did this.

Dr. Gleason also asked the prosecutor to provide complete records from Jeffrey's fifteen years of incarceration at the state prison. He heard that Jeffrey was a model prisoner, but that didn't seem entirely possible. The prison records were extensive, mostly routine checks and medical contacts, but in the twelfth year of his sentence, Jeffrey's unit was searched for suspicion of drugs, which Jeffrey did not have or use. However, some items were found in Jeffrey's locker that raised concern. Among them were two shanks, improvised knives made by prisoners, one from a plastic toothbrush sharpened on the handle's end and another from a filed-down metal spoon tightly wrapped around a makeshift wooden handle. Jeffrey's explanation for making these shanks was simply that he had an interest in seeing if he could do it, but not for violent use. He added that prisons are dangerous, and it is good to have something for self-defense. In addition, however, Jeffrey's locker had a notebook of his drawings depicting sadistic sexual torture scenes, some with dismembered body parts, gouged-out eyes, and decapitated heads. The drawings included captions.

"Master, I love how you make me feel. I love how you hurt me."

"He drank her blood like fine wine, savoring every drop, letting it soothe his mind, his tension flowing out from his body."

"Give her the pain she's afraid to ask for."

Jeffrey said his drawings were only for creative expression—his way of passing the time.

With the consent of Jeffrey's lawyer, Dr. Gleason conducted an extended personal interview with Jeffrey over two days. He went over Jeffrey's life history in detail, from year to year, and discussed the new information from Chris Donahue and the prison records. Jeffrey was surprisingly candid and unaffected as he acknowledged the new reports. Afterward, Dr. Gleason produced his comprehensive psychiatric report in which he diagnosed Jeffrey as having an antisocial personality disorder,[9] which he said was not a mental illness and was insufficient for a finding of not guilty by reason of insanity. At a deposition requested by Jeffrey's lawyer, Dr. Gleason explained his opinions further.

Dr. Gleason: My opinion is that Mr. Forbes suffers from an antisocial personality disorder; by that I mean he is a psychopath who does not conform to social norms or lawful behaviors. He is deceitful, impulsive, and aggressive, and he has a reckless disregard for others. He also has no remorse for his unlawful behaviors. Individuals with antisocial personality disorder are self-centered and manipulative and have a lack of concern for the feelings or problems of others. They have no guilt. And, as in Mr. Forbes's case, they can be preoccupied with violent and sadistic fantasies about others, including getting satisfaction from another's pain or death. The most severe psychopaths are serial murderers.

Jeffrey's Lawyer: Objection. There is no evidence that Jeffrey is a serial murderer; that is prejudicial.

Prosecutor: Save your objections for trial; this is a deposition.[10]

Jeffrey's Lawyer: You bet I will.

Dr. Gleason: I apologize. I was testifying to the extremes of the condition. Mr. Forbes does have this striking lack of remorse that, as Dr. Wallace says, is quickly noticed when you talk to him. That is a hallmark of psychopaths, and one reason why they don't learn from their mistakes—they never feel guilty.

Furthermore, an antisocial personality disorder is not a mental illness, and a mental illness is required for an insanity defense. An antisocial personality disorder doesn't keep individuals from knowing what they do is wrong; they just don't care that it's wrong. An antisocial personality disorder doesn't prevent people from controlling their actions; they just don't control them. Mr. Forbes's violence does not come out of nowhere like a seizure. It's based on anger and a disregard for the other person. That's what happened when he stabbed the old man who was chasing him from the convenience store; when he beat up his girlfriend, Diane, for being out late after he had prepared a dinner for the two of them; or when he killed his mother because she insulted him and demeaned him one too many times. People with mental illness have hallucinations or delusions or are out of contact with reality. There is no evidence that was the case when Mr. Forbes killed his mother. And, in my opinion, there is no evidence that his violence is out of character for him or unexpected. My review of his friend Chris Donahue's statements, after their arrest for stealing beer from the convenience store and then stabbing the clerk, shows that Mr. Forbes had a longstanding problem with angry and violent behaviors. Records from the state prison show that Mr. Forbes made two shanks, obviously for violent use, and created a notebook of drawings that show his preoccupation with violence, even sadistic violence. This is most consistent with a psychopathic person, not a mentally ill person.

JEFFREY'S LAWYER: Dr. Gleason, you obviously disregard Dr. Ruddick's opinions that Mr. Forbes suffers from a traumatic brain injury. Since you are not a neurologist, would you concede that Dr. Ruddick is in the best position to make that diagnosis?

DR. GLEASON: If Mr. Forbes did have any significant brain damage following his head injury, it would be unusual that no one picked it up for thirty years. The attentional deficits that are described in Mr. Forbes's pediatric records are very common among youngsters. By the way, they are not uncommon in individuals with antisocial personality disorder—in the absence of any brain damage at all. Even neurological soft signs are not specific to traumatic brain injury. You know, Dr. Wallace reported that these signs can be found in individuals who have schizophrenia too.

JEFFREY'S LAWYER: You also disregard Dr. Ruddick's diagnosis of subclinical seizures. Isn't that correct?

DR. GLEASON: Dr. Ruddick has not shown any brainwave evidence of a seizure disorder; that's why they're called *subclinical*, because objective evidence does not exist for a seizure. In addition, Dr. Ruddick is attributing Mr. Forbes's violent behavior to seizures because Mr. Forbes claims he does not remember what happened. Claims of not remembering a crime are very unreliable. Many criminal defendants say they do not remember their criminal behavior for a variety of reasons, including that they may not want to remember. Dr. Ruddick thinks otherwise because he assumes that Mr. Forbes's violence was out of character for him. Well, now we know that it wasn't out of character. He was preoccupied with violence and sadistic fantasies even when he was not having, so to speak, seizures.

JEFFREY'S LAWYER: You also dismiss Dr. Wallace's diagnosis of simple schizophrenia. Is that right?

DR. GLEASON: I do, because the diagnosis of simple schizophrenia is no longer used in our current diagnostic manual, and in fact the last time that it was used was 1968. Therefore, this outdated diagnosis to explain Mr. Forbes's lack of remorse is misleading.

JEFFREY'S LAWYER: Would you agree, however, that there is scientific research that shows that subgroups of psychopaths, like certain autistic individuals, lack the neurological ability to have empathy?

Dr. Gleason: Yes, there is scientific research to that effect.

Jeffrey's lawyer: And psychopaths may lack an ability for emotional reciprocity. Isn't that true?

Dr. Gleason: Yes, that is also true.

Jeffrey's lawyer: If they do not have the ability for emotional reciprocity, they may not mature morally and ethically, right?

Dr. Gleason: Yes, hypothetically, that is so.

Jeffrey's lawyer: So regardless of whether we call it simple schizophrenia or antisocial personality disorder, what's wrong to everyone else may not be wrong to those individuals. Isn't that true?

Dr. Gleason: I think that is difficult to prove and basically says that they have no capacity to know what's wrong, even though they understand that society, religion, the law, and most everyone else do not agree with them. I think it's more that they don't care it's wrong.

Jeffrey's lawyer: But you would agree, Doctor, that neuroscience in recent decades is showing professionals like yourself that one's behavior cannot be easily separated from what's going on in one's brain, wouldn't you?

Dr. Gleason: Yes, I would agree with that, but today we are where we are, and as a society we are not ready to say that all the wrong things that happen in the world are because of a bad brain and not a bad person.

Jeffrey's trial lasted over two weeks and flushed out his history of troubled interpersonal relationships and violence. Evidence of prior crimes was allowed to be introduced, since he was raising his mental state at issue for an insanity defense, and his past behaviors were relevant to that. Dr. Ruddick and Dr. Wallace each testified for almost a full day and were subject to tough cross-examination by the prosecutor. Dr. Gleason also testified for much of the day and acknowledged the same points that he did during his deposition with Jeffrey's lawyer. Jeffrey did not take the witness stand because his lawyer was afraid that his lack of emotions and remorse would come through to the jury and blind them to the neurological and psychiatric aspects of the case, even though the case for insanity was built on those personal characteristics. The jury deliberated for over three days, during which they sent a number of questions back to the judge for clarification. It showed that they were interested in the professional evidence presented and were deliberating on it. Aunt Joan testified about the conflictual relationship that Jeffrey had with his mother and how he had always been a strange boy. However, she also acknowledged that at times she was afraid of him but could not explain why. She did not attend the trial other than for her testimony, and there was no one else at trial on Jeffrey's behalf.

Jeffrey was found not guilty by reason of insanity and was committed to the state psychiatric facility for the criminally insane. Did the jury believe his neurology and psychiatry experts, or did they have difficulty understanding how someone could show no emotion or remorse for such extreme violence without being insane? Since Jeffrey's mental condition is not new, does that mean he should have been found insane for stabbing the old convenience store clerk? Or beating up his girlfriend, Diane? No one testified that Jeffrey's mental illness can be successfully treated, so when should he be released from the state psychiatric facility? What if he is a model patient and shows no more signs of dangerousness? Typically, after a designated period of time, the prosecution has to prove that the person is still dangerous, or he will be gradually given increasing privileges toward eventual release.

Do you agree with the verdict? Does it mean that Jeffrey couldn't control his behavior? What additional information would be helpful? Would that be scientific information or factual information? If factual information would be more helpful, is that because the narrative of what happened is not that clear? Or is it clear? Was there sufficient evidence showing that Jeffrey suffered from a mental illness? Or was it the story that his experts told using the scientific information? Which was the best story—the one closest to the truth?

Conclusions: Narratives and Science

Figure 15. "Gear Head," Digital Vision Vectors, credit FR86. Getty Images #165790881.

Forensic psychiatrists are often challenged in court by lawyers who say that psychiatry is an "inexact science." They point to dramatic disagreements by psychiatrists on the diagnosis of a mental disorder, the cause of that disorder, and to what extent the person was impaired by the disorder. They say that the diagnosis of a mental disorder is based almost entirely on symptoms and not objective signs, and the symptoms cannot be verified. The *Diagnostic and Statistical Manual of Mental Disorders* 5th ed. *(DSM-5)*[1] which psychiatrists use has also been an easy target for criticism, because the number of disorders described in the *DSM-5* has grown substantially over the past fifty years and many symptoms of those disorders may be just normal variation in human experience, not a sickness. In defense of forensic psychiatry, however, let me point out that experts testifying on matters other than psychiatry also may disagree dramatically. This includes pathologists, arson and ballistics experts, computer scientists, criminologists; as well as experts in DNA evidence, fingerprints, hair follicle analysis, and other areas of forensic identification. Furthermore, the science of mental disorders, as in other medical specialties, has a vast body of research subject to peer review and scientific scrutiny, and extensive psychological tests which have been developed to help corroborate signs and symptoms of a mental disorder. Over the last fifty years there have also been significant advances in identifying the genetic and hereditary basis of mental disorders, as well as neurochemical and neuroanatomical changes associated with mental disorders.[2] In decades to come, diagnostic tests showing those changes will no doubt be developed for clinical use with patients, rather than remaining in a scientific laboratory.

However, criticism of psychiatry may not be entirely off base when it comes to testimony in a criminal trial. With severe mental disorders such as schizophrenia, bipolar disorder in manic phase, and other psychotic conditions, symptoms may be so characteristic of the mental disorder, and observations of the defendant may show such typical abnormalities in behavior and speech, that the diagnosis is clinched. But, the symptoms of less severe mental disorders such as depressive disorder, anxiety disorder, or posttraumatic stress disorder - not that a person isn't genuinely suffering - may be harder to corroborate. Defendants facing criminal charges are typically distressed; and may intuitively know the type of symptoms that could be part of a disorder, can suggest those symptoms to themselves, and can endorse those symptoms if asked about them in the interview or on questionnaires administered as part of the evaluation. More importantly is the question of what the mental disorder had to do with the crime. This is where the science of mental disorders, and often the science of non-psychiatric experts, is not enough. The defendant claiming a mental disorder also knows it is not enough and could construct a narrative to show how the mental disorder, their disturbed state of mind, was responsible for the crime. The story provides a meaning for the science.

Advances in science and technology, staggering amounts of information stored in computers, and the speed of information processing suggest that hard science is the future of our understanding of the world that we live in and of ourselves. Yet, interest in narrative as a research tool has grown in virtually all intellectual disciplines.[3] It challenges the belief that science is the only means of arriving at objective truth. A few examples help illustrate the need for narratives in a world of hard science.

In recent years, some scientists have used "haikus," in Japanese a short poem to express meaning for more complex scientific works, alongside the scientific title. For example, a scientific paper entitled, "The Effects of Shock and Raman Laser Irradiation on the Maturity of Organics in Martian Meteorites" added the haiku: "Look at falling sky, rock from big red rock in black sky, to find life signs."[4] Or in a course on addiction at a Boston university, the topic, "Negative Reinforcement Model of Addiction," generated this student haiku: "I know I must stop, withdrawal holds me captive, my drug is my cure." [5]

Despite the importance of storytelling as part of the human experience, computers still cannot reliably create and tell novel stories, nor understand stories told by humans. This has led to ways of creating or increasing "computational narrative intelligence."[6] In addition to information that computers store, they are taught common sense knowledge, i.e., a set of socially and culturally shared beliefs about how the world works. This is a challenge. Computers need to absorb stories that reflect values and beliefs from which to draw meaning for their information. It is how humans develop their intelligence. Feeding computers stories, such as "television soap operas," has been found helpful in the learning process.[7] Or introducing a "story generation system" for the computer to move from a model which is taught to generate new stories based on the model.[8] Regardless of how it is implemented, narrative learning is required.

Big data is now sweeping across sciences, business, and just about every field of knowledge, and promises to answer the toughest social questions. Here too, however, it has been noted that the implication of big data in everyday life may miss things that are true and worth knowing. There is increasing recognition that data and story go hand in hand. Some have described it as: "Data is to storytelling as the brick is to building"; the two comprise "the central pillar of communication and arguably the foundation of human civilization."[9]

Storytelling and our need for stories also drives technical information and imagination. This connection is seen by the impact of Facebook, Microsoft and Apple on our lives. We have more ways to generate, present, and consume data than ever before, but also to apply it to everyday experiences. Someone recently said: "We are quite literally drowning in data and a story helps us find the signal through the noise."[10]

In forensic psychiatry evaluations, the data presented can become overwhelming. It includes police investigation reports, physical evidence documentation, computer generated data in emails and texts, interviews of multiple witnesses, and mental health information from medical records and associated documents. There are also narratives of the defendant and other parties to the crime, often inconsistent or conflicting. The psychiatrist retained by the defendant's lawyer first sifts through the data, evaluates the defendant, and offers a scientific narrative to explain the data as it relates to the defendant and the crime. The prosecutor may or may not retain a psychiatrist to corroborate that narrative or to offer a different one, from a review of the same data. The science of mental disorders does not stop where the data ends, but weaves through the story which is told, backing up the story or refuting it.

In every story in this book, except Dougie's in *Little Saints*, and Ronald's in *Pops*, the defendant or the defendant's lawyer claimed that the defendant had a mental illness and the mental illness was an excuse for the crime. In most jurisdictions, both of those issues must be proved by the defendant. The first issue, whether the defendant had a mental illness, is more scientific. The second issue, whether the mental illness is an excuse for the crime, is more narrative. Neither issue is purely scientific or purely narrative.

In *Blessed Death*, Warren was suffering with depression which could be just a state of mind or a depressive disorder with characteristic symptoms, e.g., insomnia, fatigue, poor concentration, lack of appetite, feelings of hopelessness and suicidality. Warren would not need a psychiatrist to testify that he was depressed if the depression was just a state of mind, but he would need a psychiatrist if it was a diagnosed depressive disorder. A psychiatrist would know what questions to ask Warren to determine if he had a mental disorder and, by taking a careful history of when the symptoms began and how they impacted his life, a psychiatrist could determine the severity of the depressive disorder. Warren would not have to think hard to know what the symptoms of a depressive disorder are, since he is likely depressed because of what he has done but may be having symptoms now which he didn't prior to killing his wife Ann and his twin boys. A psychiatrist could administer questionnaires to help identify the symptoms of a depressive disorder, and if the questionnaire had built in validity scales the results might show that Warren was exaggerating his symptoms. Yet, since Warren is undoubtedly depressed, exaggeration does not mean that there is no depressive disorder. Making a diagnosis of a depressive disorder is important for Warren's defense, since a disorder implies that he was impaired and is more likely to show that Warren has an excuse for the crime. Of course, merely suffering with a mental disorder is not an excuse unless it explains the defendant's actions. Here, the narrative is more important. Most people with a depressive disorder will not kill their wife and children, so what else was going on? That must be determined by carefully walking through a timetable of Warren's actions. Although he denies it now, he had a history of anger and violence. On the day of the killings, he was not depressed but hopeful that he could re-establish a relationship with Anne. Then he discovered that his hope was pointless. Anne deceived him, continued seeing her new lover, and then rejected and humiliated him during his lovemaking. The series of events is a narrative of anger more than depression. His attempt at suicide because by then he was depressed, may have been because of what he had done. The insanity defense in the jurisdiction where the killings occurred was by definition quite liberal, but his actions were too outrageous for his depressive disorder to be an excuse. His narrative was not accepted by the jury.

In *The Prince of Wales*, Frankie did suffer from a mental disorder before he killed Ron and years afterward when he killed himself. His mental disorder was corroborated by psychiatric treatment records as a bipolar disorder in which there were times when he was psychotic and out of contact with reality. The science of mental disorders acknowledges that individuals who are psychotic can commit violent crimes because of their delusional thinking and misinterpretation of reality. The jury was told this in psychiatric testimony, but they rejected Frankie's insanity defense on a narrative analysis regardless of the science. Just because someone is psychotic does not mean everything they do is necessarily psychotic. The insanity defense in that jurisdiction was also conservative so that in spite of Frankie's psychotic disorder, he had to prove that he did not know what he was doing. Frankie's delusion that he was royalty, even if he believed it, doesn't make killing right. The jury may also have doubted that the delusion was real since Frankie had an acting background and his claims about being royalty were not always consistent. In addition, the timeline of when the killing occurred, i.e., three days after Frankie had been desperately waiting for Ron to return home and being upset about it, was not coincidental. The science of mental disorders gave way to Frankie's inconsistent narrative.

The Witch is Dead shows how pure science is almost of no value without a narrative to explain or excuse criminal behavior. A renowned scientist testified about extreme negative effects of LSD on a person's mind and behavior, but with an incomplete narrative and no personal evaluation of Dennis who killed his girlfriend Sally. Just because someone who ingested LSD may hallucinate and act violently on those hallucinations, does not mean that Dennis' violence was necessarily because of LSD. There was no proof that Dennis had ingested LSD except for his story of hallucinations. The narrative implied by the scientist did not work because it was inconsistent with the timeline. However, the strategy by Dennis' lawyer was not entirely without value because Dennis did not plead insanity. The scientist was introduced simply to muddy the waters and make it more difficult for the prosecutor to prove wrongful intent on Dennis' part even if there was clearly a wrongful act. Perhaps the jury did take into account the scientist's testimony and gave Dennis the benefit of a doubt sufficient to convict him only of second degree murder and not first degree. He probably would not have been successful pleading insanity.

In *Firefly*, Roxie's lawyer introduced psychiatric testimony about a condition scientifically called "reward deficiency syndrome," but only speculatively applicable to Roxie's fire setting. Scientific theory which does not yet have a general acceptance in the scientific community, and insufficient peer review research to validate the theory, may be challenged by the prosecution as inadmissible. The trial judge ultimately decides if the testimony can come in or not, and must follow a number of criteria established in case law.[10] The final decision, however, is totally up to the judge. Here, although there is no way to scientifically know that Roxie suffered from this condition, the testimony was still allowed as evidence, but with an opportunity for the prosecution to impeach it, i.e., discredit it. Fire setting behaviors and other compulsive acts can be associated with a variety of mental conditions, psychological factors, and personal motives, so that no one cause is enough to explain the behavior. With Roxie, the science falls short as an excuse when the timeline surrounding the crime was considered. The most significant problem for her was overcoming evidence of planning the crime. This suggests something more than a sudden, impulsive act which was not well thought out. Some of Roxie's prior fire setting incidents may have been impulsive, but many if not all were also a response to her anger. Setting fire to the tire warehouse was clearly an angry response to the owner's inappropriate sexual advances and, indirectly, to her husband for making her work at the tire warehouse. Roxie did not set the fire when she left her work that day, but went back home, and returned with a plan of what she will do and how she was to do it. It may be that "instinctive" behavior can involve planning but, for human beings, time to plan also offers time to consider what they are doing and whether or not they should do it. The jury might have been more sympathetic to Roxie if the tire warehouse hadn't burned down especially because she had been a victim of its owner. However, the horror of a massive fire was too unsettling to dismiss as excusable. Regardless of how it was labeled, Roxie did suffer with a mental disorder, the earliest signs of which were in childhood. With a less dramatic consequence for her actions, she might have received more sympathy.

Jill's story in *The Goodnight Motel* is sad because of the devastating effects of a well-known mental disorder, i.e., postpartum depression or psychosis, experienced by many mothers. The more common form is postpartum depression which usually does not lead to violence, even if the mother is suffering. The delusional symptoms Jill displayed and her desperation are scientifically recognized as postpartum psychosis, and need to be pointed out by experts so that more ordinary motives in her behavior are not suspected. Her delusions were not so absurd that they could not be real, and Jill concocted her own story to explain what she was feeling and why - not realizing that it was caused by the mental disorder. The outcome to Jill's charges, i.e., a negotiated insanity plea with the prosecution, is not typical. Similar cases go to trial and insanity will have to be proved by the defendant. Indeed, every case needs to be assessed not only by establishing a diagnosis, but by showing consistencies and inconsistencies with the diagnosis and the timeline. If the mother's delusions are not so absurd and the timeline shows other motives, e.g., anger or revenge, an alternative explanation to postpartum psychosis may be justified. In Jill's case, the quick disposition of the case as to guilt, and what appeared to be successful treatment in the years that followed, can mislead families, and at times psychiatrists, to believe there is no further concern. Unfortunately, episodes of postpartum depression or postpartum psychosis can be the start of a recurrent mental disorder, including bipolar disorder, with subsequent mental breakdowns with or without other pregnancies. Psychiatrists are not always accurate in predicting further episodes of psychosis or violent behavior, and with every episode the risk of more episodes increases. However, long-term psychiatric follow-up of the mother is still necessary.

In *Pops*, Ronald did not place his mental state at issue or claim insanity for killing his brother Martin. His deteriorating brain disease made him incompetent to stand trial. The mental disorder was his brain disease which could be established by very characteristic orientation and memory problems, confabulation, and decline in functioning. Neurological testing might have corroborated a brain disease. Because Ronald's brain disease could not be treated successfully, his competency could not be restored in order for him to go to trial ever. However, if he had gone to trial, the science of mental disorders would have been strong evidence of impairment for an insanity defense. The narrative may also have been consistent to the extent that Ronald had become delusional, erroneously believed Martin was dying, and was so dependent and afraid that without his brother he could not survive - all of which became a distorted justification for a mercy killing. On the other hand, early resentment toward Martin, the successful brother, and disinhibited rage may have also been a factor. The timeline might have shown a mixed narrative of fear and rage but the portion that was rage would never have come to the surface were it not for the impairment of his mental filter for random and impulsive behaviors. Diagnostic imaging of Ronald's brain, i.e., magnetic resonance imagery (MRI) likely showed shrinking of brain tissue and other structural signs of dementia, helping to confirm scientifically the nature of his mental disorder. Unfortunately, diagnostic imaging to date does not clinically confirm other mental disorders. However, it may in years to come with advances in imaging of the brain for how the brain works (functional MRI), not just how it is structured.

Nice Shoes presents thorny sociological and psychiatric problems: What is a sexual crime? What is a sexual disorder? In the early part of the 20th century, for example, adultery, sodomy, and homosexuality were crimes; and sexual aggression towards women was too often considered just part of the chase. Psychiatrically, homosexuality was defined as a mental disorder in the *Diagnostic and Statistical Manual of Mental Disorders* 2nd ed. (*DSM-2*) until 1973,[11] and sexual fetishes of all kinds were also disorders. Today, most consensual sexual activity between adults is not a crime, although insistent sexual advances can be considered a criminal assault. So what about Kenny? Was his sexual fascination with shoes a mental disorder? Today's DSM says that if Kenny is not bothered by his fetish, and does not hurt anyone else, then it would not be a mental disorder.[12] If Kenny had been caught parking near Veronica's car every day, he might have been charged with stalking, and his sexual fascination for shoes would have been no excuse. The science of mental disorders and sexuality may explain how Kenny did not mature sexually and how shoes were his safe alternative. Veronica just happened to be in the way. But, it did not stop with parking near her car. Kenny discovered where Veronica lived, broke into her home, planned encountering her there, and finally confined her out of sexual excitement. Most people who find sexual excitement from shoes would not do that, but some like Kenny do. What began as a private matter extended to criminal behavior and followed the same type of distortion which most serious sexual offenders use, i.e., they think the victim likes it or could like it. If a psychiatrist would have evaluated Kenny for stalking Veronica, parking near her car every day, the psychiatrist might have concluded that this is just a private fetish not meant to hurt anyone. No doubt Kenny would have then claimed that he did not want her to know he was there or to fear him in any way. The psychiatrist may have testified in Kenny's behalf and told the story of his sexual immaturity implying that Kenny is basically harmless. Part of the difficulty in evaluating individuals like Kenny is that they do not tell the truth about their sexual activities. They minimize or deny more dangerous sexual fantasies, and do not admit to the extent of their sexual behaviors.[13] Frequently, their sexual immaturity is part of an overall social immaturity, an inability to make adult social and intimate connections. They feel lonely and isolated. They may be depressed. Kenny no doubt was depressed once he was sentenced to prison and likely was a target of inmate harassment if not abuse. He likely suffered with a depressive disorder which led to his suicide, and may have been suffering from low-grade depression for years. The depression, however, does not explain his behavior prior to imprisonment. Then, he was relishing in his new found sexual delights. While it is not inevitable that sexual offenders will continue offending, they are difficult to treat psychiatrically and the likelihood of similar behaviors is high. Society has responded to this by creating sex offender registries, and in some jurisdictions by requiring psychiatric re-evaluation after a sentence is completed to assess the potential for dangerousness. Predicting this kind of behavior accurately, however, is very difficult.

Out of Africa is a story told hundreds of times every day in this country with a flurry of scams as fantastic as the ones to which Bruce responded, but also countless less dramatic attempts to solicit and ensnare vulnerable individuals through flim flam schemes. Most people having been duped once would learn their lesson. But some respond with the promise of easy money, a dynamic perfectly known by the scammer. Bruce's story is different, however, because he incorporated the scams to fill a hole in his life. He was an intelligent man who once operated a successful architect business and missed the financial means he once had but mostly missed the identity which had been taken away from him. This allowed for a delusion to develop which filled the hole. Individuals with a delusional disorder believe in something that is patently absurd and cling to it no matter what the contradicting evidence is or the harm they come to because of it.[14] In Bruce's circumstances, greed was not the main motivation, but a new life as a financier, when his old life had crumbled. Because delusions have a semblance of truth, they are hard to refute individually. Here, though, the delusion was compounded and expanded. The process of accepting preposterous suggestions over and over shows why it was a mental disorder. It may be difficult to conceive how Bruce refused to accept reality, but numerous studies have shown how once a narrative forms, particularly one that is needed, people stick to it. This may be one of the reasons delusional disorders are among most difficult mental disorders to treat successfully. They do not respond well to psychiatric medications or psychotherapy. Patients may seem troubled by the delusion but they also find a psychological benefit that outweighs the harmful reality.

Dougie in *Little Saints* was not suffering from a mental disorder which he used as an excuse for a crime. He may have had posttraumatic stress disorder due to sexual abuse by Eugene Burke years earlier in his childhood, or he may have talked himself into believing he had posttraumatic stress disorder even if there had been no sexual abuse. If his story that Eugene Burke abused him was not true, because it was not true for Mark and Darrell, then he may have made all of it up. More likely, though, something did happen that was traumatic and his narrative served a purpose for him, not just financially from civil litigation, but as an explanation for his own difficulties in life. It is not uncommon to repress painful memories from childhood. In fact, we never remember everything about our childhood and some things are best forgotten. The problem is how and under what circumstances we remember them later. The longer it has been from the time of the incident, the more likely that the memory will be distorted either by how the person was reminded of it and/or what the memory means to the person. If a psychiatrist or psychologist diagnoses Dougie with posttraumatic stress disorder, that assumes that a trauma did occur but the diagnosis itself can't prove it. When there is civil litigation and the possibility of financial gain, memories are distorted even more easily and, like in criminal matters, need to be viewed within a timeline. Dougie's early history of emotional and behavioral problems prior to any contact with Eugene Burke must be compared to problems he claims to have had afterward. What other factors in his personal life before or after contact with Eugene Burke may have also played a role? In his civil litigation, Dougie won a large jury award for the abuse by Eugene Burke. Eugene Burke did not testify, and Dougie was believed. His narrative was not new or unusual. In fact the narrative of childhood abuse being discovered or disclosed later in life is now a frequent topic in the news and in court proceedings. This creates a larger social narrative from which a jury assessed Dougie's narrative and which improved Dougie's chance to be credible. How a jury would have acted on Mark and Darrell's testimony, if they had gone through civil litigation, is not known. Would the timeline that shows Eugene Burke was not there when they said he abused them be convincing or would Mark and Darrell have been given the benefit of a doubt, by the strength of Dougie's testimony for them. The details may not be exactly right but something must have happened. It is likely, however, that Mark and Darrell grew to believe that they were abused, just as Dougie said he was, and they would not accept any contradictory facts. Once again, our memories are as strong as the need we have for them, even if erroneous.

Jeffrey's story of *Insanity* is particularly complicated because Jeffrey did not appear normal since he did not show normal emotions to his horrendous act of violence. It is not unusual for violent acts, sadistic cruelty, and disregard for another's suffering to be viewed as abnormal and, therefore, "insane." Here, two reputable psychiatrists came to that conclusion about Jeffrey, even though they had entirely different mental disorders to explain it. The reason for Jeffrey's lack of normal emotions is, however, more likely based on what we call "psychopathic" personality traits in which a person shows callous emotionality and indifference to others.[15] It is the extreme form of antisocial personality disorder and tends to be a lifelong condition.[16] The mental disorders which the psychiatrists diagnosed Jeffrey as having could not be verified by objective means and yet they were compelling to the jury. Scientific research into psychopathic personalities has shown neuropsychological deficits in brain function which are associated with the person's behavior, especially how they understand and regard others.[17] Curiously, people with neurodevelopmental disorders from childhood, e.g., autism, also have difficulty understanding and regarding others, and they are said to show similar neuropsychological deficits.[18] The difference is that people who are psychopaths don't feel what another is feeling, and those who are neurodevelopmentally disordered don't know what the other is feeling. With further research, and improved diagnostic methods, it may be possible someday to identify these deficits more conclusively. For now, however, it is still too speculative to conclude that the deficits suspected actually exist from behavioral manifestations alone. Referring to the categories of insanity, such individuals do not have a problem with "thinking rationally," but they may have a problem "controlling their behavior." On the other hand, maybe they don't care about controlling their behavior because others are not important to them. Jeffrey's story is, therefore, still being told and may not be completed for decades to come. It appears that the jury, by finding him not guilty by reason of insanity, must have intuitively determined that there is something abnormal about Jeffrey, or else how could his actions be explained.

Acknowledgments

I am grateful to my wife, Jura, and Elite Authors for editing this book of stories and showing me what I didn't see in style and substance, no matter how many changes I had already made. I am also grateful to Michelle Skrzysowski and Barbara Dziura for their tireless preparation of the manuscript. Finally, a special thanks goes to the scores of individuals who shared their stories with me during my thirty-five years of practicing forensic psychiatry.

Notes

Introduction

1. O. B. Wielk and R. Becker, "What Is the Difference between Story and Narrative?" Beemgee (May 2015), accessed October 12, 2019, https://www.beemgee.com/blog.

2. M. Biesele, *Women Like Meat: The Folklore and Foraging Technology of the Kalahari Ju/'hoan* (Bloomington: Indiana University Press, 1983), 19–20.

3. E. M. Thomas, *The Old Way: A Story of the First People* (New York: Picador, 2006), 208–9 (adaptation).

4. Thomas, 200–201 (adaptation).

5. J. Campbell, *The Power of Myth with Bill Moyers*, ed. S. F. Flowers (New York: Doubleday, 1988), 42–43 (adaptation).

6. "Pablo Picasso > Quotes > Quotable Quotes," accessed April 27, 2019, https://www.goodreads.com/quotes/67884.

7. "Symphony No. 5 (Beethoven)," accessed October 12, 2019, https://en.wikipedia.org/wiki/Symphony_No._5_(Beethoven).

8. Merle Kilgore and June Carter, "Ring of Fire," featuring Johnny Cash, Amazon Music, accessed October 12, 2019, http://www.azlyrics.com/lyrics/johnnycash/ringoffire.html.

9. J. Gottscheall, *The Storytelling Animal: How Stories Make Us Human* (New York: Houghton Mifflin Harcourt, 2012).

10. L. R. Beach, *The Psychology of Narrative Thought: How the Stories We Tell Ourselves Shape Our Lives* (Lexington, KY: Xlibris, 2010); D. Herman et al., *Narrative Theory: Core Concepts and Critical Debates* (Columbus: Ohio State University Press, 2012).

11. S. E. Worth, "Narrative Understanding and Understanding Narrative," *Contemporary Aesthetics* 4 (2004), accessed February 22, 2020, https://contempaesthetics.org/ newvolume/pages/article.php?articleID=237; T. D. Wilson, *Redirect: The Surprising New Science of Psychological Change* (New York: Little, Brown and Company, 2011).

12. B. Bernard, *In the Theater of Consciousness* (New York: Oxford University Press, 1997).

13. J. Joyce, *Ulysses, the 1922 Text* (New York: Oxford University Press, 2008), 357.

14. E. Hemingway, *For Whom the Bell Tolls* (New York: Scribner, 1940), 53.

15. P. Briant, *Alexander the Great and His Empire: A Short Introduction* (Princeton, NJ: Princeton University Press, 2012).

16. D. L. Schacter, *Memory Distortion: How Minds, Brains and Societies Reconstruct the Past* (Cambridge, MA: Harvard University Press, 1995).

17. R. C. Schank, *Tell Me a Story: Narrative and Intelligence* (Evanston, IL: Northwestern University Press, 1990); C. J. Brainerd and V. F. Reyna, "Fuzzy-Trace Theory: Dual Processes in Memory, Reasoning, and Cognitive Neuroscience," *Advances in Child Development and Behavior* 28 (2001): 41–100.

18. C. G. Jung, *The Red Book: A Reader's Edition* (New York: W. W. Norton, 2009).

19. P. K. Cross, "Not Can, but *Will* College Teaching Be Improved?" *New Directions for Higher Education* 17 (Spring 1977): 1-15, accessed April 21, 2019, https://doi.org/10.1002/ he.36919771703.

20. L. K. Miller, "The Savant Syndrome: Intellectual Impairments and Exceptional Skill," *Psychological Bulletin* 125, no. 1 (1999): 31–46.

21. B. Korkmaz, "Theory of Mind and Neurodevelopmental Disorders of Childhood," *Pediatric Research* 65, no. 5, part 2 (2011): 101R–8R.

22. T. Kuran, *Private Truths, Public Lies: The Social Consequences of Preference Falsification* (Cambridge, MA: Harvard University Press, 1995); R. W. Kurzban, *Why Everyone Else Is a Hypocrite: Evaluation and the Modular Mind* (Princeton, NJ: Princeton University Press, 2011).

23. E. S. March, "Is Facebook Making Us Lonely?," *The Atlantic*, May 2012.

24. N. Pennington and R. Hasti, "A Cognitive Theory of Juror Decision Making: The Story Model," *Cardozo Law Review* 13 (1991): 519–42.

25. Jacob A. Stein, Esq., Suffolk University Law School, 1984.

26. C. L. Scott, "Evaluation of Criminal Responsibility," in *Textbook of Forensic Psychiatry*, eds. L. H. Gold and R. L. Frierson, 3rd ed. (Arlington VA: American Psychiatric Association Publishing, 2018): 281–82. Under common law, criminal responsibility requires a guilty mind (mens rea), as well as a guilty act (actus reus); more commonly, these elements are called "wrongful intent" and "wrongful act," respectively. They are independent considerations from insanity and typically do not involve psychiatric testimony.

27. C. L. Scott, 292–93. "Diminished capacity" is referred to as a defense, but it is actually the failure of the prosecution to prove specific intent of a crime "beyond reasonable doubt." It is most applicable to crimes that potentially have more than one specific intent or a lesser included intent that the jury could choose. For example, first-degree murder typically requires the specific intent

of premeditation and deliberation; lacking that, the defendant may still be found guilty of second-degree murder, voluntary manslaughter, or involuntary manslaughter. Psychiatric testimony is typically not presented, and in some jurisdictions not allowed, since this is considered the role of the fact finder—that is, the jury or judge.

28. J. S. Janofsky et al., "AAPL Practice Guidelines for Psychiatric Evaluation of Defendants Raising the Insanity Defense," *Journal of the American Academy of Psychiatry and the* Law 42, no. 4 (2014): S1–S76. The "insanity defense" is raised when, in spite of intending the wrongful act and being the one who committed the wrongful act, defendants claim that a mental defect or disease impacted their behavior, so that they should not be found guilty of a crime. Unlike the elements of the crime that the prosecution has to prove beyond a reasonable doubt, in most instances with the insanity defense, defendants have to prove that they were insane. Every jurisdiction by statute or case law defines insanity or its parameters.

29. "Jurisdiction" is the territory over which the court's authority extends. Typically, it is the state where the crime was committed, unless it is a federal crime, which would put it in federal court. Civil cases can be brought to federal court if parties are from different jurisdictions and if greater monetary damages are sought.

30. C. L. Scott, "Evaluation of Criminal Responsibility," 282–84. "Unable to think rationally" is a simplified way of discussing one of the two prongs that make up the insanity defense in most jurisdictions. This one is called the cognitive prong and has to do with what someone knows, understands, or appreciates about the wrongful act or crime.

31. C. L. Scott, 282–84. "Unable to control him—or herself" is a simplified way of discussing the other, or volitional, prong, which is derived from an earlier concept of irresistible impulse. Was the impulse so strong that the person would have committed the crime even if a policeman were standing there? The more technical language, if included for the insanity defense, is the ability or inability to conform one's actions to the requirements of the law.

32. R. Charon et al., *The Principles and Practice of Narrative Medicine* (Oxford, UK: Oxford University Press, 2017).

33. A. M. Drukteinis, "Forensic Historiography: Narratives and Science," *Journal of the American Academy of Psychiatry and the Law* 42 (2014): 427–36.

34. "Reasonable medical certainty" or "reasonable medical probability" is the standard by which an expert provides an opinion in court. Another way to put it is "more likely than not," which essentially means just a little over 50 percent certainty. This has nothing to do with the standard of proof that the court requires (e.g., "beyond a reasonable doubt," which is a separate and secondary issue for the jury or judge).

35. P. A. Zapf and T. Grisso, "Use and Misuse of Forensic Assessment Instruments," in *Coping with Psychiatric and Psychological Testimony*, ed. D. Faust, based on the original work by Jay Ziskin (New York: Oxford University Press, 2012), 488–510. Except for cognitive tests, which require the subject to perform various tasks, most psychological tests are in questionnaire form, so the subject greatly controls the information provided and the degree of symptoms and impairment that the test measures. Many psychological tests have built-in validity measures that show by the manner of response that the subject is exaggerating or unusually denying mental problems. But these tests are not foolproof, especially if the subject is facing serious criminal charges. Therefore, the results of psychological tests should always be viewed in combination with clinical and factual information as to their consistency and usefulness.

Blessed Death

1. Police may not question a person in custody without first giving Miranda warnings: that the person has a right to remain silent, that any statements made can be used in court, that a lawyer can be consulted first and provided to the person if necessary, and so on (Miranda v. Arizona, 384 U.S. 436 [1966]). However, if the police ask no questions and do not prompt the person, spontaneous statements are not protected by the Miranda rule.

2. See Introduction note 28 above.

3. See Introduction note 30 above.

4. See Introduction note 31 above.

5. A. Moskowitz, "Dissociation and Violence: A Review of the Literature," *Trauma Violence Abuse* 5, no. 1 (2004): 21–46. Individuals who are not normally violent or aggressive but commit a violent act will often make statements that suggest "dissociation," in which they claim to have had a separation of conscious awareness from the act committed or a lack of intention even while committing the act. Sometimes they claim amnesia for the act entirely, and it is difficult to distinguish what they cannot remember from what they do not want to remember. The frequency of such reports in homicide is provocative and cannot be easily dismissed; American Psychiatric Association (APA), *Diagnostic and Statistical Manual of Mental Disorders*, 5th ed. (*DSM-5*) (Arlington VA: American Psychiatric Association, 2013), 291–307. "Dissociative disorders" are characterized by a disruption in the normal integration of consciousness, memory, identity, emotion, perception, body representation, motor control, and behavior. They can include dissociative amnesia, but also depersonalization and derealization (i.e., the person is not sure who they are or what is real around them) and dissociative identity disorder (previously known as multiple personality disorder), in which they claim to have two or more distinct personalities.

6. See J. S. Janofsky et al., "AAPL Practice Guidelines," S5. "Product of mental illness" is an insanity definition from New Hampshire cases in the nineteenth century but reaffirmed more than one hundred years later (Abbott v. Cunningham, 766 F. Supp. 1218 [D.N.H. 1991]); the District of Columbia adopted the language in 1954 by what would be known as the Durham rule (Durham v. United States, 214 F. 2d 862 [D.C. Cir. 1954]). In 1972 it was abandoned for more traditional tests of insanity. It continues to be used in New Hampshire and in the British Virgin Islands.

7. See APA, *DSM-5*.

8. New Hampshire Bar Association, *Criminal Jury Instructions* (Insanity), Drafting Committee Version (September 2010): 278. In New Hampshire, juries are instructed to consider any evidence of insanity that they choose, regardless of psychiatric testimony, and there is no legal definition. They may consider whether the defendant was suffering from delusions or hallucinations, knew the difference between right and wrong and the nature of their acts, had the power to choose between right and wrong, could recognize acquaintances and transact business or manage his affairs, and so on. Although the jury may consider any of these issues, they are not compelled to do so and may rely on anything that they feel is pertinent to whether the defendant was sane or insane at the time of the crime.

9. A "delusion" is a psychotic symptom in which an individual has a fixed false belief about something that is not true, and the person refuses to recognize the false belief in spite of incontrovertible evidence against it. In many cases, there is no bright line that separates delusions from distortions or from variable beliefs that are held by substantial groups of people as cultural differences or ordinary variances of thinking.

10. This definition has no legal weight and is somewhat ambiguous because the words "impairs an individual's ability to perceive or understand reality" suggest that this is a "psychosis" where someone is out of contact with reality, but does not use the term psychosis. It also excludes "voluntary intoxication" when there are cases in which voluntary intoxication can lead to severe unexpected mental changes, particularly if those changes persist after the expected time for sobriety; this is sometimes referred to as "settled insanity"; American Psychiatric Association (APA), *Position Statement on the Insanity Defense* (Arlington, VA: American Psychiatric Publishing, 1982). More recent support for the insanity defense by the APA expanded the definition to "serious mental disorders [that] can substantially impair an individual's capacities to reason rationally and to inhibit behavior that violates the law"; it can also include "developmental disabilities and other causes of impaired mental functioning." American Psychiatric Association (APA), Position Statement on the Insanity Defense (Arlington, VA: American Psychiatric Publishing, 2007, reaffirmed 2014).

11. H. Kohut, *Thoughts on Narcissism and Narcissistic Rage in the Search for the Self*, vol. 2 (Madison, CT: International Universities Press, 1972), 615–18. "Narcissism" and its corresponding reaction of narcissistic rage are psychoanalytical terms in which there is a threat to one's self-esteem or self-worth with accompanying dysregulation of behaviors that can lead to violent or homicidal attacks. It may be one of the most common dynamics in domestic violence.

12. J. Katz, "Seductions of Crime," *Crime, Law, and Social Change* 28, no. 2 (1997), 175–80. "Righteous slaughter" often accompanies narcissistic rage, in which the humiliation is of such intensity that it must be rectified, often a "last stand in defense of one's basic worth." The attack aims at obliterating the source of the humiliation and, paradoxically, recovering respectability no matter the consequence.

13. L. Peter-Hagene, A. Jay, and J. Salerno, "The Emotional Components of Moral Outrage and Their Effect on Mock Juror Verdicts: The Jury Expert," *The Art and Science of Litigation Advocacy* 26, no. 2 (2014): 1–20. While jury instructions may identify technical aspects of decision-making in insanity cases, the greater factor that juries consider may be the balance between their feelings of outrage and sympathy for the defendant or the victims. Those feelings may be easier to understand than the instructions given to juries and may be more influential.

14. Historically, "personality disorders" differed from other mental conditions and were seen as maladaptive patterns of behavior for which the individual is responsible (i.e., not an affliction). However, *DSM* criteria have changed in the most recent version (*DSM-5*); there is now no threshold of distinction between personality disorders and other mental disorders as to classification. This change has been in response to the belief that individuals with personality disorders are also suffering and should not be discriminated against in terms of understanding and treatment, even though successful treatment is much harder. A personality disorder must be diagnosed by a pattern that is apparent over the adult lifetime of an individual and in varied life circumstances. Most psychiatrists continue to believe that the behaviors of someone with a personality disorder are in their

control even though their perspective about their world and their relationships is distorted. See APA, *DSM-5*, note 5 above, 645–49, 761–63.

15. See Scott, "Evaluation of Criminal Responsibility," 292-93, Introduction note 27 above.

The Prince of Wales

1. "Psychosis" refers to a mental condition in which someone has lost contact with reality, typically because of hallucinations in which they perceive things that are not there or delusions in which they believe things that are clearly not true.

2. See Blessed Death note 9 above.

3. See J. S. Janofsky et al., S1-S76, Introduction note 28 above.

4. See C. L. Scott, "Evaluation of Criminal Responsibility," 282-84, Introduction note 30 above.

5. This definition is based on one of the oldest laws for insanity, which evolved in the mid-1800s to become the M'Naughten Rule, one form of which is used in many US jurisdictions, including federal cases. The actual wording was "The party accused was laboring under such a defect of reason, from disease of the mind as not to know the nature and quality of the act he was doing; or if he did know it, that he did not know he was doing what was wrong." See also J. S. Janofsky et al., "AAPL Practice Guidelines," S5, Introduction note 28 above.

6. Temporary insanity is claimed even though the person is no longer suffering from the mental illness or perhaps never suffered before the crime from a mental illness. The main problem is how to prove temporary insanity without evidence before or after the illness.

7. U.S. Department of Justice, *U.S. Lawyers' Criminal Resource Manual: Section 638. Burden of Proving Insanity*, 18 U.S.C. Section 17(b) (US Department of

Justice, October 2017). In most jurisdictions, the burden is placed on the defendant to prove his or her insanity. Often it is only by a preponderance of the evidence (51 percent, more likely than not), but some states require a higher burden (clear and convincing evidence). In a few states, however, once the defendant raises the issue of insanity, the burden remains on the prosecution to prove sanity beyond a reasonable doubt.

8. See C. L. Scott, "Evaluation of Criminal Responsibility," 281-282, Introduction note 26 above.

9. C. Cirincione, H. J. Steadman, and M. A. McGreevy, "Rates of Insanity Acquittals and the Factors Associated with Successful Insanity Pleas," *Bulletin of the American Academy of Psychiatry in the Law* 23, no. 3 (1995): 399–409.

10. A shank is a self-made, knife-like weapon, typically fashioned in prison where knives are not available. Shanks are regularly used in violent attacks against other prisoners, but they are also used in suicides.

11. This question suggests dissociation, a mental phenomenon often claimed to occur in violent acts. See A. Moskowitz, "Dissociation and Violence," 21-46, Blessed Death note 5 above.

The Witch is Dead

1. See C. L. Scott, "Evaluation of Criminal Responsibility," 292-93, Introduction note 27 above.

2. See C. L. Scott, 281-82, Introduction note 26 above.

3. Once someone is found not guilty by reason of insanity, most jurisdictions will conduct a hearing to determine if the person is dangerous, and new evidence may be introduced. If the crime was violent, there may be a presumption of dangerousness. When dangerousness is established, a person may be committed to a mental institution; the length of time is variable.

4. Under the Fifth Amendment, a defendant does not have to provide any information to the police or prosecution, and remaining silent is not a presumption of guilt during the trial. Once a person raises his or her mental state as an issue (e.g., claims insanity), however, he or she may forfeit some of these Fifth Amendment rights, especially if the person has been evaluated by a psychiatrist who will testify as to his or her insanity. The prosecution can then retain a psychiatrist for an evaluation as well, and what the defendant says to both psychiatrists will be disclosed to the prosecution.

5.. See APA, *DSM*-5, 10–15. A "substance-induced psychotic disorder" refers to a condition in which a substance or medication produces delusions or hallucinations (i.e., psychosis with the person out of control with reality) with no indication that the person would have become psychotic in the absence of such effects.

6. Toxicology screening of urine or blood can identify the presence of a drug or its metabolites and can suggest a degree of impairment, but alone it does not confirm that someone was out of contact with reality or did not know what he or she was doing.

7. See C. L. Scott, "Evaluation of Criminal Responsibility," 292-93, Introduction note 27 above.

Firefly

1. See APA, *DSM*-5, 461–80. "Disruptive, impulse control, and conduct disorders" include conditions with problems in self-control of emotions and behaviors. They may also involve problems in emotional or behavioral regulation.

2. See C. L. Scott, "Evaluation of Criminal Responsibility," 282-84, Introduction notes 30, 31 above.

3. H. Lodish et al., "Section 21.4: Neurotransmitters, Synapses, and Impulse Transmission," in *Molecular Cell Biology*, 4th ed. (New York: W. H. Freeman, 2000). Neurotransmitters are chemical substances found in the brain, such as

epinephrine or norepinephrine, serotonin, dopamine, and others, that conduct impulses (messages) from one cell to another.

4. K. Blum et al., "Reward Deficiency Syndrome: A Biogenetic Model for the Diagnosis and Treatment of Impulsive, Addictive, and Compulsive Behaviors," Supplement i–iv, *Journal of Psychoactive Drugs* 32 (November 2000): 1–112.

5. P. Katz and J. Rabinowitz, "A Retrospective Study of Daughters' Emotional Reversal with Parents, Attachment Anxiety, Excessive Reassurance Seeking and Depressive Symptoms," *American Journal of Family Therapy* 37 (2009): 185–95. The concept is known as "parentified child" an unhealthy family dynamic where the child takes on a parental role in the absence, physically or emotionally, of the parent.

6. Scientific evidence can only come into court if it is reliable. The earlier standard was whether the principle or the procedure was generally accepted in the scientific community (Frye v. United States, 293 F. 1013 [D.C. Cir. 1923]). More recently, a more comprehensive standard is used, which mainly asks whether there is also research to support this principle or procedure (Daubert v. Merrell Dow Pharmaceuticals, 509 U.S. 579 [1993]).

The Good Night Motel

1. This is a less technical term for a person who is psychotic and paranoid. While not an actual disorder in *DSM-5*, since it is absorbed in other diagnoses, it usually reflects a serious mental illness.

2. V. Bergink, N. Rasgon, and K. L. Wisner, "Postpartum Psychosis: Madness, Mania, and Melancholia in Motherhood," *American Journal of Psychiatry* 173, no.12 (2016): 1179–88. *Postpartum psychosis* is a term focusing less on specific symptoms but rather on when the illness develops (i.e., following the birth of a child). There are many forms, the most common of which may be a brief psychotic disorder, but it also may represent the start of a more serious and chronic illness such as bipolar disorder.

3. Bergink, Rasgon, and Wisner, 1179–88.

4. Defense lawyers like to call a treating psychiatrist as an expert in court because the jury might believe the treating psychiatrist has more of an understanding of the patient than a retained expert who only conducts an evaluation for trial. However, this creates potential conflicts, especially if the psychiatrist might provide an opinion that is not favorable for the patient. Also, a treating psychiatrist would typically not have access to all the medical records and criminal evidence, so that would be a disadvantage and could make the treating psychiatrist's testimony in trial less credible.

5. See C. L. Scott, "Evaluation of Criminal Responsibility," 282-84, Introduction note 30 above.

6. See The Prince of Wales note 5 above.

7. Not infrequently, prosecutors may accept the findings of a defense psychiatrist on the issue of insanity, particularly if the psychiatrist has a good reputation in the community, and the facts of the case are compelling for insanity.

Pops

1. See APA, *DSM*-5, 591–644. *Cognitive impairment* refers to dysfunction of the brain, manifest by disorientation, poor memory, difficulty with concentration and mental focus, and problems with judgment and reasoning. When this occurs because of temporary factors such as intoxication or brain infection, it is called *delirium*; when it is caused by the deteriorating condition of the brain with permanent impairment, it is called *dementia*.

2. A. D. Thomson and E. J. Marshall, "The Natural History and Pathophysiology of Wernicke's Encephalopathy and Korsakoff's Psychosis," *Alcoholism* 41, no. 2 (2006): 151–58.

3. C. L. Scott, "Evaluation of Competencies in the Criminal Justice System," in *Textbook of Forensic Psychiatry*, eds. L. H. Gold and R. L. Frierson, 3rd ed.

(Arlington VA: American Psychiatric Publishing, 2018), 263–80. Competency to stand trial is a basic right in criminal proceedings and for fairness requires that the defendant be able to rationally work with his or her lawyer and rationally follow the proceedings; otherwise, the trial itself would be a mockery. Unlike insanity in which the focus is the mental state of the defendant at the time of the crime, competency to stand trial has to do with the mental state of the defendant at trial. As such, it is fluid, and someone can be competent at one point during the court proceedings and incompetent at another. Once it is determined that someone is incompetent, the next question is whether competency can be restored, typically by treatment.

4. Known as *anosognosia*.

5. Known as *Anton's syndrome*.

6. *Nervous system* in this context refers to the central nervous system, which means the brain and spinal cord structures.

Nice Shoes

1. Sex offender registry websites track convicted sex offenders in all fifty states and US territories, as well as by the federal government. They also track residences of sexual offenders, and the public has access to that information—for example, the United States Department of Justice, *National Sex Offender Public Website*, accessed November 2, 2019, https://www.nsopw.gov/en/registries/all registries.

2. See APA, *DSM-5*, 685–706.

3. APA, *DSM-5*, 700–702.

4. See B. Korkmaz, "Theory of Mind," 101R–8R. This is similar to those individuals with neurodevelopmental disorders who have a defect in theory of mind, they don't recognize what another is feeling.

5. See APA, *DSM-5*, 659–63, 764–65. *Antisocial personality disorder*, sometimes known as *sociopathic personality*, refers to an individual with a pervasive pattern of disregard for and violation of the rights of others, who is self-centered, focuses on personal gratification, lacks empathy, and can't form intimate relationships.

6. Some states require an additional evaluation for sex offenders following the completion of their sentences. Psychiatrists may be asked to predict whether the individual is still a danger to the public and whether he or she is likely to commit further sexual crimes. This is a controversial issue, since the individual has already served a full sentence, and the predictive ability of psychiatrists in this regard is not well established.

Out of Africa

1. See C. L. Scott, "Evaluation of Competencies," 263-80, Pops note 3 above.

2. See Prince of Wales note 9 above.

3. See J. S. Janofsky et al, AAPL Practice Guidelines," S1-S76, Introduction note 28 above.

4. Since competency to stand trial means that the defendant must be able to work rationally with his or her lawyer, if the defendant refuses to consider a plea of not guilty by reason of insanity, that may not be rational. This does not mean that a defendant cannot refuse an insanity defense, and some courts say that is the prerogative of the defendant no matter what, so the evidence of a compelling mental illness with no other rational defense but insanity has to be well established.

5. E. S. Person, *By Force of Fantasy* (New York: Penguin Books, 1995).

Little Saints

1. See APA, *DSM-5*, 271–80. *Posttraumatic stress disorder* is a condition that can develop from exposure to one or more traumatic events, in which a person

continues to reexperience the event, avoids situations that are reminders of that event, experiences negative changes in thinking and mood, and is much more easily aroused and reactive emotionally.

2. The *statute of limitations* refers to a period of time for bringing a criminal prosecution (in criminal cases), after which it can no longer be done. Although it differs from one jurisdiction to another, a ten- or twelve-year statute of limitations is typical, except for more serious crimes such as murder, in which there may be no statute of limitations. The statute of limitations for civil cases is much less time.

3. This is known as *respondeat superior*, in which a person with oversight for another may be held responsible too, even if he or she did not directly contribute to the wrong that occurred.

4. See APA, *DSM-5*, 591-644, Pops note 1 above.

5. See C. L. Scott, "Evaluation of Competencies," 263-80, Pops note 3 above.

6. See Introduction note 29 above.

7. J. Le'Merrer et al., "Reward Processing by the Opioid System in the Brain," *Physiological Review* 89, no. 4 (2009): 1379–412. There is evidence that narcotic analgesics, as well as other abused substances, can shut off a person's natural chemical pathways for pleasure; in essence they "hijack" the pleasure system so that only more of the substance seems to allow pleasure.

8. These conditions, found in childhood, involve neurodevelopmental problems, as well as impulse control problems. Attention deficit hyperactivity disorder is a persistent pattern of inattention or hyperactivity-impulsivity that impacts learning and social behavior, often coupled with an independent learning disorder sometimes unrecognized. See APA, *DSM-5*, ref. 46, 59–74; oppositional defiant disorder is a pattern of angry or irritable mood, argumentativeness, and vindictiveness that typically persists over many years and includes particular difficulty with authority figures. See APA, 462–66.

9. See note 1 above. Posttraumatic stress disorder was formerly classified as a type of anxiety disorder, but with specific characteristics as a result of a traumatic event. It is now reclassified in a chapter for trauma and stressor-related disorders and can include dissociation as a symptom in which the person traumatized learns to separate him-or-herself from conscious awareness of the horrible experience.

10. Dr. Webber is not saying that Dougie Stengler is lying, since that would be a factual determination left to the judge or jury. She is just raising factors in his personality and psychological makeup that could impact his credibility and need to be considered.

11. It may seem that if a person is diagnosed with posttraumatic stress disorder, it establishes that trauma occurred, but posttraumatic stress symptoms are intuitively known to people and can be reported or endorsed even by an imagined trauma. Therefore, every diagnosis of posttraumatic stress disorder must meet the criteria for having been exposed to trauma, but it does not mean that the diagnosis by a psychiatrist verifies the trauma, especially if there is a dispute as to what occurred or did not occur.

12. A well-known study asked shoppers in a department store to select which nylon stockings they preferred. All pairs of stockings were identical, but the shoppers nonetheless gave a variety of reasons for their choices. Even when later told that the stockings were identical, they insisted on their earlier explanations. R. E. Nisbett and T. D. Wilson, "Telling More Than We Can Know: Verbal Report on Mental Processes," *Psychological Review* 84 (1977): 231–59.

Insanity

1. See C. L. Scott, "Evaluation of Criminal Responsibility," 282-84, Introduction note 30 above.

2. See Prince of Wales note 5 above.

3. A traumatic brain injury, if sufficiently severe, can lead to epileptic seizures that have specific characteristics (e.g., loss of consciousness, generalized shaking, biting of the lips or tongue) and can be verified by electroencephalogram (EEG) studies. Less common are seizures that do not have typical characteristics but include odd behaviors of which a person may be unaware. These are more controversial but should be proved by EEG evidence or other objective means.

4. A traumatic brain injury does not necessarily have to show signs of brain contusion or bleeding on diagnostic studies, but typically the prognosis is much better, with most people eventually recovering without those signs. In the absence of clear evidence of a brain insult, abnormal behaviors that are attributed to alleged traumatic brain injury months or years after the injury took place are speculative.

5. See APA, *DSM-5*, 59–66. Attention deficit disorder, or the more technically correct diagnosis of attention deficit hyperactivity disorder, is a neurodevelopmental condition and not one brought on by traumatic brain injury. However, individuals with a traumatic brain injury can demonstrate attentional problems, and at times they are also treated with stimulant medication.

6. J. M. Cromer, "After Brain Injury: The Dark Side of Personality Change, Part 1," *Psychology Today*, (March 9, 2012). Damage to the frontal lobes of the brain from injury or disease can result in disinhibition (i.e., a lack of control over one's actions or a change in personality with seeming disregard for the consequences of what a person says or does). However, most individuals with those types of behaviors do not have identified damage to the frontal lobes, so the behaviors do not confirm the damage.

7. Neurological soft signs are called *soft* because they may be subtle, temporary, or equivocal. They have value but do not necessarily confirm a diagnosis of traumatic brain injury or brain dysfunction.

8. See APA, *DSM-5*, 87–122. Earlier concepts of schizophrenia included such core characteristics. But in recent decades, psychiatrists focus more on typical symptoms such as hallucinations, delusions, and disorganization of thoughts and behavior, coupled with chronic mental impairment.

9. See Nice Shoes note 5 above.

10. In depositions, there is no judge, so lawyers usually agree to limit objections because there is no one to make a ruling on the objection. Depositions are usually for discovery purposes, not for final testimony—as in trial—unless the deposition is specifically conducted in place of a trial (e.g., the witness may not be available for trial).

Conclusions

1. See APA (*DSM-5*).

2. E. R. Kandel, *The Disordered Mind: What Unusual Brains Tell Us About Ourselves*. (New York: Farrar, Straus and Giroux, 2018).

3. J. A. Holstein and J. F. Gubrium eds., *Varieties of Narrative Analysis*. (Los Angeles: Sage Publications, 2012).

4. D. Hernandez, "Haikus About Space/Make Science Less Tedious/So Hope Scientists," *Wall Street Journal*. (March 25, 2019), accessed January 26, 2020, https://www-wsj-com.cdn.ampproject.org/v/s/wsj.com/ amp/articles/haikus-about-space-make-science-less-tedius-so-hope-scientists-11553527816?amp_js_v=a2&amp_gsa=1&usqp-mq331AQCKAE%3D#aoh=15800588992964&&referrer= https%3A%2.

5. A. E. Pollack and D. L. Korol, "The Use of Haiku to Convey Complex Concepts in Neuroscience," *Journal of Undergraduate Neuroscience Education* 12 (1) (October 15, 2013): A42-A48, accessed January 26, 2020, https://www.ncbi.nlm.nih. gov/pmc/articles/PMC3852870/#_ffn_sectitle.

6. M. Riedl, "Computational Narrative Intelligence: Past, Present, and Future." *10th Workshop on Intelligent Narrative Technologies* (October 24, 2017), accessed January 26, 2019, https://medium.com/@mark_riedl/computational-narrative-intelligence-past-present-and-future-99e58cf25ffa.

7. A. Flood, "Robots Could Learn Human Values by Reading Stories, Research Suggests." *The Guardian* (Feb 19, 2016), accessed January 26, 2019, https://amp-theguardian.com/books/2016/feb/18/robots-could-learn-human-values-by-reading-stories-research-supggests?amp_js_v=a2&amp_gsa=1&usqp=mq331 AQCKAE%3D#aoh=15800622372219&referrer=https%3A702.

8. B. Kybartas and R. Bidarra, "A Survey on Story Generation Techniques for Authoring Computational Narratives," IEEE *Transaction on Computational Intelligence and AI in Games* 9, no.3 (September 2017): 239-253.

9. R. Genauer, "The Story of Data Driven Storytelling," *Towards Data Science* (June 13, 2017), accessed January 20, 2019, https://towardsdatascience.com/the-story-of-data-driven-storytelling-65a02aac9d4.

10. Daubert v. Merrell Dow Pharmaceuticals 509 U. S. 579 (1993).

11. American Psychiatric Association, *Diagnostic and Statistical Manual of Mental Disorders* 2nd ed. (*DSM-2*) (Washington DC: American Psychiatric Association, 1968): 44-45.

12. See APA (*DSM-5*).

13. L. S. Grossman, B. Martis, and C. G. Fichtner, "Are Sex Offenders Treatable? A Research Overview, *Psychiatric Services* 50, no.3 (1999): 349-361.

14. See APA (*DSM-5*): 90-93

15. See APA (*DSM-5*): 746-765.

16.   See APA (*DSM-5*): 659-663.

17.   H. Soderstrom et al., "Reduced Frontotemporal Perfusion in Psychopathic Personality," *Psychiatric Research Neuroimaging* 114 (2002): 81-94.

18.   C. A. Pardo and C. G. Eberhart, "The Neurobiology of Autism," *Brain Pathology* 17, no.4 (October 2007): 434-47, accessed January 27, 2020, https://doi.org/10.1111/j.1750-3639.2007. 00102.x.

Bibliography

American Psychiatric Association (APA), *Diagnostic and Statistical Manual of Mental Disorders*, 5th ed. (*DSM-5*) (Arlington VA: American Psychiatric Association, 2013).

American Psychiatric Association, *Diagnostic and Statistical Manual of Mental Disorders* 2nd ed. (*DSM-2*) (Washington DC: American Psychiatric Association, 1968).

American Psychiatric Association (APA), *Position Statement on the Insanity Defense* (Arlington, VA: American Psychiatric Publishing, 1982).

American Psychiatric Association (APA), Position Statement on the Insanity Defense (Arlington, VA: American Psychiatric Publishing, 2007, reaffirmed 2014).

American Psychiatry Association, Position Paper, 1982

Beach, L. R., *The Psychology of Narrative Thought: How the Stories We Tell Ourselves Shape Our Lives* (Lexington, KY: Xlibris, 2010).

Bergink, N., Rasgon, and K. L. Wisner, "Postpartum Psychosis: Madness, Mania, and Melancholia in Motherhood," *American Journal of Psychiatry* 173, no.12 (2016): 1179–88.

Bernard, B., *In the Theater of Consciousness* (New York: Oxford University Press, 1997).

Biesele, M., *Women Like Meat: The Folklore and Foraging Technology of the Kalahari Ju/'hoan* (Bloomington: Indiana University Press, 1983), 19–20.

Blum, K., et al., "Reward Deficiency Syndrome: A Biogenetic Model for the Diagnosis and Treatment of Impulsive, Addictive, and Compulsive Behaviors," Supplement i–iv, *Journal of Psychoactive Drugs* 32 (November 2000): 1–112.

Brainerd, C. J., and V. F. Reyna, "Fuzzy-Trace Theory: Dual Processes in Memory, Reasoning, and Cognitive Neuroscience," *Advances in Child Development and Behavior* 28 (2001): 41–100.

Briant, P., *Alexander the Great and His Empire: A Short Introduction* (Princeton, NJ: Princeton University Press, 2012).

Campbell, J., *The Power of Myth with Bill Moyers*, ed. S. F. Flowers (New York: Doubleday, 1988), 42–43 (adaptation).

Charon, R., et al., *The Principles and Practice of Narrative Medicine* (Oxford, UK: Oxford University Press, 2017).

Cirincione, C., H. J. Steadman, and M. A. McGreevy, "Rates of Insanity Acquittals and the Factors Associated with Successful Insanity Pleas," *Bulletin of the American Academy of Psychiatry in the Law* 23, no. 3 (1995): 399–409.

Cromer, J. M., "After Brain Injury: The Dark Side of Personality Change, Part 1," *Psychology Today*, (March 9, 2012).

Cross, P. K., "Not Can, but *Will* College Teaching Be Improved?" *New Directions for Higher Education* 17 (Spring 1977): 1-15. accessed April 21, 2019, https://doi.org/10.1002/ he.36919771703.

Daubert v. Merrell Dow Pharmaceuticals 509 U. S. 579 (1993).

Drukteinis, A. M., "Forensic Historiography: Narratives and Science," *Journal of the American Academy of Psychiatry and the Law* 42 (2014): 427–36.

Flood, A., "Robots Could Learn Human Values by Reading Stories, Research Suggests." *The Guardian* (Feb 19, 2016), accessed January 26, 2019, https://amp-theguardian.com/books/ 2016/feb/18/robots-could-learn-human-values-by-reading-stories-research-supggests?amp_js_v =a2&amp_gsa =1&usqp=mq331AQCKAE%3D#aoh=15800622372219&referrer=https%3A702.

Genauer, R., "The Story of Data Driven Storytelling," *Towards Data Science* (June 13, 2017), accessed January 20, 2019, https://towardsdatascience.com/the-story-of-data-driven-storytelling-65a02aac9d4.

Gottscheall, J., *The Storytelling Animal: How Stories Make Us Human* (New York: Houghton Mifflin Harcourt, 2012).

Grossman, L. S., B. Martis, and C. G. Fichtner, "Are Sex Offenders Treatable? A Research Overview, *Psychiatric Services* 50, no.3 (1999): 349-361.

Hemingway, E., *For Whom the Bell Tolls* (New York: Scribner, 1940), 53.

Herman D., et al., *Narrative Theory: Core Concepts and Critical Debates* (Columbus: Ohio State University Press, 2012).

Hernandez, D., "Haikus About Space/Make Science Less Tedious/So Hope Scientists," *Wall Street Journal*. (March 25, 2019), accessed January 26, 2020, https://www-wsj-com.cdn.ampproject.org/v/s/wsj.com/ amp/articles/haikus-about-space-make-science-less-tedius-so-hope-scientists-11553527816?amp_js_v=a2&amp_gsa=1&usqp-mq331AQCKAE%3D#aoh=15800588992964&&referrer= https%3A%2.

Holstein, J. A., and J. F. Gubrium eds., *Varieties of Narrative Analysis*. (Los Angeles: Sage Publications, 2012).

Janofsky, J. S. et al., "AAPL Practice Guidelines for Psychiatric Evaluation of Defendants Raising the Insanity Defense," *Journal of the American Academy of Psychiatry and the* Law 42, no. 4 (2014): S1–S76.

Joyce, J., *Ulysses, the 1922 Text* (New York: Oxford University Press, 2008), 357.

Jung, C. G., *The Red Book: A Reader's Edition* (New York: W. W. Norton, 2009).

Kandel, E. R., *The Disordered Mind: What Unusual Brains Tell Us About Ourselves.* (New York: Farrar, Straus and Giroux, 2018).

Katz, J., "Seductions of Crime," *Crime, Law, and Social Change* 28, no. 2 (1997), 175–80.

Katz, P. and J. Rabinowitz, "A Retrospective Study of Daughters' Emotional Reversal with Parents, Attachment Anxiety, Excessive Reassurance Seeking and Depressive Symptoms," *American Journal of Family Therapy* 37 (2009): 185–95.

Kohut, H., *Thoughts on Narcissism and Narcissistic Rage in the Search for the Self*, vol. 2 (Madison, CT: International Universities Press, 1972), 615–18.

Korkmaz, B., "Theory of Mind and Neurodevelopmental Disorders of Childhood," *Pediatric Research* 65, no. 5, part 2 (2011): 101R–8R.

Kuran, T., *Private Truths, Public Lies: The Social Consequences of Preference Falsification* (Cambridge, MA: Harvard University Press, 1995).

Kurzban, R. W., *Why Everyone Else Is a Hypocrite: Evaluation and the Modular Mind* (Princeton, NJ: Princeton University Press, 2011).

Kybartas, B. and R. Bidarra, "A Survey on Story Generation Techniques for Authoring Computational Narratives," IEEE *Transaction on Computational Intelligence and AI in Games* 9, no.3 (September 2017): 239-253.

Le'Merrer, J. et al., "Reward Processing by the Opioid System in the Brain," *Physiological Review* 89, no. 4 (2009): 1379–412.

Lodish, H. et al., "Section 21.4: Neurotransmitters, Synapses, and Impulse Transmission," in *Molecular Cell Biology*, 4th ed. (New York: W. H. Freeman, 2000).

March, E. S., "Is Facebook Making Us Lonely?," *The Atlantic*, (May 2012).

Miller, L. K., "The Savant Syndrome: Intellectual Impairments and Exceptional Skill," *Psychological Bulletin* 125, no. 1 (1999): 31–46.

Miranda v. Arizona, 384 U.S. 436.

Moskowitz, A., "Dissociation and Violence: A Review of the Literature," *Trauma Violence Abuse* 5, no. 1 (2004): 21–46 (1966).

New Hampshire Bar Association, *Criminal Jury Instructions* (Insanity), Drafting Committee Version (September 2010): 278.

Nisbett, R. E., and T. D. Wilson, "Telling More Than We Can Know: Verbal Report on Mental Processes," *Psychological Review* 84 (1977): 231–59.

Pardo, C. A. and C. G. Eberhart, "The Neurobiology of Autism," *Brain Pathology* 17, no.4 (October 2007): 434-47, accessed January 27, 2020, https://doi.org/10.1111/j.1750-3639.2007. 00102.x.

Pennington, N. and R. Hasti, "A Cognitive Theory of Juror Decision Making: The Story Model," *Cardozo Law Review* 13 (1991): 519–42.

Person, E. S., *By Force of Fantasy* (New York: Penguin Books, 1995).

Peter-Hagene, L., A. Jay, and J. Salerno, "The Emotional Components of Moral Outrage and Their Effect on Mock Juror Verdicts: The Jury Expert," *The Art and Science of Litigation Advocacy* 26, no. 2 (2014): 1–20.

Pollack, A. E. and D. L. Korol, "The Use of Haiku to Convey Complex Concepts in Neuroscience," *Journal of Undergraduate Neuroscience Education* 12, no.1 (October 15, 2013): A42-A48, accessed January 26, 2020, https://www.ncbi.nlm.nih.gov/pmc/articles/ PMC3852870/#_ffn_sectitle.

Riedl, M., "Computational Narrative Intelligence: Past, Present, and Future." *10th Workshop on Intelligent Narrative Technologies* (October 24, 2017), accessed January 26, 2019, https://medium.com/@mark_riedl/computational-narrative-intelligence-past-present-and-future-99e58cf25ffa.

Schacter, D. L., *Memory Distortion: How Minds, Brains and Societies Reconstruct the Past* (Cambridge, MA: Harvard University Press, 1995).

Schank, R. C., *Tell Me a Story: Narrative and Intelligence* (Evanston, IL: Northwestern University Press, 1990).

Scott, C. L., "Evaluation of Criminal Responsibility," in *Textbook of Forensic Psychiatry*, eds. L. H. Gold and R. L. Frierson, 3rd ed. (Arlington VA: American Psychiatric Association Publishing, 2018): 281–82.

Soderstrom, H. et al., "Reduced Frontotemporal Perfusion in Psychopathic Personality," *Psychiatric Research Neuroimaging* 114 (2002): 81-94.

Thomas, E. M., *The Old Way: A Story of the First People* (New York: Picador, 2006), 208–9 (adaptation).

Thomson, A. D. and E. J. Marshall, "The Natural History and Pathophysiology of Wernicke's Encephalopathy and Korsakoff's Psychosis," *Alcoholism* 41, no. 2 (2006): 151–58.

U.S. Department of Justice, *U.S. Lawyers' Criminal Resource Manual: Section 638. Burden of Proving Insanity*, 18 U.S.C. Section 17(b) (US Department of Justice, October 2017).

Wilson, T. D., *Redirect: The Surprising New Science of Psychological Change* (New York: Little, Brown and Company, 2011).

Worth, S. E., "Narrative Understanding and Understanding Narrative," *Contemporary Aesthetics* 4 (2004), accessed February 22, 2020, https://contempaesthetics.org/ newvolume/pages/article.php?articleID=237

Zapf, P. A. and T. Grisso, "Use and Misuse of Forensic Assessment Instruments," in *Coping with Psychiatric and Psychological Testimony*, ed. D. Faust, based on the original work by Jay Ziskin (New York: Oxford University Press, 2012), 488–510.

Made in United States
North Haven, CT
28 September 2023

42083461R00153